Ecofeminist Literary Criticism

The Environment and the Human Condition

An interdisciplinary series edited by
Eric T. Freyfogle and John Tallmadge

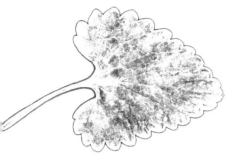

Ecofeminist Literary Criticism:
Theory, Interpretation, Pedagogy

Edited by Greta Gaard and Patrick D. Murphy

University of Illinois Press
Urbana and Chicago

1 2 3 4 5 C P 5 4 3 2 1

This book is printed on acid-free paper.

Library of Congress Cataloging-in-Publication Data
Ecofeminist literary criticism : theory, interpretation, pedagogy /
edited by Greta Gaard and Patrick D. Murphy.
p. cm. — (The environment and the human condition)
Includes bibliographical references (p.) and index.
ISBN 0-252-02373-0 (acid-free paper). —
ISBN 0-252-06708-8 (pbk. : acid-free paper)
1. American literature—Women authors—History and criticism.
2. Ecology in literature. 3. American literature—Women authors—
History and criticism—Theory, etc. 4. American literature—Women
authors—Study and teaching. 5. Feminism and literature—United
States. 6. Women and literature—United States. 7. Human ecology in
literature. 8. Feminist literary criticism. 9. Ecofeminism in literature.
10. Nature in literature. I. Gaard, Greta Claire. II. Murphy, Patrick D.,
1951– . III. Series.
PS169.E25E25 1998
810.9'355—DC21 97-45322

CIP

Contents

Introduction

Greta Gaard and Patrick D. Murphy

This volume began as a special session that Greta Gaard had proposed for presentation at the annual convention of the Modern Language Association. When that proposal was denied, Gaard approached Patrick D. Murphy with several fine conference papers and the idea for a special issue of *ISLE: Interdisciplinary Studies in Literature and Environment,* which Murphy had founded and was editing at the time. Murphy was receptive and suggested other essays for inclusion in the volume; thus began our three-year-long collaboration, conducted via every mechanized medium available to us—fax machine, stamp machine, and electronic mail. We spoke on the telephone once and met for the first time after the contents of the special issue had been finalized.[1] Even though we were largely unknown to each other—as were the contributors to this volume—we believe our collaboration, including its snags and its successes, has been effective because of our shared foundation in ecofeminism.

Feminist and ecofeminist theories shaped the collaboration between editors in a number of ways: for example, we both believed that the essays would be enriched by the dialogue that evolves between two editors and the writers, rather than just one. We shared decisions at each step of the way. We talked about the collaborative process. We were pleased that our collaboration would provide another example of men and women working together to build ecofeminism, thereby undermining the misconception that ecofeminism is the province of women alone. Our different disciplinary backgrounds were perceived as strengths rather than as limitations: Murphy is primarily a literary scholar and ecocritic, whereas Gaard is primarily an ecofeminist scholar/activist and composition instructor, with an education in literature and literary theory. Hence, our readings were thus somewhat different, but complementary. Finally, in the process of collaboration, we were attentive to the contexts of our lives that inevitably influenced the pace and the process of our communication. These uniquely feminist aspects of our collaboration made our work both productive and pleasurable.

This volume consists of essays in ecofeminist literary theory, criticism, and pedagogy. Our criteria for selecting particular essays and the common ground that unites them implicitly articulates our conception of ecofeminism and its relationship with the study of literature, as well as the role of literary production and analysis within ecofeminism. In the next few pages, then, we will provide a brief overview of the diversity that constitutes ecofeminism, explain our sense of the relationships between ecofeminism and literary study, and conclude with introductory remarks about each of the chapters that follow.

⌒

Ecofeminism is a practical movement for social change arising out of the struggles of women to sustain themselves, their families, and their communities. These struggles are waged against the "maldevelopment" and environmental degradation caused by patriarchal societies, multinational corporations, and global capitalism. They are waged for environmental balance, heterarchical and matrifocal societies, the continuance of indigenous cultures, and economic values and programs based on subsistence and sustainability. The foundation and ground of ecofeminism's existence, then, consists of both resistance and vision, critiques and heuristics. Ecofeminism is not a single master theory and its practitioners have different articulations of their social practice. For the most part, those who set out to articulate its philosophy and worldview do so in the belief that such theorizing will assist specific movements, actions, and practices. Such theorizing will do so through increasing the self-consciousness of its participants and representing its beliefs to those who are open to it. As Irene Diamond and Gloria Feman Orenstein note in their introduction to *Reweaving the World,*

> Ecofeminist politics does not stop short at the phase of dismantling the androcentric and anthropocentric biases of Western civilization. Once the critique of such dualities as culture and nature, reason and emotion, human and animal has been posed, ecofeminism seeks to reweave new stories that acknowledge and value the biological and cultural diversity that sustains all life. These new stories honor, rather than fear, women's biological particularity while simultaneously affirming women as subjects and makers of history. This understanding that biological particularity need not be antithetical to historical agency is crucial to the transformation of feminism. (xi)

Transformation may very well be the single term to which all adherents of ecofeminism would assent. Hazel Henderson, for example, believes that "to-day's eco-feminism is restoring [the] earlier pre-*history* [of goddess worship and matriarchal societies], and its art and rituals, which celebrate Nature as an order that is, *in principle* not fully knowable precisely because humans are a part of it. Eco-feminism once more views Nature as sacred" (207). Starhawk defines the spiritual wing of ecofeminism in terms of its being based on a goddess tradition, nature theology, indigenous spirituality, and immanence rather than transcendence. She goes on to state that "these principles—immanence, interconnection, and community—call on us to do something. . . . When we start to understand that the earth is alive, she calls us to act to preserve her life" (74). Further, she claims that "ecofeminism challenges all relations of domination. Its goal is not just to change who wields power, but to transform the structure of power itself" (77). To accomplish such a task, activists need to realize that "environmental issues cannot be intelligently approached without the perspectives of women, the poor, and those who come from other parts of the globe, as well as those of all races and cultural backgrounds" (83). For Starhawk and many other ecofeminists, then, ecofeminism is based not only on the recognition of connections between the exploitation of nature and the oppression of women across patriarchal societies. It is also based on the recognition that these two forms of domination are bound up with class exploitation, racism, colonialism, and neocolonialism.

Such a belief in the interconnections of forms of oppression does not require an adherence to any particular belief in spirituality or in goddess worship. Rather, the spiritual wing of ecofeminism is linked to other wings, such as the radical and social wings, by means of a fundamental starting point, which Ynestra King defines: "In ecofeminism, nature is the central category of analysis. An analysis of the interrelated dominations of nature—psyche and sexuality, human oppression, and nonhuman nature—and the historic position of women in relation to those forms of domination is the starting point of ecofeminist theory" ("Healing" 117). King has articulated a set of basic principles that has been quoted extensively and generally embraced as a sound orientation:

1. The building of Western industrial civilization in opposition to nature interacts dialectically with and reinforces the subjugation of women, because women are believed to be closer to nature. Therefore, ecofeminists take on the life-struggles of all of nature as our own.

2. Life on earth is an interconnected web, not a hierarchy. There is no natural hierarchy; human hierarchy is projected onto nature and then used to justify social

domination. Therefore, ecofeminist theory seeks to show the connections between all forms of domination, including the domination of nonhuman nature, and ecofeminist practice is necessarily antihierarchical.

3. A healthy, balanced ecosystem, including human and nonhuman inhabitants, must maintain diversity. Ecologically, environmental simplification is as significant a problem as environmental pollution. Biological simplification, i.e., the wiping out of whole species, corresponds to reducing human diversity into faceless workers, or to the homogenization of taste and culture through mass consumer markets. Social life and natural life are literally simplified to the inorganic for the convenience of market society. Therefore, we need a decentralized global movement that is founded on common interests yet celebrates diversity and opposes all forms of domination and violence. Potentially, ecofeminism is such a movement.

4. The survival of the species necessitates a renewed understanding of our relationship to nature, of our own bodily nature, and of nonhuman nature around us; it necessitates a challenging of the nature-culture dualism and a corresponding radical restructuring of human society according to feminist and ecological principles. ("Ecology" 19–20)

Some from within and others from without have criticized ecofeminism because it refrains from consolidating itself around a single ideological orientation. Lee Quinby, however, views the philosophical plurality and ongoing theoretical dialogue within ecofeminism as one of its marked strengths. She wants

to argue against these calls for coherence, comprehensiveness, and formalized agendas and to cite ecofeminism as an example of theory and practice that has combated ecological destruction and patriarchal domination without succumbing to the totalizing impulses of masculinist politics. Ecofeminism as a politics of resistance operates against power understood, as Foucault puts it, as a "multiplicity of force relations," decentered and continually "produced from one moment to the next." Against such power, coherence in theory and centralization of practice make a social movement irrelevant or, worse, vulnerable, or—even more dangerous—participatory with forces of domination. (123)

And further, ecofeminism "suggests that theory in the interrogative mode— as opposed to theory in the prescriptive mode—asks difficult questions; that is, it asks questions that pose difficulties, even, perhaps especially, for one's own practices. In fact, the we of ecofeminism is most formidable in its opposition to power when it challenges its own assumptions" (124). Quinby and many others do not want ecofeminism to be used to dictate how a particular people in a specific place, particularly indigenous peoples, should determine the parameters of human-nonhuman reciprocity. Further, not believing in mechanistic theories of progress and development, they want ecofeminism to open a space for future generations to work out their relationships with the rest of nature. Our children should be free from the idea that such relationships will necessarily build on or advance from current cultural and political practices.

In brief, then, these are some of the key features of ecofeminism. In terms of academic discourse, and attention within the university, at least in the United States, ecofeminism was initially discussed almost exclusively in departments of philosophy and women's studies and on the fringes of environmental studies, where any inroads made by feminism were almost always allied with ecology, as in the work of Sandra Harding, Evelyn Fox Keller, and Donna Haraway. In more recent years, ecofeminism has begun to turn up in other departments, such as criminology, in conjunction with environmental justice in terms of both racial and gender oppression; political science, in terms of social movements and community politics; cultural studies, almost exclusively to the degree to which it engages postcolonial considerations; and English departments, in terms of women's and environmental literatures.

~

Since 1990 there has been an eruption of ecofeminist literary analysis. Although individuals have been working in this vein for decades, the majority of ecofeminist literary criticism is being practiced by younger academics who have received their degrees since 1990 and doctoral students who are building on the wealth of materials. One task that feminism has accomplished in the past three decades is its revelation of the range and quantity of women's writing that had been excluded from serious literary study and ignored in canon formation. But feminists in literature departments tended with rare exceptions to overlook the interpenetration of ecology and feminism as it was developing throughout the 1970s and 1980s. In the 1990s ecofeminism is finally making itself felt in literary studies. Critics are beginning to make the insights of ecofeminism a component of literary criticism. They also are discovering a wide array of environmental literature by women being written at the same time as ecofeminist philosophy and criticism is being developed.

We can relate ecofeminist principles and interpretation to existing literary study by building on feminist attention to the concept of the "other." This concept is prevalent in literary study as a result of the influence of psychoanalytic theory and feminist critique. But the "other" must be rethought through grounding it in physical being. One aspect of such grounding is to reject the notion of absolute difference and the binary construct of inside and outside. The discipline of ecology challenges any such dichotomy. Ecology is not a study of the "external" environment we enter—some big outside that we go to. Ecology is a study of interrelationship, with its bedrock being the recognition of the distinction between things-in-themselves and things-for-us. The latter entities result from intervention, manipulation, and transformation. Any entity that has been rendered as a *thing* for human use began its existence as an entity-in-itself. And, at least in the case of other sentient beings, as an entity-for-itself, since the impetus of any species is to survive and reproduce. Feminism demands male recognition of the "other" as not only different but also of equal ontological status. Such an ontology would indicate the need to view the self/other distinction as one of relative difference on the basis of heterarchy rather than hierarchy (see Henderson; Murphy).

Usually, when humans ask, What good is it? they really mean, What good is it to me or to my society? Maria Mies and Vandana Shiva have demonstrated the ways in which this question, when asked by the technological elite from First World countries, often leads to ecological disaster for people of the Third World. Such destruction occurs because the "me" that the technologists treat as a universal does not fit the needs, perspectives, or environmental relationships of the indigenous peoples to which it is applied. Ecofeminism takes this critique further by pointing out that a better question is, What good is it within its ecosystem, and what is the relationship of humans to the maintenance or degradation of that good within that system? Using the health of the ecosystem and the relationship among all life forms within that ecosystem as the fundamental criterion for judgment enables the recognition of diversity as a necessary dimension of individual species and ecosystemic survival. Cultural diversity, for example, is one dimension that enhances the survival of the human species. Difference, then, is not only relative and interrelated but also necessary.

And so with the recognition and positive identification of otherness—not just among people but also among people and other natural entities—as non-alien, healthy diversity becomes a fundamental recognition of ecofeminism. But recognizing the "other" as a self-existent entity is only one step. Another step is to perceive the self-other relationship as one of interanimation, as mutual co-creation, which has parallels in many Buddhist, animistic, and indigenous beliefs and practices. Static categories that define nature or individuals can be only distortions. Likewise, definitions of literature, its genres, and its canons that attempt to establish timeless universals by relying on a few male authors and ignoring the contextual, historical, thematic, and aesthetic dimensions of literary production can also be only distortions. Just as women's writing has historically been marginalized, so too has environmental writing. Ecofeminist analysis provides both an explanation for this phenomenon in literary analysis and the philosophical orientation for developing an ecofeminist literary theory to guide new criticism.

Donna Haraway has noted that "ecofeminists have perhaps been most in-sistent on some version of the world as active subject, not as resource to be mapped and appropriated in bourgeois, Marxist, or masculinist projects. Ac-knowledging the agency of the world in knowledge makes room for some unsettling possibilities" (199). Such unsettling can certainly be extended to literary studies. It can be done by critiquing the traditional canon and the male tradition of nature writing in American literature. It can also be done by re-covering, exploring, and promoting environmental literature by women.

∽

In selecting the essays for this volume and in offering comments to the writ-ers, we brought to bear these ideas about the parameters of ecofeminism and the intersection of ecofeminist and literary theories. For instance, we were both familiar with the intersection of feminism and literary criticism and the kinds of questions that arise from that intersection; ecofeminist literary criticism, however, would need to do more. It could not be confined to performing a litmus test to determine the percentage of a text's ecofeminist content; such an approach would be both arrogant and, in more cases than not, anachro-nistic. Instead, it seemed ecofeminist literary criticism would involve reading literary texts through the lens of ecofeminist theory and practice and asking questions: What previously unnoticed elements of a literary text are made visible, or even foregrounded, when one reads from an ecofeminist perspec-tive? Can this perspective tell literary critics anything new about a text in terms of the traditional elements of style and structure, metaphor and narrative, form and content? How might an ecofeminist perspective enhance explorations of connections and differences among "characters" in a text—between humans and animals, between culture and nature, and across human differences of race, class, gender, and sexual orientation—connections and differences that affect our relationships with nature and with each other? How could this perspec-tive be applied to classroom teaching situations? And finally, Do we really need to do this? That is, could literary criticism—and its newest development, eco-criticism—get along without an ecofeminist perspective, or does ecofeminist literary criticism have something vital to offer? The essays that follow exem-plify ecofeminist literary criticism in that they articulate and address one or more of these questions.

We begin the volume with Barbara T. Gates's "A Root of Ecofeminism: *Ecoféminisme*," which offers a closer look at the writings of François d'Eau-bonne, a French feminist widely credited with first writing the term *ecoféminis-me*. Gates provides a helpful summary of the central points in d'Eaubonne's two books, which were published in French in the 1970s and have been known to U.S. readers primarily through d'Eaubonne's translated excerpt in Elaine Marks and Isabelle de Courtivron's *New French Feminisms*. While ecofeminist theories and practices have developed and diversified in the twenty years following d'Eaubonne's first book, her work remains an important part of the history of ecofeminism's Western articulation.

Patrick D. Murphy in "'The Women Are Speaking': Contemporary Literature as Theoretical Critique" explores literary examples of women speaking about the relationships of wilderness, nature, home, and identity. Murphy's analysis uses as a departure point Ursula K. Le Guin's famous 1986 statement, "where I live as a woman is to men a wilderness. But to me it is home." Murphy studies a multicultural selection of works of nonfiction, fiction, and poetry published since 1986 in order to consider the theoretical implications of such literature for the further development of ecofeminist literary criticism. Murphy echoes Quinby's concern not only for the benefit of plurality in theorizing but also for theory in the interrogative mode, allowing the literature to critique the theory.

While Murphy starts with literature to question theory, Deborah Slicer in "Toward an Ecofeminist Standpoint Theory: Bodies as Grounds" offers an ecofeminist philosophical approach to the woman/nature connection. Drawing on feminist standpoint theory and ecofeminist philosophy, Slicer explores the potential constructions of an ecofeminist standpoint as grounded in specific physical bodies, thereby reinforcing Diamond and Orenstein's argument that recognizing "that biological particularity need not be antithetical to historical agency is crucial to the transformation of feminism" (xi). Continuing with the emphasis on particularity, Slicer then offers an ecofeminist critique of Jane Smiley's novel *A Thousand Acres* to ground her thesis in situated women's experiences and in the sort of politically reflexive context afforded by fiction that standpoint theorists and contemporary postmodernists alike endorse.

Josephine Donovan's "Ecofeminist Literary Criticism: Reading the Orange" uses the concept of the absent referent, an idea developed in structuralist and poststructuralist language theory, along with the theories of Martin Buber and Mikhail Bakhtin to analyze the ontology of domination as depicted in literary texts. Drawing examples from Dorothy Wordsworth, Sarah Orne Jewett, and Clarice Lispector, which allows for an ecofeminist reconsideration of these authors, Donovan argues that ecofeminist literary and cultural criticism can and should encourage a kind of "epistemological awakening" whose purpose is to sensitize dominators to the realities of the dominated. In such a practice, the text is not reduced to an "it" but rather recognized as a "thou" where the absent referent (the thou) is restored, and where new modes of potentially transformative relationships—dialogue, conversation, and meditative attentiveness—are developed.

One project of ecofeminism has involved a critique of the dualisms of white Western patriarchal culture, dualisms such as self/other, culture/nature, man/woman, human/animal, and white/nonwhite, which construct white male human identity as separate from and superior to the identities of women, people of color, animals, and the natural world. Through challenging the problems with philosophical dualism, Karla Armbruster in "'Buffalo Gals, Won't You Come Out Tonight': A Call for Boundary-Crossing in Ecofeminist Literary Criticism" posits a number of questions about identity and difference that can be helpful to the development of ecofeminist literary criticism. Reading Ursula Le Guin's short story "Buffalo Gals, Won't You Come Out Tonight" as a test case, Armbruster combines poststructuralist and ecofeminist theories to illuminate ways that an author can create a conception of human and nature intersubjectivity, a relation involving a human identity shaped by an acknowledgment of both connection and difference.

In "'Skin Dreaming': The Bodily Transgressions of Fielding Burke, Octavia Butler, and Linda Hogan," Stacy Alaimo examines the way that Butler and Hogan create human bodies not as static sites of cultural inscription alone, but as "threshold[s] where nature and culture dissolve," sites where domination can be constantly resisted, where transformations can continuously occur, and where constructions of race, gender, environment, and society can be transgressively critiqued. Reclaiming the body is important work for ecofeminism, particularly since human (male) identity has been equated with the mind alone, and the body has been variously raced, animalized, feminized, and naturalized in order to be seen as inferior and antagonistic to the progress of culture. Alaimo's discussion reveals the body as itself a locus of knowledge transmission and reception, a source of information just as valuable as the intellect, at the same time that it emphasizes the differences and particularities of the perspectives of the body presented in writing by women of color.

Continuing an emphasis on the interrelatedness of gender, race, and ecology, Kamala Platt examines the relationship between ecofeminist and environmental justice movements through a reading of a contemporary Chicana novel in "Ecocritical Chicana Literature: Ana Castillo's 'Virtual Realism.'" Even though ecofeminism, like feminism itself, has tended to emphasize gender over race in its analyses, Platt demonstrates through her reading of So Far from God the inseparability of race, class, and gender in exploring issues of environmental racism. She argues persuasively that "neither those within ecofeminism nor the environmental justice movement have taken full advantage of the possibilities which an alliance of agendas addressing the junction of gender and race would allow. Such an alliance would expand both groups' understandings of the causes and effects of global and local environmental degradation and would empower their struggles against environmental racism." Environmental classism needs to be emphasized simultaneously with environmental racism, Platt observes, since each reinforces and upholds the other.

In "Rethinking Dichotomies in Terry Tempest Williams's *Refuge*" Cassandra Kircher examines the ways that culture/nature and male/female dualisms are both utilized and rendered problematic in a text many have described as ecofeminist. While Williams's narrator critiques the patriarchal institutions of culture that are destructive to both women and nature, her critique is complicated by her awareness—and lack of awareness—of the way that she too participates in those cultural institutions. Kircher contrasts the linearity of polarized dualisms with the organizing trope of the circle, which describes the book's structure as well as the narrator's sense of family and personal identity. Because Williams seeks but does not find a reconciliation between culture and nature that will preserve the integrity of each, Kircher argues, *Refuge* is a complicated and often paradoxical book. Kircher's critique exemplifies the ways in which an ecofeminist perspective can introduce new dimensions to a literary analysis of a well-known work and the importance of using ecofeminist critique to understand, and not simply to judge, particular works about women.

While most of the authors treated in this volume are from the United States, "In Search of Common Ground: An Ecofeminist Inquiry into Christa Wolf's Work" turns our attention to another European feminist. Deborah Janson addresses the continuing relevance of the East German writer Christa Wolf by drawing parallels between her work and that of well-known ecofeminists from the capitalist West, including Susan Griffin, Starhawk, and Riane Eisler. Using Wolf's novels *No Place on Earth, Cassandra: A Novel and Four Essays,* and *Accident,* Janson compares ideas in Wolf's texts with ecofeminists' views on peace and antinuclear issues, on the desirability of a partnership-based society, on the preference for an immanent rather than a transcendent spirituality, and on the detrimental effects of certain types of science and technology on human and environmental health.

Many of the contributors in this volume argue that ecofeminist literary criticism needs to address theory and practice, scholarship and pedagogy. In conceptualizing the purpose for this volume, we felt very strongly not only that the practice of pedagogy should be represented in this volume but also that more direct forms of activism that utilized literary criticism needed to be included. In "Grass-Roots Ecofeminism: Activating Utopia," Cathleen McGuire and Colleen McGuire describe their work bringing ecofeminism to life in the center of New York City through a reading, discussion, and activist group called EVE (Ecofeminist Visions Emerging). The group met monthly for three years (1991–94), each time discussing a topic based on readings from various ecofeminist writers. These discussions became the tool for developing grass-roots ecofeminist theory and action. After each session, the McGuires summarized the discussion and actions, distributing their reports in the form of a newsletter that had international circulation. To illustrate their discussions, the McGuires detail EVE's comparative reading and discussion of two ecofeminist utopian novels, Marge Piercy's *Woman on the Edge of Time* and Starhawk's *The Fifth Sacred Thing*. In their chapter they describe the organization, functioning, and activities of EVE and suggest ways for bringing ecofeminist theory out of the academy and into the streets.

In "Deep Response: An Ecofeminist, Dialogical Approach to Introductory Literature Classrooms," John Paul Tassoni describes a teaching method that works to dismantle the authoritarian, monological stance of the teacher, a stance that has imposed the teacher's values on the students instead of encouraging students to think critically. Tassoni argues that ecofeminism—a theory that values egalitarian, noncoercive relations among humans and nonhumans alike—is best introduced to students through dialogue with the instructor, with small groups, with readings, and with the students' written responses to texts and discussions. Presenting literature "as a point of departure," ecofeminist teachers using a dialogical approach can encourage discussions in which students will "critically examine the attitudes and beliefs that influence them and the world around them." By allowing students to participate in the text selection, and by opening up the standards of grading for discussion, Tassoni offers new ways of creating an ecofeminist, democratic classroom.

Greta Gaard, in "Hiking without a Map: Reflections on Teaching Ecofeminist Literary Criticism," explores various applications of ecofeminist theory to literary criticism through the example of a specific course design. Ecofeminist theories offer strategies rather than rules, so although the intersection of ecofeminism and literary criticism is largely unmapped, scholars have a number of guidelines to follow. Gaard discusses the text selection, grading methods, and pedagogical strategies she used in her class and the considerations that influenced her choices. Next, she presents an overview of the class discussions and the texts studied. In her conclusion she offers a series of questions for ecofeminist literary criticism that were articulated in dialogue with her students.

Many of the works discussed in these chapters contain some of the new stories being written as part of the cultural critique necessary to resist oppression and the visionary projection required to supplant those wreaking havoc and destruction across the planet. They are also part of the process of rewriting the old stories, including those about literary canons, artistic quality, aesthetics, and thematics. Their discussion contributes to both a rewriting and a new writing of the relationships of theory to practice, literary theory to literary criticism, and of the foregoing to pedagogy and community activism. At the same time that we praise these accomplishments, we also must be forthright about what this volume has not considered.

In answering the question, Where do we go from here? we must recognize that in this volume we have not addressed sufficiently the particularities and differences that need to be recognized and understood in an international cross-cultural study of ecofeminist theory and criticism and world literature. Nor have we tackled whether there is ecofeminist literature written by men. And while spirituality in ecofeminism has been raised, the spiritualist wing of ecofeminism and its literary representations deserve far more attention than could possibly be given in these pages. But, then, these are areas to explore in developing a comprehensive ecofeminist literary criticism, and, as a first volume on the subject, this book is necessarily introductory in its scope and in the ambition of its editors. If it inspires such comprehensive work, it will have succeeded.

For those who are already working in tandem with us, but were not represented here, and for those who would follow let us emphasize in closing that ecofeminist literary criticism need not accept the role of younger sister to other ecofeminist and ecocritical theories simply because its development has lagged behind. It has the potential to develop side by side in dialogue with ecofeminist theories, ecocriticism, literary criticism, feminist and ecofeminist pedagogy, and community activism. To the extent that ecofeminist literary criticism illuminates relationships among humans across a variety of differences and between humans and the rest of nature, exploring ways that these differences shape our relationships within nature; to the extent that it offers a critique of the many forms of oppression and advocates the centrality of human diversity and biodiversity to our survival on this planet; and to the extent that it emphasizes the urgency of political action aimed at dismantling institutions of oppression and building egalitarian and ecocentric networks in their place—to the extent that it does all these things, ecofeminist literary criticism has a vital contribution to make.

Note

1. We mention this primarily because, as Gaard noted in her foreword to the *ISLE* special issue, "it's a curious way for ecocritics to collaborate; certainly, I would have preferred to meet over an organic vegetarian meal, followed by a walk in the woods, a

workshop on building labor-environment coalitions, or a protest against GATT, environmental racism, or the Contract on America."

Works Cited

Diamond, Irene, and Gloria Feman Orenstein, eds. *Reweaving the World: The Emergence of Ecofeminism.* San Francisco: Sierra Club Books, 1990.

Haraway, Donna J. *Simians, Cyborgs, and Women: The Reinvention of Nature.* New York: Routledge, 1991.

Harding, Sandra. *The Science Question in Feminism.* Ithaca: Cornell University Press, 1986.

Henderson, Hazel. "The Warp and the Weft: The Coming Synthesis of Eco-Philosophy and Eco-Feminism." *Reclaim the Earth: Women Speak Out for Life on Earth.* Ed. Léonie Caldecott and Stephanie Leland. London: Women's Press, 1983. 203–14.

Keller, Evelyn Fox. *Reflections on Gender and Science.* New Haven: Yale University Press, 1985.

King, Ynestra. "The Ecology of Feminism and the Feminism of Ecology." *Healing the Wounds: The Promise of Ecofeminism.* Ed. Judith Plant. Philadelphia: New Society Publishers, 1989. 18–28.

———. "Healing the Wounds: Feminism, Ecology, and the Nature/Culture Dualism." *Reweaving the World: The Emergence of Ecofeminism.* Ed. Irene Diamond and Gloria Feman Orenstein. San Francisco: Sierra Club Books, 1990. 106–21.

Marks, Elaine, and Isabelle de Courtivron, eds. *New French Feminisms: An Anthology.* Amherst: University of Massachusetts Press, 1980.

Mies, Maria, and Vandana Shiva. *Ecofeminism.* London: Zed Books, 1993.

Murphy, Patrick D. *Literature, Nature, and Other: Ecofeminist Critiques.* Albany: State University of New York Press, 1995.

Quinby, Lee. "Ecofeminism and the Politics of Resistance." *Reweaving the World: The Emergence of Ecofeminism.* Ed. Irene Diamond and Gloria Feman Orenstein. San Francisco: Sierra Club Books, 1990. 122–27.

Starhawk. "Power, Authority, and Mystery: Ecofeminism and Earth-Based Spirituality." *Reweaving the World: The Emergence of Ecofeminism.* Ed. Irene Diamond and Gloria Feman Orenstein. San Francisco: Sierra Club Books, 1990. 73–86.

1

A Root of Ecofeminism:
Ecoféminisme

Barbara T. Gates

SITTING ON MY DECK translating Françoise d'Eaubonne, one of the early exponents of ecofeminism, with the help of a French exchange student, Roxanne, I felt I had found the appropriate outdoor space for the enterprise. The phone rang. It was Michiyo, a young Japanese scholar whom I once taught, calling from Tokyo. "Should I," she asked, "translate Terry Tempest Williams, or is it better to rewrite my dissertation on modern drama for publication? I think Williams is an ecofeminist." I advise the former; everything is pointing to an international movement whose moment has come. And Roxanne and I had set out to recapture a moment of its past.

If ecofeminism as a movement has indeed come into its own in the United States in the 1990s, ecofeminist historians have most often given credit for its intellectual and theoretical spadework to a Frenchwoman writing in the early 1970s. Generally they cite a word or two about the books of Françoise d'Eaubonne and then go on—as they should—with their own agendas.[1] But now, some twenty years after the publication of d'Eaubonne's first book on *ecoféminisme*, it seems past time to review d'Eaubonne's contribution to ecofeminist thought in an effort to trace one of the central European roots of a growing world movement. I would nevertheless like to reemphasize the often repeated fact that ecofeminism involves activism as well as ideology and that both of these aspects of ecofeminism arose simultaneously worldwide. As d'Eaubonne was publishing her books, women in the United States were protesting the atrocities at Love Canal and analyzing the shock waves of the nuclear leak at Three Mile Island as women in northern India were initiating the Chipko movement, hugging trees to save them from felling.

This essay is not, then, a "culturist" attempt to privilege European written discourse or theory over political activism or other legitimate manifestations of ecofeminism. Rather, I aim to give more access to d'Eaubonne's pioneering work by offering a summary, a commentary, and a brief repositioning of it in the context of 1990s ecofeminism. D'Eaubonne's books are hard to find and her work all but inaccessible to those who do not read French. My hope is to provide something more wide-ranging than the brief, translated selection published in *New French Feminisms: An Anthology* but not to fulfill a need for a fully fledged translation. This essay may also serve to remind those of us who use English readily just how anglicized ecofeminist writing has become; English is the current *lingua franca* of ecofeminism. Finally, I hope the essay will be a small contribution to the enterprise that Patrick D. Murphy called for in the special ecological feminism issue of *Hypatia:* the need to "refine our conception of ecofeminism's relationship to literature" (154). After all, writing is the medium through which many of us continue to learn about the cultural complexities of ecofeminism.

What d'Eaubonne was suggesting in the Europe of the 1970s was what others like Rosemary Radford Ruether in *New Woman/New Earth* (1975) were also recognizing as a new way of seeing old problems: the linking of the devaluation of both women and the earth. "Practically everybody," d'Eaubonne claimed, "knows that today the two most immediate threats to survival are overpopulation and the destruction of our resources; fewer recognize the complete responsibility of the male System, in so far as it is male (and not capitalist or socialist) in these two dangers; but even fewer still have discovered that each of the *two* threats is the logical outcome of one of the *two* parallel discoveries which gave men their power over fifty centuries ago: their ability to plant the seed in the earth as in women, and their participation in the act of reproduction" (qtd. in Marks and Courtivron 66).[2] This excerpt, the one most familiar to English speakers, directly joins women and the environment, in this case through reproduction. D'Eaubonne, as all acknowledge, also coined the word *ecoféminisme.*

In the 1970s, d'Eaubonne wrote two books that dealt with aspects of *ecoféminisme.* The first, *Le Féminisme ou la mort* (1974), offers a background and an explanation for her newly coined word. D'Eaubonne begins her book and prepares the stage for her theorizing by summarizing the central European political movements related to ecofeminism. The first, the Front Reformiste, developed an ecological component in 1973, basing this in part on Shulamith Firestone's allusions to the ecological context of U.S. feminism mentioned briefly in *The Dialectic of Sex* (1970). The Front soon renounced its ecological manifesto, however, and concentrated on its original interests—abortion, divorce rights, and equal opportunity. Some of its members then split off to found a second group and sponsored the Ecologie-Feminism Centre. Work at the center led to the movement *l'ecologie-féminisme*. What d'Eaubonne set out to do was to refine and redefine this movement, hence *ecoféminisme*.

Le Féminisme ou la mort offers a capsulized view of many of the issues later discussed and developed in greater detail in *Ecologie féminisme: Révolution ou mutation?* (1978). Women, d'Eaubonne suggests in the earlier book, have been reduced to the status of a minority by a male-dominated society, although their importance in terms of numbers, and even more significantly in terms of reproduction, should have permitted them a dominant role. Nevertheless women have not even been allowed to control births without hindrance from men, in particular male theologians and legislators. Throughout most of recorded time, men have consistently desired power over women's reproductive functions. Even male scholars have colluded in this. They have, for example, paid little attention to the conjuring rites ancient women evolved to stop conception and birth but have overemphasized ancient fertility rites. Now it is imperative to stop this fallacious thinking. Overpopulation is ruining both humanity and the earth, for the earth is treated with the same disregard as are women. Urbanized, technological society, which is male-driven, has reduced the earth's fertility, while overbreeding, also male-driven, has increased the population. Women must act to save themselves and the earth simultaneously. The two needs are intimately linked.

D'Eaubonne describes that linkage in terms of both the past and the present. In the past, women gathered from and tilled the earth; they were the world's gardeners. According to d'Eaubonne, unlike many contemporary nonorganic agriculturalists, many women of the past used ecologically sound methods. D'Eaubonne suggests that this bond between women and earth remains and frequently manifests itself in the present, as when women have taken the lead in protests against nuclear power. Yet such women do not demand personal power when they protest. They are concerned with others: other people, other women, other species, the planet itself. Their work, their protests also cross gender lines in ways that men's work, men's protests usually do not. Like Carol Gilligan in *In a Different Voice* (1982), d'Eaubonne believes that women have historically been wedded to other people and nature through a social imperative requiring caring and consideration and that this acculturation in caretaking persists. Give ecofeminists what they are asking for, says d'Eaubonne, and "human beings would finally be regarded as persons and not first and foremost as males or females. And our planet, close to women, would become verdant again for everyone" (251).

These thoughts form the backbone of d'Eaubonne's arguments in both of the texts I have mentioned, although in *Ecologie féminisme* they are more carefully spelled out. The book's subtitle, *Révolution ou mutation?* suggests d'Eaubonne's deepening concern by the later 1970s. *Mutation*—alteration through time—seems insufficient to effect what needs to be done. The pressing problems raised by inattention to women's and the earth's well-being demand a revolution in Western thought. According to d'Eaubonne, "since 1974, that is when I started to write [this book], the events that have followed one another in the field of ecological struggle—as well as women's struggle—have confirmed—more than I thought—the emergency of the double problem" (11). She goes on: "I am far from writing something trendy in juxtaposing these two questions, two problems, two struggles. . . . I am also far from putting together, in an uncertain way, two myths—that of the eternal woman and of the inexhaustible Earth, or aiming at a romantic idealism, or at an unrealizable utopia, or demobilization of violence. It is important to establish how deeply revolutionary the link [between feminism and ecology] can be, and I mean revolutionary in the word's most authentic sense" (13). What d'Eaubonne questions here is the failure of nineteenth- and early twentieth-century political movements, like socialism, to truly alter the state of things. "The aim," she states about the necessity for an ecofeminist revolution, "is not that of 'building a better and a fairer society.' It is that of living, of allowing history to continue, rather than our disappearing like some of the ante-diluvian animals did, or like certain species of birds, whose spermatozoic capacity went on decreasing because of overpopulation" (14). Thus the extinction of people and planet is at stake and only a revolution in thought and action can prevent it.

D'Eaubonne does not follow a Marxist line in her arguing. Pollution is attributable not only to capitalism but also to communism. To her mind, both the United States and the Soviet Union have been motivated by profit and have polluted and destroyed to implement this motivation. The Soviets must buy wheat from the Americans because they can no longer produce enough on their land to sustain their population. According to d'Eaubonne, this is a perfect example of the intimate link between reproduction of humans and the destruction of the earth. Moreover, "classic" Marxists refuse to grant women the status of a social class. Yet because of the ways in which Western cultures function, to redress the world's current condition women must be considered as a class.

D'Eaubonne believes that the Soviet Union and the United States have still more in common, particularly with respect to researching and implementing birth control. If in the Soviet Union the government approved of abortion, little research was done on contraception. If in the United States women are proud of their freedom in comparison with Europeans, they should recall that they could have had a contraceptive pill more than a century ago. Research in this area was done in the nineteenth century, but then foregone. Native Americans were also known for their ability to control birth, but white males seem not to have been interested in this. Yet, d'Eaubonne recalls, the American government has tried to stop reproduction in developing countries. "How," she wonders, "can they talk about the dangers of overpopulation when the American people are known for consuming 45 percent of the natural resources of the planet?" (45).

Such contradictions between stated attitude and policy make up the bulk of d'Eaubonne's examples in the first part of *Ecologie féminisme,* in which she finds the profit motive inherent in the policy of most governments. "The problem," d'Eaubonne posits, "is that governments take into account the economy but nothing more. They think that if it is flourishing, people will have access to happiness. Why," she queries, "don't they care about the destruction of nature, the inequality of rights?" (72). Her conclusion is predictable: such things can be "realized [only] by ecological and feminist parties which would allow society to get into the 'post-industrial era'" (83).

The second part of *Ecologie féminisme* retraces the history of why we have not moved into this kind of postindustrial era. Here d'Eaubonne briefly reviews the history of domination of women and planet from paleolithic times to the 1960s. In rediscovering ecologically sound practices, like *ecobuage* —the ancient burning of shrubs and returning their ashes to the soil—d'Eaubonne wonders at the discarding of such practices in favor of fertilization with chemicals. In reexamining the work of the nineteenth-century Swiss anthropologist Johann Jakob Bachofen on matriarchy, she queries the rush by his contemporaries to discredit his theories by suggesting that matriarchy was merely a legend. Her final expression of disgust is reserved for what she calls "unlimitism" (*i'illimitisme,* 172), which typifies male-dominated political systems and institutions. Unlimitism sets no bounds to patriarchal power—power over other countries and other people. It will, d'Eaubonne believes, continue unchecked until the planet runs out of food or a new movement like ecofeminism effects a revolutionary change in mentalities or attitudes.

This briefly summarizes d'Eaubonne's message, in two of the first book-length considerations of the necessity for ecofeminism. How, then, do they square with directions the movement has taken in the 1990s? In some ways they still seem fully central. Many of the problems d'Eaubonne saw and foresaw remain—particularly the depth of resistance of patriarchal political and cultural structures to change. And d'Eaubonne's initial diagnosis of the "double problem" is of course the reason she is so often cited as a founder of ecofeminism. Yet in other ways d'Eaubonne's work seems passé. D'Eaubonne was writing not long after the student riots and political ferment of the 1960s. Her concerns and her language, especially the desire for revolution, are in part related to the discourse of that time. So, too, is her preoccupation with the population explosion and reproductive rights. Recall the work of Barry Commoner and the feminist focus in the seventies on the right to abortion. Contemporary ecofeminists, for all their concern with reproductive choice, have focused far more on other issues: establishing a theoretical base for ecofeminism, healing the breach between theory and practice, looking more deeply at complex local issues in all parts of the world instead of attempting to solve global issues through reductivist overviews or even earth summits.

In addition, the global nature of 1990s ecofeminism has made some of d'Eaubonne's 1970s ideas seem culturally confined. Her insistence, for example, on the nonorganic nature of contemporary agriculture was not based upon a consideration of Third World means of production and consumption or on a consideration of the importance of Third World peoples to the success of First World consumerism. Reminding us that "development" has been a patriarchal project, Vandana Shiva has subsequently shown how women have suffered as a result of what she calls "maldevelopment." If d'Eaubonne saw that women's ancient work with the soil was replaced by contemporary agriculture, Shiva sees how such work in the Third World continues to be supplanted by systems that both split the family and impoverish the land. In Shiva's words: "The ideology of development is in large part based on a vision of bringing all natural resources into the market economy for commodity production. When these resources are already being used by nature to maintain her production of renewable resources and by women for sustenance and livelihood, the diversion of resources to the market economy generates ecological instability and creates new forms of poverty for women" (196–97).[3]

Moreover, contemporary ecofeminism has itself had to face several significant challenges that have evolved since d'Eaubonne's texts were written. The first has been a challenge to ecofeminist philosophy. Primarily because of their misconceptions of its intent, critics have insisted that ecofeminism is essentialist, that it purports that women have a biological closeness to nature that men do not have. On the contrary, inherent in ecofeminism is a belief in the interconnectedness of all living things. Since all life is nature, no part of it can be closer than another to "nature." A second challenge to ecofeminism has come through dissension among those in the contemporary environmental movement. Deep ecologists, proponents of altering the anthropocentric view of nature by asking humans to think more biocentrically, have questioned the feminist bias in ecofeminism; ecofeminists have in turn faulted deep ecologists for retaining androcentrism while claiming to have discarded anthropocentrism. And as I indicated at the outset, women involved in the environmental movement have been at odds when defining its parameters. Janet Biehl, for example, a social ecologist, has criticized ecofeminism for being so diverse as to have no center.

Although I strongly disagree with Biehl, I must say that when I began teaching ecofeminist literature, for weeks my students quested for a firm definition of *ecofeminism*. Then they built individual definitions, eclectically taken from their perceptions of readings in the subject. Soon they came to argue vehemently with one another over literary texts: whether any given text could be called ecofeminist. They then began to form a workable within-the-class definition of the concept. Was only a poem like Janice Mirikitani's "Love Canal"—about the dying of the land in upstate New York and the simultaneous dying of a woman poisoned by her proximity to Love Canal—to be considered ecofeminist? Or could an older piece, like Sarah Orne Jewett's "A White Heron," be ecofeminist, too? After all, it was about women and nature and species preservation and against hunting and killing beautiful specimens of non-human nature in the name of science.

Nevertheless, like my students by the end of their course, ecofeminists have come to share a number of beliefs, and some of them do hark back to d'Eaubonne. Janis Birkeland has gathered ideas she thinks ecofeminists have in common, which I believe help circumscribe a contemporary ecofeminist ideology. They include the necessity for social transformation by moving beyond power politics and an equivalent necessity for less "management" of the land—both central ideas in d'Eaubonne's work. They also include an appreciation of the intrinsic value of everything in nature—a biocentric rather than an anthropocentric viewpoint; an end to dualisms like male/female, thought/action, and spiritual/natural; and a trust in process, not just product (20). Future ecofeminist literature will, I believe, be most deeply concerned with these issues. As I write these words, I must admit to a strong pull to join ranks with anyone working to effect such changes. Nor can I help recalling d'Eaubonne, with her earnestness: "I am far from writing something trendy in juxtaposing these two questions. . . . I am also far from putting together, in an uncertain way . . . a mere romantic idealism . . . or unrealizable utopia" (*Le Féminisme ou la mort* 13). Now, more than twenty years after d'Eaubonne published her first book on *ecoféminisme,* her desires have found company in ecofeminists around the globe who are working diligently to effect changes in attitudes toward women and nature that may in turn promote the survival of all people, other living creatures, and the earth.

Notes

With special thanks to Roxanne Petit-Rasselle for a semester's hard work with unfamiliar texts.

1. See, for example, Merchant 100 or Adams 126, where d'Eaubonne comes to us via a Boston classroom, or Mies and Shiva 13.
2. The remainder of the translations of d'Eaubonne's works are courtesy of Roxanne Petit-Rasselle; page numbers refer to the original French texts.
3. Shiva's work in "Development as a New Project of Western Patriarchy" and with Maria Mies has completely revisioned development from an ecofeminist perspective. She and Mies both recapitulate and extend d'Eaubonne's ideas about population in "People and Population," chapter 19 of *Ecofeminism*.

Works Cited

Adams, Carol J. "Ecofeminism and the Eating of Animals." *Hypatia: A Journal of Feminist Philosophy* 6.1 (1991): 125–45.

Biehl, Janet. *Rethinking Ecofeminist Politics*. Boston: South End Press, 1991.

Birkeland, Janis. "Ecofeminism: Linking Theory and Practice." *Ecofeminism: Women, Animals, Nature*. Ed. Greta Gaard. Philadelphia: Temple University Press, 1993. 13–59.

Commoner, Barry. *The Closing Circle: Nature, Man, and Technology*. New York: Knopf, 1971.

d'Eaubonne, Françoise. *Ecologie féminisme: Révolution ou mutation?* Paris: Les Editions A.T.P., 1978.

———. *Le Féminisme ou la mort*. Paris: Femmes en Mouvement, 1974.

Firestone, Shulamith. *The Dialectic of Sex: The Case for Feminist Revolution*. New York: Morrow, 1970.

Gaard, Greta, ed. *Ecofeminism: Women, Animals, Nature*. Philadelphia: Temple University Press, 1993.

Gilligan, Carol. *In a Different Voice: Psychological Theory and Women's Development*. Cambridge: Harvard University Press, 1982.

Marks, Elaine, and Isabelle de Courtivron, eds. *New French Feminisms: An Anthology*. Amherst: University of Massachusetts Press, 1980.

Merchant, Carolyn. "Ecofeminism and Feminist Theory." *Reweaving the World: The Emergence of Ecofeminism*. Ed. Irene Diamond and Gloria Feman Orenstein. San Francisco: Sierra Club Books, 1990. 100–105.

Mies, Maria, and Vandana Shiva. *Ecofeminism*. London: Zed Books, 1993.

Murphy, Patrick D. "Ground, Pivot, Motion: Ecofeminist Theory, Dialogics, and Literary Practice." *Hypatia* 6.1 (1991): 146–61.

Ruether, Rosemary Radford. *New Woman/New Earth: Sexist Ideologies and Human Liberation*. New York: Seabury, 1975.

Shiva, Vandana. "Development as a New Project of Western Patriarchy." *Reweaving the World: The Emergence of Ecofeminism*. Ed. Irene Diamond and Gloria Feman Orenstein. San Francisco: Sierra Club Books, 1990. 189–200.

2

"The Women Are Speaking":
Contemporary Literature as Theoretical Critique

Patrick D. Murphy

WHEN I BEGAN WRITING this chapter in the early months of 1996, the presidential caucuses and primaries had just gotten underway and Patrick Buchanan was scoring victories with a message attacking multiculturalism, attacking international dialogue, attacking immigration, attacking sexual diversity, espousing a single religious tradition as informing all that is truly "American," and promising a return to family values based on a singular image of what constitutes a family. Such rhetoric has been building for some time, and the other candidates, including Bill Clinton, responded by blasting Buchanan's extremism but adopting modified versions of many of his platform planks. Is it coincidental that such attacks on cultural diversity are occurring at the same time that the United States is experiencing a backlash against environmentalism, environmental regulations, and long-range environmental planning? I think not. Efforts are being made continuously to separate conceptions of nature and decisions about environmental problems and planning from cultural constructions and the relationship of cultural practices to environmental effects. It seems that as the linkages between the values that shape how we live and the shape that such living imposes on the land become increasingly apparent, the rhetoric depicting a static, perpetual, true "America" becomes more shrill and intense. Yet many people know better and are listening to someone else: women who speak of gender, of nature, and of culture.

Ecofeminism from its inception has insisted on the link between nature and culture, between the forms of exploitation of nature and the forms of the oppression of women. While these linkages have been most fully explored in philosophy and practiced through a variety of means in the streets and forests, an increasing body of literature identified as ecofeminist has emerged, as has an even larger number of works recognized as demonstrating or containing significant elements of a feminist ecological sensibility. But anyone working with theory has to guard against the danger of trusting the theory and testing only the practice, whether that practice consists of acts of civil disobedience, behavioral changes, or the production of literary works. With literature, readers need to be asking themselves constantly what the texts in their hands can offer to enhance the theories that shape their lives.

For that purpose I have chosen works by seven authors: Pat Mora, Sallie Tisdale, Jane Brox, Marnie Mueller, Edna Escamill, Lori Anderson, and Nora Naranjo-Morse. Three are nonfiction, two are novels, and two are collections of poetry. All are works by women, but they are not necessarily all feminist works, either in terms of an authorial self-expressed ideology or a position easily definable as such by a reader. All of them demonstrate a significant awareness of the interdependence of women's oppression and environmental degradation. They also tend to emphasize the relationship of cultural diversity and natural diversity, or what might be termed an ecological multiculturality. In the next three sections of this essay I want to focus on works that raise questions about, or help us extend, certain theoretical issues and activist concerns.

Nonfiction

The literary nonfiction essay is the prose genre that has come to define nature writing in the United States, in part because it appears to combine a personal voice with factual and accurate description. The generally accepted Enlightenment binary construct of "the subjective" and "the objective" seem to meet in a blend of the best of each. Belief in such a blending justifies the presentation of universalizing general philosophical statements that are often based on an author's very specific and relatively minute experiences. For the most part, such nonfiction has been written by white males yet treated as if it were speaking for everyone. Increasingly, however, white women and women of color have taken up writing in this genre and in doing so have increased its potential for discursive variety and a broadening of the voices expressing the freedom to evaluate natural and cultural phenomena.

Pat Mora, poet, essayist, and children's author, hails from the southwestern desert of North America, part of the U.S.-Mexico borderlands. Too often feminist critics who are not ecologically literate tend to fail to recognize the specificity of place and the bodily reality of individual experience that situate a woman's life, preferring instead to establish a disembodied mind or an uninhabited body as the locus of their analysis. Mora continuously resists such dematerializing of women's experiential lives. She reminds her readers that what is known as the Southwest is a particular type of borderland situation that has generated many *mestiza* cultures with varying class structures and economic formations on both sides of the nation-state boundary. One common feature of these cultures is their indigenous heritage, which provides ethnic roots far older than the four hundred years since the Spanish invasion. In choosing a Nahuatl word for the title of her essay collection, *Nepantla: Essays from the Land in the Middle* (1993), Mora invokes just such a heritage.

Mora writes early in *Nepantla* that "nurturing [cultural] variety is central, not marginal to democracy" (19).[1] Mora's claim links her ideas directly with a foundational tenet of ecofeminism: diversity is a necessary basis for a balanced ecosystem. Often, however, diversity is understood only in regard to animal and plant species variety and rarely is the diversity of humanity addressed in like manner. Human culture, however, is a component of biological diversity every bit as significant as the shape of a hummingbird's bill or the tail of an Amazonian primate. Therefore, Mora's emphasis on the nurturing of cultural variety is as ecological as the animal diversity championed by wildlife conservationists. Seeing culture and ecology as intersystemic phenomena, Mora calls for emphasizing cultural conservation as much as "historical preservation" and "natural conservation" (18).

In fundamental ways, such cultural conservation is situated and ecoregional in character:[2] "a true ethic of conservation includes a commitment to a group's decisions, its development and self-direction" (30). Just as biological diversity is crucial to biotic survival, cultural diversity, Mora warns, is crucial to human survival: "Pride in cultural identity, in the set of learned and shared language, symbols, and meanings, needs to be fostered not because of nostalgia or romanticism, but because it is essential to our survival. The oppressive homogenization of humanity in our era of international technological and economic interdependence endangers us all" (36). Melding ecoregional awareness and commitment to place with multiculturalism challenges much of the masculinist theorizing and master-theory building practiced by various leaders of environmental organizations.

Many of the essays in *Nepantla* focus precisely on the issue of cultural conservation, as Mora defines the term, even as they embody such a practice. Mora rightly emphasizes the conservation of Mexican, Central American, South American, and Caribbean cultures, but also addresses respect for many other cultures around the world. Further, she calls for an understanding of the differing degrees and kinds of effects that dominant U.S. culture has on subordinated cultures within the United States and worldwide. For many readers, *Nepantla* would not fit their definitions of nature writing or even the broader category of environmental literature because it is so focused on human culture. Yet through her recognition of the interconnectedness of cultural and political practices, particularly in terms of the homogenization of cultures globally to meet the needs of multinational corporations, Mora also identifies the relationship between local cultural preservation and the defense of biological diversity. She demonstrates such connections in part through reaffirming the situatedness of cultures, and within that situatedness the relationship of beliefs, practices, and character to the place from which they stem and in which they continue to be lived and worked out.

Preservation needs to be understood precisely as an ongoing working out of relationships and process rather than as a static condition of existence. Among environmentalists and ecologists, particularly through the growth of the field of restoration biology, a debate is occurring about the propriety of restoring various habitats to earlier, allegedly pristine, states. Much of the argument within the restoration movement, and against it as well, is taking place over the contradiction between images and ideals of particular ecosystemic stability and the reality of continuous process. At what point do people continue to restore and then fine tune a habitat area, and at what point do they let it go its own way? Mora addresses this same dilemma in relation to the restoration of oppressed cultures, which must either renew themselves to a certain level of cohesion and stability or be wiped out by the advance of consumerist uniformity. She speaks against the illusions of nostalgia and stasis by arguing for the need to criticize the historical flaws of one's own culture and to question continuously what ought to be renewed and what ought to be transformed within a given culture. As she states it, cultural conservationists must "question and ponder what values and customs we wish to incorporate into our lives, to continue our individual and our collective evolution" (53). For example, in *Nepantla* she critiques dominant Mexican culture's suppression of indigenous peoples and languages (28–29, 40). Such suppression there, as in the United States, means the loss of knowledge about indigenous plants and crops, herbs and medicines, as well as rituals and practices that define and renew spiritual relationships to the land.

Mora also helps us understand the role of art in cultural and ecological conservation. She links in the essay "Poet as *Curandera*" the art of the traditional healer with her own poetic artistry as an act of healing through "witnessing" to her culture. In "The Border: A Glare of Truth," Mora defines the origin of her being as poet-*curandera:*

> When I lived on the border, I had the privilege accorded to a small percentage of
> our citizens. I daily saw the native land of my grandparents. I grew up in the Chi-

huahua desert, as did they, only we grew up on different sides of the Rio Grande. That desert—its firmness, resilience, and fierceness, its whispered chants and tempestuous dance, its wisdom and majesty—shaped us as geography always shapes its inhabitants. The desert persists in me, both inspiring and compelling me to sing about her and her people, their roots and blooms and thorns. (10)

Clearly, Mora believes that place is not determined by national boundaries because such boundaries often cut apart ecosystems and watersheds, even dividing lakes between states and countries. Cultures can and must traverse political boundaries to remain true to their places of existence. So, too, understanding ecoregions and their implications for sustainable human inhabitation requires ignoring political and property boundaries based on abstract and universalist legal and political codes in favor of acknowledging the situated experience of changing environmental contours.

Mora's sensibility is one of ecological multiculturality. I conceptualize "ecological" here in two related ways. One, the concept of ecosystem functions as metonym and metaphor for a set of necessary human-land relationships. As Mora contends, "because humans are part of this natural world, we need to ensure that our unique expressions on this earth, whether art forms or languages, be a greater part of our national and international conservation effort" (25). Two, specific ecologies are a component of cultural heritage and continuity. The very concept of *la mestiza* that Mora employs defines an ecological multiculturality.[3] It is based on a cultural melding occurring in a specific region that need not efface difference between peoples, but can recognize multiplicity within the individual, the community, and the communities of the region. As Mora emphasizes, "the inheritors of culture [are] those who remain in contact with nature and tradition," in all their diversity (*Nepantla* 121).

When reviewing Mora's arguments throughout *Nepantla* from an ecofeminist perspective, one finds that she holds the basic tenets that a theorist like Ynestra King would define as fundamental ecofeminist principles (119–20), and she engages in "*reconceptualizing* ourselves and our relation to the nonhuman natural world in nonpatriarchal ways," which Karen J. Warren identifies as a strength of ecofeminism (7). Further, she also recognizes the necessity for claiming "a space for women to be heard *speaking on their own terms*" (Salleh 97). But Mora takes such recognition further by contending that women's terms must not be limited to only or even primarily an individual female voice but must also include their cultural community. With this recommendation she evokes the kind of orientation Alice Walker has defined as part of being "womanist": "Committed to survival and wholeness of entire people, male *and* female" (xi). Mora's conceptualization of the ecologically responsible practice of cultural conservation as carried out by marginalized and suppressed groups, particularly indigenous peoples, suggests ways to enhance ecofeminism.

Mora's *Nepantla* can help advance ecofeminist theory and practice in at least three ways. First, ecofeminism can learn from a womanist sensibility about the cultural and racial dimensions of situated knowledge and integrate those into any decision-making process about political action. Second, it can evaluate the implications of Mora's cultural preservation sensibility for the further and more sophisticated elaboration of an ecofeminist commitment to place and locale. Third, it can conceptualize an ecological multiculturality that will more fully enable women and men to advance ecofeminist transformation without consciously, or even inadvertently, imposing political, economic, and environmental solutions on ecosystems continuously ravaged in the interests of rampant consumerism.

While Mora's *Nepantla* focuses on cultural preservation, Sallie Tisdale's *Stepping Westward: The Long Search for Home in the Pacific Northwest* (1991) chronicles the efforts of Anglo-European immigrants to create culture by attempting to determine how to live in this particular region of the United States. A first point to note is that Tisdale continuously refers to the numerous tribal peoples inhabiting this region prior to the slow but inexorable onslaught by easterners and other immigrants. She emphasizes the diversity and locally appropriate inhabitory practices of the various native communities, as well as criticizing the racism to which they have been subjected historically and contemporaneously. The organicism of their diversity becomes an ideal that Tisdale holds up in her hopes for the possibility of a contemporary settlement that is ecologically viable, economically sustainable, and inclusive of Native Americans.

Another point to note is Tisdale's gender balancing of her examples of individual lives and authorities. Where in another text of this type one would expect a reference to a male pioneer or scientific authority—because that is how most of these nonfiction books are written—Tisdale is more likely to refer first to women, such as Mary Ellicott Arnold and Mabel Reed, who in 1908 "were among the first white women to appear in Karuk country" (32). Here Tisdale does not simply provide the reader with female examples who conform to masculinist stereotypes of pioneer women, but also provides counterstereotypic examples: Arnold and Reed "had come west looking for adventure of some undefined kind, knowing only that settling down into marriage and motherhood had to wait until more of the huge world had been seen" (32). She then often follows such a presentation with an example of the male frontier stereotype: destructive, ecologically insensitive, and bent on subduing the land and the natives to his own designs. But again, Tisdale does not limit herself to male stereotype versus female counterstereotype; she also provides frequent examples of male counterstereotypes, whose ideas and actions align ✳ them more with the values of the pioneering women than with the gold rush, timber harvest, exploitative men (see, for example, 165–75). In these accounts Tisdale demonstrates, not only along cultural but also along gender lines, what rancher-writer Linda Hasselstrom philosophizes: "we have tried to change nature to fit not only our needs and desires but our whims. We should seriously consider a period of adapting ourselves to nature's laws, before our damage is irreversible" (197).

Tisdale makes a poignant case for the necessity of an ecoregional orientation toward inhabitation. If those who have migrated to the Pacific Northwest, displacing its first human inhabitants, are ever going to be able to settle down and make a home, rather than just a profit or loss, they will have to create a culture adapted to the region's characteristics instead of continuing to render the land in the image of some other place. Through her repeated calling forth of women from the past to speak again of the wilderness in which, and of which, they made their homes, she demonstrates the necessity for any regional, ecologically responsible agenda to be an ecofeminist one, to include the true diversity of human experience of habitation through ensuring that the women who have been speaking are now being heard. She also, by implication, demands of ecofeminism that it further articulate its position on regionalism as an agenda and organizing principle, that its practitioners and theorists continue to define and redefine their conceptions of community-in-place.

On the opposite shores of the United States, Jane Brox has written in *Here and Nowhere Else: Late Seasons of a Farm and Its Family* (1995) a very different type of nonfiction from either *Nepantla* or *Stepping Westward*. It is a frequently meditative narrative, written not so much for its audience as for the author and then shared with others. While Mora and Tisdale treat large, sweeping regions of the United States, Brox focuses on a single family farm in Massachusetts. She too addresses its regional ecological particularities, doing so in the context of the passing of an agrarian way of life whose values need to be preserved even as the historical means of practicing them continue to be plowed under by agribusiness. While *Here and Nowhere Else* does not read as if it were written to be a feminist polemic, or is particularly gender emphatic, it nevertheless weaves themes of nature, gender, and culture into a single fabric that the reader feels compelled to appreciate by not only looking at it but also by feeling its texture and reflecting on its frayed ends.

In her narrative, Brox makes it clear that she feels compelled to return home. She is pulled homeward by the appeal of place, the memories of childhood, the rewards of working with her hands in addition to working with her words.

But the compulsion comes from the plight of her parents as they try to maintain their agrarian, homesteading way of life in the face of suburban sprawl, economies of scale, their own aging, and, most important for Brox, the incapacity of their son and heir to the farm. Of her siblings only her brother has remained to practice the arts of farming, but he is a drug addict incapable of full participation in the work or the family, and so she returns home, moves into an abandoned house on the property, and once more takes up helping with the farm. But hers is no nostalgic trip home, although there are nostalgic moments of memory and common labor. Rather, she feels the contradictory demands of her desires and life work, the expectations of being a dutiful daughter, and the obligations of a descendant through whom the traditional family farm lore must pass or become extinct.

The strength of Brox's narrative, in addition to the sensuous beauty of her precise, descriptive prose, lies in the tension and anguish that she records. She recognizes that there is no simple, separatist, or autonomous decision to be made. She perceives the obligations of family tradition and continuity, of lineage and heritage as real ones, not to be shrugged off so that she can pursue her personal dream. But she also recognizes the need to avoid being trapped by traditional gender roles, by the image of the dutiful daughter who will become mother to her parents and brother.

In the end, she continues to live in her house on the farm, but withdraws from its daily operations, realizing that becoming the head of the farm is not the life that she must lead: "I can still feel that my returning here has only delayed what was inevitable, and that we've all returned to our old places. . . . Still, I can't imagine this place as anything other than a farm" (142–43). Brox knows that the issue is not inheriting the land, but inheriting a working farm and a specific way of life, one that she respects but is unable to pursue. That inability does not come from weakness, however, but from difference and the unwillingness to accept the paring down of her possibilities as a woman that would be required as part of inheriting the farm. In a sense, Brox is caught in the dilemma that Mora addresses. The culture needs to be preserved, but it cannot be continued without change. Because of who she already is, the impossibility of breaking down traditional gender roles within this specific environment precludes Brox from inheriting the farm's way of life, which in turn places the future of the land at risk. Community needs are set against individual growth. Brox makes a choice but does not imagine that it is without cost, knowing that interdependence rather than autonomy defines her identity.

As a result of Brox's personal anguish and her recognition of the price of her choosing, *Here and Nowhere Else* is strongly elegiac in tone. This tone is particularly strong in her recording of her meditative walks through the woods.

During these walks she develops a philosophy of change and continuity based on the second growth processes of the previously cleared but long abandoned farmland-returned-to-woodland. She finds an ancient oak standing alone surrounded by second or third growth trees, threaded by collapsing stone walls of forgotten fields: "Maybe spared by sentiment or reverence, this one outlived them all" (138). This line is, of course, appropriate for the family farm as well. Her hope lies not with the new trees, but with the very process of succession itself: clear-cutting giving way to second growth, softwoods giving way to hardwoods, abandoned fields reaching toward a forest climax state.

In such hope Brox reveals that she does not have the answers for the larger cultural questions that her meditations provoke: What is our obligation toward the protection of sustainable family farming in lieu of a viable alternative at this point in time? Can the traditional gender roles of traditional family farming be transformed, or must we wait for the second growth following the catastrophes attendant upon agribusiness and exploitative extraction, which Tisdale catalogs and warns against, to try anew? What will or can replace the nuclear family that will support the liberation of women from gender oppression and maintain or renew community and mutual responsibility? While a significant body of literature by women on and in agriculture and ranching is developing, ecofeminist theory and ecofeminist literary criticism has not yet addressed such literature. This gap suggests that critics have not yet thought through the complexities that writing such as Brox's raises in regard to agrarian ways of life in industrialized, agribusiness-driven countries, but that they need to do so and soon with the same intensity that others have practiced in addressing women and agriculture in traditional agrarian cultures.

Some ecofeminists, however, have attempted to address at least part of the problem depicted in *Here and Nowhere Else*. Linda Vance, in "Ecofeminism and the Politics of Reality," has spoken to the dilemma Jane Brox faces and addresses it in necessarily contradictory ways. Vance states that while ecofeminists cannot expect to see "huge demographic transitions within our lifetimes," ecofeminists can "make the need for responsible cooperation with the land known, and use our own lives to model the possibilities" (137). Brox undertakes the first of these actions by describing in detail the example of her family's "responsible cooperation with the land," but finds that she cannot "model" its continuation because of the limitations of gender roles that have developed along with that cooperation. Brox does experience what Vance says women have learned historically: "a type of attentiveness that allows us to move back and forth between seeing the needs of an individual and seeing the needs of a larger community" (139), but the attentiveness does not enable Brox to generate a solution that mediates those needs. Instead, she feels compelled to choose and undertakes what Vance also calls for: "to take on the challenge of exploring our own reality as free as possible from the constraints of masculinist ideology" (140). But that will mean letting the farm die, letting the lone example of an alternative to creeping suburbia in her locale go under the blades of the bulldozers.

It must be remembered, however, that while Brox's father is a good farmer, he is still a patriarch, and it is the role of patriarch more than farmer that his son wants to assume. All the good farming in the world will not be good enough within that logic of domination. Men in ecofeminism and men who are willing to read ecofeminist criticism and women's literature with ecological and feminist sensibilities must avoid a convenient identification with the victimized—Brox and the farm here—and admit instead the degree of identification between our lives and behavior and the male antagonists of this text and others. We men with feminist consciousnesses have a special responsibility to work out the implications of how we can persuade and transform the other men who are the culture bearers of the oppression that ecofeminism is committed to transforming.

Brox assumes the responsibility for choosing her freedom from familial patriarchal domination at the likely cost of local agrarian tradition, but only because she cannot refuse to be a victim and at the same time protect the farm from victimization. Why? Because the men will not change; because her brother will not relent or enter into recovery; because her father cannot turn over the farm to anyone other than his son, no matter how unfit. The elegiac tone of *Here and Nowhere Else: The Late Seasons of a Farm and Its Family,* then, results not from Brox's limitations—although she engages in some self-blame—but from the resistance of men heavily invested in patriarchal ideology and traditional male-dominant behavior.

Fiction

Fiction is probably the terrain in which the least codification of a nature writing canon or mode of representation has occurred. Even so, traditional realism tends to be emphasized, in part due to an opposition to the philosophical implications of postmodernist forms and in part due to a penchant for seeing the fiction approximate the factuality of nonfiction nature writing. A major problem with such an orientation is its failure to acknowledge the popularity of different genre conventions across cultures and that "traditional realism" is largely an Anglo-American invention of the nineteenth century.

In the first novel I want to treat, the protagonist visits a place that has a deep and lasting impact on her life. *Green Fires: Assault on Eden: A Novel of the Ec-*

uadorian Rainforest (1994) by Marnie Mueller chronicles the return to Ecuador in late 1969 of an American woman who had been a Peace Corps volunteer there six years earlier.[4] In this novel Ana travels through a tropical forest well inhabited by people facing extinction as a result of the merciless economic exploitation of their country by hers. The crisis of the novel is generated by her and her husband's discovery that the country's government, with the complicity of various U.S. agencies, is bombing the villages of indigenous peoples to clear the way for multinational oil exploration within the rain forest.

In the novel Mueller clearly supports the continuity of indigenous cultural practices while emphasizing their degree of difference from other cultures. Mueller focuses attention on the human-human relationships of the various characters and the cultures they represent rather than on the human-nature relationships because the latter are imperiled by the former. Defining one's responsibility to others, both the alien and the familiar, and determining the proper location for fulfilling such a responsibility is the root of the crisis for Ana as well as for several other characters. To demonstrate the complexity, difficulty, and risk involved in such self-defining, Mueller has various characters reach different and, at times, contradictory conclusions about their relationship with and responsibility toward the indigenous peoples and their environment. Almost invariably, the construction of such relationships renders the indigenous peoples *objects* of attention, either for protection or exploitation, rather than as mutually speaking *subjects* involved in the determination of their own future.[5]

The dilemma is not resolved as the novel ends, and readers are encouraged to recognize that although the novel is set in 1969, the events are not past history but part of an ongoing process as deforestation of the Amazon region and displacement of its indigenous inhabitants continues. The importance and the difficulty of establishing a sense of "anotherness"—recognition of a relationship based on a combination of differences and similarities rather than on identity and alienation—is highlighted as Ana attempts to avoid the pitfalls of both assuming too much similarity with the indigenous peoples and experiencing too great a sense of difference to see relatedness. Mueller emphasizes that recognition of the right of indigenous peoples to continue their cultural and economic practices is fundamental to this struggle. This recognition provides the intellectual and psychological foundation for developing new cultural formations that will discontinue the global ecocide spearheaded by multinational corporations and centralized state governments. Mueller understands the significance of remembering one's position as an outsider, one's limited, noninhabitory, visitational awareness, even in the process of establishing relationships with others. She never lets the reader forget that the wild jungle she describes is already well inhabited. She also indicates a significant dimension of the reader's responsibility toward others by having Ana realize that assuming responsibility for the continuation of Amazonian peoples means returning home to propagandize, not remaining in the jungle.

When teaching this novel in the summer of 1995 to graduate students who were mostly experienced teachers, I heard several of them complain that there was no really likable or heroic character with which to identify. They also agreed with one student who emphasized how realistic Ana's inner turmoil and the uncertain and nonvictorious conclusion seemed to be. They resisted having a female protagonist who was not modeled on the traditional masculinist hero in terms of plot resolution and superior inner strength. They also resisted the degree to which *Green Fires* insists that each of us is working through a quagmire of conflicting necessities and probabilities in trying to chart a path for pursuing our goals and desires while meeting the imperatives of our recognition of ecological crisis.

Mueller's hard-edged realism about the limitations of epiphanies and crisis-induced revelations in *Green Fires* challenges the kind of bright-eyed, revolution-around-the-corner idealism prevalent in the United States in the 1960s and typical of the novel's protagonist and her peers. In this regard, *Green Fires* bears striking similarities to *Here and Nowhere Else* in its representation of Ana's developing self-awareness, despite the tremendous differences in setting and plot. Mueller's protagonist is keenly aware of her own psychological repression and highly self-reflective about the implications of her return to Ecuador. At novel's end, Ana is enlightened yet still conflicted and more committed but even less programmatic about her future course of action. In this novel, the indeterminacy of postmodernism has entered the thematic representation of women's recognition of ecological and multicultural responsibility, producing a more realistic and less triumphant ecofeminist hero, one who knows that baggage cannot just be dumped in a single pile at the trail's edge. In terms of the theoretical development of ecofeminism, *Green Fires* calls for an intensification of the efforts to integrate multicultural and postcolonial critiques of class, race, and nationality with those of women's oppression and environmental degradation. It also suggests the need to continue to think through subject construction in terms of not only social gender hierarchies but also psychological factors and the degree to which culture constructs the psyche's perceptions of identity and difference, alienation and relatedness.

In contrast to the irresolute resolution of *Green Fires,* Edna Escamill's *Daughter of the Mountain: Un Cuento* (1991) depicts a successful synthesis of mundane and spiritual experience that soothes the internal conflict and turmoil that its protagonist undergoes. Structured as a coming-of-age novel, *Daughter* portrays the rise of *mestiza* Maggie's spiritual unity with the land of her birth, tribal ancestry, and cultural continuity, even as it depicts the decimation of her family, community, and closest friend.

That the knowledge, rituals, and practices of traditional ways holds out hope for Maggie's survival and continuation is suggested by the narrative structure. The main narrative is preceded by two framing devices. The first is a mythic story told in direct address in Spanish and then translated. Other such stories are interspersed throughout the main narrative. Following the first mythic story is a tale of Adela Sewa, Maggie's grandmother, and her experience of recovery and rebirth from alcoholism by embracing the spiritual pathway of isolation in the sacred space on the mountain slope of La Madre. The reader realizes that this chapter is a second telling of the mythic story in real time narration, and that Adela Sewa is the mythic voice. Only then does Maggie's narrative begin. At the end of the novel, Maggie ascends the mountain slope and meets with Adela Sewa's spirit to consolidate her understanding of how to survive in the white-dominated world by embracing her heritage and the promise of its spirituality. This final narrative chapter is followed by the framing of the mythic voice of the grandmother, who says: "You see, my daughter, the road going is also the one coming back" (211).

Maggie's family is suggestive of the composition of the population in the southern Arizona borderland where she is born. Her grandmother is a Yaqui Indian, who knows the traditional ways of the *curandera* as well as deeper and more mystical spiritual ways. Although Maggie's mother is a *mestiza* she adheres to Mexican American culture more than Native American or white culture, but is little informed or informing of her heritage. Maggie's absent father and stepfather are white. Yet Maggie is largely unaware of the ethnic and racial diversity that comprises her heritage until the rapid arrival of white suburbanites after World War II. They and their school system inform her that she is poor, that she is mixed rather than melded, that she is from a lower class of people doomed to be removed and relegated to subservient work. They also decide to adapt the desert to their way of life with air conditioning, unsuitable housing, and high energy consumption and destroy the environmentally adaptive economy and culture of the residents.

Maggie's story, then, is largely a quest for identity in the face of oppressive deculturation and racism. I use *deculturation* here instead of *assimilation* because it is more accurate. While the suburbanite invaders practice urban renewal on a semi-rural community, they make no attempt to integrate the residents into the "American dream," but rather attempt to intensify their economic exploitation by stripping residents of the mechanisms that would enable them to maintain community autonomy, such as customs, language, and subsistence agriculture.

While *Daughter of the Mountain* is very much a tale of individual triumph, Escamill nevertheless embodies in fiction Mora's fundamental concern with cultural preservation. Escamill does so by emphasizing spirituality and native heritage. But it is also a story of rejection of the denigrating values and consumerist lifestyle of white culture. And in this theme it is not an individual's story at all, but one of entire communities. Withdrawal from interaction with the dominant culture is not posed as a viable option for Maggie or her friends—or for some Native American communities. Rather, Escamill has Maggie learning white ways to subvert them, as she does when she learns how to shoot from her stepfather and then threatens him with a pistol. Her pilgrimage to the mountain to meet with Adela Sewa's spirit is a ritual undertaken before she leaves for college. Escamill indicates, then, that the road "coming back" is not sudden, the result of a single epiphany, or immediately realizable. Rather, the epiphany of spiritual union is a preparation and a protection for a much longer travail than she has experienced in her first eighteen years. The difference between Ana at the end of *Green Fires* and Maggie at the end of *Daughter of the Mountain* is, therefore, not one of resolution to achieve, support, or protect inhabitory ways of life but one of support for that enterprise. Ana knows that as a member of the oppressor's culture she must transform it without an alternative heritage to draw on. Maggie, however, knows not only what she must oppose but also what she must embrace—the spirituality of her grandmother's Yaqui heritage, which she must preserve and adapt while she seeks to overcome the alien culture that oppresses her.

The path presented for Maggie by Escamill is not one that all readers will be able to imitate. Those with such a heritage may do so; the rest must discover how to support resistance, how to intensify the appreciation of difference that would evoke validation from members of the dominant culture, how to search for the mythopoeia and practices of a viable alternative culture from within the dominant culture of which they, and I, are a part. At present, most ecofeminists are in a position more similar to Ana's than to Maggie's and must not only avoid the temptation to appropriate that other position for their own needs but also develop ecofeminist practice in such a way that it articulates alternatives to the dominant culture, which is necessary for an end to oppression. In other words, ecofeminists must propose general alternatives to end patriarchy and the dominant U.S. culture without generating universalist theories that suppress difference and reinscribe cultural hierarchies.

For those in literary criticism, the necessity for integrating different voices into courses and reading lists is reinforced by the power of Escamill's novel, which in turn indicates the ease with which multicultural texts that promote ecological sensibilities and embody values that ecofeminist theory upholds can be embraced, introduced, and promoted. At the same time, individuals must remain vigilant in supporting such voices instead of presuming to represent them with culturally situated interpretations and perceptions. Louis Owens indicates what is at stake here: "There seems to be a widespread sense that a new kind of critical-theoretical approach is needed if multiculturalism is to be more than another aspect of the familiar discourse of dominance, what has been called critical imperialism" (53).

Poetry

Contemporary critics have tended to align poetry addressing humanity's relationship with the rest of the natural world with British Romanticism and American Transcendentalism. Further, the "I" of poetry is generally identified as no more fictional than that of the naturalist essay, while both are treated as qualitatively distinct from the "I" of prose fiction. Proceeding from these bases and relying on many of the attributes for which nonfiction nature writing is praised, critics often place significant emphasis on solitude, meditation, non-participant observation, accurate detail, ego dissolution or expansion, and personal epiphanies.[6] The two poetry volumes I will discuss here, both published in 1992, do not work along these lines. As the title of Lori Anderson's collection, *Cultivating Excess*, suggests, the poems tend to be short on most of these attributes and long on attitude, action, and immersion. Nora Naranjo-Morse's collection, *Mud Woman: Poems from the Clay*, combines poetry with color plates of her sculptures and pottery, which aesthetically and thematically reinforce each other as they indicate that narrative is more semiotic than linguistic. In both poems and art, symbol and metaphor articulate the weight of cultural mediation of environmentally immersed and self-aware personal experience but eschew any nostalgia for, or idealization of, unmediated interaction. Indeed, Naranjo-Morse celebrates the cultural enrichment of individual interaction with the natural elements.

As Gretchen Legler notes, *Cultivating Excess* "asks readers to challenge traditional notions of nature, of nature writing, and of human relationships with other humans and with the natural world. In this collection, Anderson deliberately, and excessively, works to turn the binary oppositions in language and philosophy upside down and inside out" (190). *Cultivating Excess* is divided into four sections: "Excess Jesus," "Silviculture," "Civilculture," and "Excess Isis." Here I will focus on the first three of these. But before doing so, I want to comment on the book's title, which signals the kind of word play to be found throughout the book, as when the "Excess Jesus" section ends with the poem "Exegesis; Her Song." The word *cultivating* foreshadows the environmental orientation of much of the book, as well as suggesting images of caring and nurturing, practices depicted in patriarchal thought as being "natural" for a woman. But Anderson ruptures such an easy and oppressive identification in two ways. One, she weds *cultivating* with the word *excess*, establishing an inversion of expectations that rescues *cultivating* from the patriarchal domain and sets it loose on the terrain of sexual politics. Two, the understanding of the word *excess* itself is also gradually reversed for readers. Anderson is not referring to something that is actually "excessive," as in too much or more than appropriate, which is frequently a relative rather than an absolute condition and a cultural rather than a natural limit. Instead, *excess* can be understood as meaning "exceeding," as in the transgression of norms.

In the "Excess Jesus" section, one sees the practice of binary inversion that Legler identifies in the five-stanza poem "Fish in Air," which may be a pun on *visionnaire*. In the opening stanza the speaker identifies herself and an unnamed "you" as "new lovers" who are visiting a park named "Eagle Something," while the second stanza reveals that both lovers are women. As Greta Gaard observed in commenting on a draft of this chapter, the phrase *new lovers* can be read in two ways: "newly in love, or newly out," as in first admitting one's sexual orientation.[7] The first stanza ends "long after," suggesting that the events of the rest of the poem happen some time after the characters' sexual initiation. In the second stanza, the "you" character recoils from the lesbian identification between the speaker and herself established in stanza one and calls on

> a holy host
> of others (your Father, your Friends)
> male trinity ensuring we
>   only look for eagles. You all
> agree on one I cannot
> see then tell a tale.
>   (9)

The holy patriarchy's story is about an eagle who grabs a sturgeon too large to haul into the sky and then allegedly drowns through the sin of covetousness. The "eagle" dies for overreaching itself for an allegedly unnatural satisfaction of its appetites, which could be understood as lesbian sexual desire. As if the triteness and convenience of the story were not enough to cast doubt upon its veracity, the use of the word *tale* signals that this story is taking place in the mind of the teller rather than in the air over the river.

This eagle allegory wielded against the speaker of the poem is a stereotypical animal story in which the other's existence is anthropomorphically expropriated for human edification. But the speaker decides that she can play the game of allegory as well and renames the eagle "she" and redefines the eagle's dive as a quest for transformation:

> But how else would eagle ever enter
>   water to such depths save
>   by an anchor of flesh? Maybe
> her longing is as ours is:
>   fish in air, bird under
>   water, man off earth (woman in
> heaven) ((heaven down under))
>   flesh needing flesh to rise
>   to delve to depths beyond/above
> our allotted home.
>   (10)

How often when the "eagle" is deployed as symbol do readers or viewers consider it female? How often is the use of "unnatural" deployed as a term to conceal the hierarchical value attached to a cultural construction of difference, particularly sexual difference?

The poem concludes with an inversion that identifies the "you" as a sturgeon with an eagle in her mouth, in sensual repartee rather than devouring hierarchy, and another inversion is suggested. Whereas the events of the second, third, and fourth stanzas portray the "you" of the poem as denying her own sexual identity and internalizing the homophobia inculcated in her by "Father" and by "Friends," the final stanza's allusion to the "you" character's "new lover" as also a woman indicates that she has in the end accepted the naturalness of her sexuality. The speaker is thus successful in reversing and refuting the patriarchal rhetoric of the dominant culture's compulsory heterosexuality that would attempt to define both what is *natural* and what is in *excess*.

In the "Silviculture" section of *Cultivating Excess*, Anderson critiques the use of mathematics and fragmenting technical vision in the poem "Self Portrait Eye to Eye with Clinometer & Prism" (see Legler 191) and then reinforces that critique in the following poem, "Berm." A clinometer is used to measure a slope or, more for Anderson's sexual ecological politics, an inclination. It is the erotic inclination throughout the poem that chafes and tongues against the commodification of the forest as timber, because, when the erotic asserts itself: "Trees about us no / longer commodities our body taking us for ride" (35). But the clinical detachment of the clinometer reasserts itself and insists on the logic of human domination over the forest and over the erotic impulse, in much the same way that the "tale" of "Fish in Air" was designed to tame lesbian desire. Out of frustration, the speaker in "Berm" offers the path of a deer trail in opposition to the straight-line bushwhacking of a forestry agent who is measuring off land for a timber sale. In her anger she would like to leave him behind forever.

Anderson, however, in "Reclaiming Slashburns," informs the reader that marking timber for sale is not nearly as painful as clearing the land for commercial tree farms. With bitter irony, she contrasts the work of the slashburn crew with popular culture's idealized image of pristine forests in *The Sound of Music*. Where theater and television audiences see the singing family hiking through unspoiled mountain vistas, Anderson images the reality of clear-cutting and subsequent tree farming that not only destroys the mountains and their forests but also poisons women and children downstream: "Pre-replanting, these chemicals leached / down into the water / where women drank and bred / and miscarried" (40). Invoking Isis and edelweiss in opposition to the film's von Trapp mythos and the trap of commercialism, the poem's speaker sings of her own "entrapment" in the "understory" of our mountains and forests. The "understory" here is both literal and metaphoric; the former in terms of the slash that is being burned off, left behind from the clear-cutting, and the latter in terms of the subversive critique that Anderson writes in opposition to our cultural illusions and corporate disinformation. As Legler observes, this entire section "echoes work done by Susan Griffin in *Woman and Nature*, where Griffin juxtaposes scientific and institutional language with the language of desire and the language of women's spirituality" (192). By placing such discourses on equal terms, Anderson validates the gender inflection and alterity of vision that can be heard in women's speaking, particularly in regard to revisioning the nature-gender-culture interrelationships.

This more general critique of the forest industry in the context of American popular culture prepares the way for the poems in the third section of *Cultivating Excess*, "Civilculture." The first poem, "If This Quilt of Names Were Made of Fire," initiates an attention to AIDS that is carried on throughout the section. This poem is not just about mourning but, like the previous sections, emphasizes action and transformation: "Navigation / charted, as always, by the shape-changers" (57). From an ecological perspective, "You Better Remember Your Own Immunization" provides the most powerful poetic expression of the interconnections between cultural perceptions and conceptions of nature and the disastrously wrongheaded depiction of nature as something out there beyond the human, rather than a process and system throughout the human body within the world body. Through this poem, Anderson traces the history of the post–World War II belief in immunizations and immunity from the illnesses of the world (as a casual review of newspapers reveals, all kinds of diseases thought conquered are returning and various new superviruses have been born from their allegedly eradicated ancestors) through the collateral belief in "antibiotics," food "additives," "herbicides," and "pesticides." Anderson uses the cultural mythos of cold war immunization as a warning against those who imagine that they are "immune" if they are not homosexuals or drug addicts, who imagine that AIDS is the only new plague on its way.

From "Fish in Air" through "You Better Remember Your Own Immunization," Anderson links the chemicals in the forests to the chemicals in our water, food, and bodies. She relates these to cultural preconceptions and misconceptions that define as *scientific,* and therefore progressive, the domination of nature, and as *unnatural,* and therefore perverse, desires that unleash feelings of identification and connection, reciprocity and renewal, between human beings and between human and other beings of the world.

In a sense, Anderson promotes a journey into excess to get out of commercial monocultural cultivation. In contrast, Nora Naranjo-Morse promotes cultivation, but of a very different kind. Naranjo Morse celebrates the cultivation of inhabitation, which is an act of spiritual and psychological survival. Such cultivation is necessary for cultural evolution, which peoples must undertake each generation to remain viable societies. Many southwestern writers of various ethnicities are today engaged in this cultivation of inhabitation. As I argued in considering Pat Mora's *Nepantla,* cultural diversity should be understood as a form of biological diversity. It should also be recognized as a component of human evolution in terms of the interactive dynamics of somatic change generating genetic change. As Gregory Cajete explains it, "Our physical make-up and the nature of our psyche are formed in direct ways by the distinct climate, soil, geography, and living things of a place" (84).

The tradition of American nature writing as it has been codified to date remains too much a monocultural monologue about the right ways to relate to nature from an already alienated position. Such alienation is reinforced particularly in its emphasis on going out to wilderness areas to experience "nature" through recreational activities or on observing seasonal cycles rather than, say, working on a local farm or feeding oneself through organic gardening—to participate and always, unavoidably, to intervene. This tradition has failed to enter into dialogue with natural diversity as manifested in the plurality of human cultures and represented in the art and literature of native writers and artists, such as the Pueblo sculptor-poet Nora Naranjo-Morse.

Naranjo-Morse's *Mud Woman: Poems from the Clay* opens with a preface that intertwines environment, culture, and art. The environment, "veins of colored earth run along the hillsides of New Mexico," gives rise to a history of integration with that place: "For hundreds of years Pueblo people have treasured their powerful relationship with clay" (9). Without the clay there would be no pueblos. As Naranjo-Morse notes, "subtle lessons from Clay Mother awaken my appreciation for daily rituals, connecting me to the Pueblo worldview" (10). The clay is neither a possession for proprietary claim nor located in a secret place so that it may be hoarded. Rather, it is part of the community, and community is reaffirmed through a relationship with it: "Even today, when a vein is located and uncovered, a prayer is offered to Nan chu Kweejo (Clay Mother), acknowledging her generous gifts to us. . . . This prayer continually renews our relationship to the earth, her gifts, and Towa [people]" (9).[8]

Naranjo-Morse's beginning her sentence with "Even today" points out that maintaining these rituals and continuing the Pueblo worldview involve a complex process of engaging and resisting the mainstream American culture in which the Towa survive and struggle to flourish. Typical of many remarks about Native American languages is the observation that "in the Tewa language, there is no word for art. There is, however, the concept for an artful life, filled with inspiration and fueled by labor and thoughtful approach" (15). While a sculpture might become a commodity, art is not a profession, or an individual career, but part of a community practice of inhabitation. The artful life is set within the inhabitory framework and unfolds in relation to it, both through received inspiration and through the cultural continuity expressed by means of artistic representation. Yet the pressures of the dominant society's values work against this community spirit and attempt to introduce and idealize individualism even in collectively evolved artistic expression.

While objects for sale may be made, it is questionable whether art can be practiced under such pressure, because the conditions and relations of production within the dominant society contradict the worldview behind the artistry, which is spiritual, communal, and ecological. As Naranjo-Morse believes, "Plant, animal and human life cycles, nurtured and guarded, are held equally in a larger vessel called earth. The symmetry of earth's vessel depends on our respect for earth's balance and our caretaking of these cycles. Gathering this knowledge as I do clay, I am impressed by the spiritual strength of these lessons" (10).

Mud Woman is organized into four sections: "Mud Woman," "Wandering Pueblo Woman," "Pearlene and Friends," and "Home." In the first section the author establishes herself as an artist, which means becoming "Mud Woman" as a result of her immersion in the earth that inspires her creativity: "This earth / I have become a part of, / that also I have grown out of" (24). Naranjo-Morse lives reciprocity. But by the fifth poem, the world of art has become complicated by the marketplace. Even so, at the end of the day in front of the museum wall, what counts is not the tally of the sales made but the relationships established between Mud Woman and the sculptors, jewelers, and artists from other pueblos and peoples. Such relationships help sustain her through the next few poems as the sculptor runs the gamut of the white-dominated art marketplace and loses her "innocence."

The "Wandering Pueblo Woman" section begins with a poem about how "Mud Woman" will return home after she has assimilated various urban sights for future art. The next poem focuses not on the individual but on the history of her people before "change disrupted night's mystery" and they lived "equal in symmetry." And it ends with the evocation of a tribal birthright. This birthright reassures the wandering woman in the next poem titled "Two Worlds" that even far away in Hawaii she is "a brown woman / who will always be a Towa" (50). Yet, Naranjo-Morse closes this section with the poem "Sometimes I Am a Sponge," in which she stakes out her place as a particular kind of Towa, a "Tse va ho, / someone not afraid to stare" (54), the kind of artist needed to represent the complex realities of these unnatural times.

The "Pearlene and Her Friends" section addresses the generation gap, if you will, in the Santa Clara Pueblo between more traditional "Tewa matriarchs" and modern young women. Here Naranjo-Morse, with poems about Pearlene, Moonlight, and Coyote, suggests that the temptations of modernity and dominant popular culture are trickster manifestations, to be countered by the artist as trickster and tribal matriarchs as tradition bearers. These poems are followed by the section "Home." Its first few poems are about Mud Woman's mother and sisters, and the fourth is about home as a vessel and a relationship, built and shared "one adobe at a time." It is built from and on the clay of the earth, and will return to it, just as Mud Woman has arisen from and is made of this earth. And her place on this earth is assured her by her father, who says, "it is going well, / it goes in beauty" (106).

The volume ends with this beauty being realized in a new work of art, a fired bowl, created within the tradition but also rendered fortuitously as a variation of it. The bowl becomes proof that the ancient art remains alive, nourishing and replenishing, rather than being a dead or sterile imitation of a lost past. This "old, new medicine bowl," like Mud Woman, inhabits the present even as, and as a representation of, the Pueblo worldview inhabits the present in a particular place and with a specific balance and continuity that needs to be artfully realized.

Greta Gaard makes the point in "Ecofeminism and Native American Cultures" that "Ecofeminism and Native American cultures have many values in common. To avoid cultural imperialism, however, ecofeminists must resist the urge to import 'convenient' pieces of Native American cultures, Middle Eastern cultures, or any other cultures to construct a mosaic of theories from varying cultural sources. Such a theory would lack the regard for context that is the common goal of all authentically feminist theories" (309–10). With such a warning in mind, one must first admit that Naranjo-Morse describes a particular interdependent relationship of life, art, and place, through the clay of soil, home, and pottery that is rarely experienced in the United States today, whether in terms of food, shelter, or usable art. And that non-Tewa people may buy both poetry and pottery, yet remain outsiders. But being outsiders does not necessarily require being alien or other to Naranjo-Morse's philosophy, aesthetics, and life. There remains the possibility of being another, but how is that to be accomplished? Not by imitation, as Naranjo-Morse indicates, since one must be born into the world that she inhabits. Imitation would only generate sterility and a parody of the attempt to renew viable cultural practices, since only the shallowness of the roots of the imitators would be revealed. Then by emulation and parallel practice one may come into a similar sensibility.

How do people experience an organic relationship with their habitats and theorize the significance of such relationships? Who sees images of the Exxon Valdez oil spill when looking at another layer of vinyl siding thinly covering the wood siding that sustained a house for one hundred years? Who sees the flooding of the First Nation Canadian lands of James Bay for hydroelectric power when they flip a light switch in New York City? Activists of various orientations have taken significant steps to define and theorize the dietary practices of the United States to bring factory farming and food processing before the eyes of consumers as they stroll the supermarket aisles, whether it be from the feminist-vegetarian position enunciated by Carol Adams or the organic cattle raising perspective of Linda Hasselstrom. Yet the true costs and the actual natural sources of the fabric of houses and apartments, transportation, and energy continue to go largely unnoticed. Often individuals are presented with the abstract data on such consumption, but rarely is it posed in terms of the alteration and destruction of the habitat of other beings, human and nonhuman. How many of Naranjo-Morse's readers can name the materials that constitute the vessel of their homes and visualize their pre-processed states? And how little of it comes from their own locale? Every new two-by-four I have purchased in the past year came from Canada. As ecofeminism continues to expand its articulations of the interdependencies of the molecular and energy pathways of daily lives on this planet, its practitioners need to learn from

Naranjo-Morse and others like her how to depict and image these lineations with the elegance and balance expected of a well-crafted poem, of an aesthetically rendered serving bowl, of a formula in physics, of the touch of a lover's hand. Let me suggest, then, that Naranjo-Morse's art, which reminds her readers of the role of story in the continuity of culture, indicates that, just as spirituality is realized in ritual, theory needs to be realized in symbol and image. That is one of the roles that the literature I have discussed here, and all the other texts deserving attention that I could not cover, can teach about extending ecofeminist theory and the ecofeminist movement.

More Work to Be Done

With the many trends in ecofeminist literary theory and its application, critics often compare its development to that of feminist literary theory and criticism. First, feminist critics reread canonical works and criticized their gender bias. Second, in extending that criticism to the entire canon, they began to recover suppressed, neglected, and lost works by women writers. Third, they began to criticize the representations of women and to uncover feminist themes in works by women. Ecofeminism, then, has come into literary criticism as the influence and continuation of an activist movement. As a result, the recovery of works by women demonstrating ecological sensibilities and proto-ecofeminist and ecofeminist themes has been, and continues to be, given high priority, particularly in women's studies and women's literature courses. Along with this has come intense debate about the degrees to which some of these recovered authors—Rachel Carson, Willa Cather, and Charlotte Perkins Gilman—are feminist or ecological or ecological feminist. Works by men that had been held up as candidates for the nature writing canon, such as Thoreau, Emerson, and Edward Abbey, have also received ecofeminist critical attention.

An area yet to be studied in depth is the degree to which contemporary male environmental writers, who have had the opportunity to learn about ecofeminism as a consciously articulated movement, are beginning to integrate ecofeminist theory and practice into their creative works, as well as responding negatively to ecofeminism. In which category, for instance, would one place Tom Robbins's *Even Cowgirls Get the Blues*? This task may very well need to be the particular responsibility of male ecofeminist critics. I would think that in such work we would especially be looking for the depiction of prominent female characters who act as speaking subjects for women's consciousness and alterity and display both the awareness and the action upon which ecofeminism is based as a movement, rather than merely a philosophy. How then, for example, would I react to, and account for, Wendell Berry's insistent romanticized, traditional depictions of farm women in his fiction? And what would I or others make of the ecologically devastated landscapes and totally artificial environments in cyberpunk fiction by male and female writers alongside of their frequent depictions of strong, independent female characters? In other words, we would need to be asking whether or not the male authors have been listening to the women who are speaking and reflecting those voices in their own work, even as we continue to promote the women who are speaking and encourage other women to give voice through literature to their beliefs and values.

More narrowly, but nevertheless as part of the transformative goals of ecofeminism, critics need to demonstrate, as feminist theory and criticism in general have done, that ecofeminist literary criticism is a necessary component of literary studies. And such critics need to develop further an understanding, and display it through critical practice, that a multicultural ecofeminist literary criticism brings the nonhuman actors and characters into prominence alongside the human ones from every ethnicity and nationality.

Notes

The title of this essay comes from Ursula K. Le Guin's quoting of Linda Hogan's poem, "The Women Are Speaking" in "Woman/Wilderness," a talk Le Guin gave at the University of California at Davis in 1986 and published in *Dancing at the Edge of the World,* 161–64.

1. For a more developed discussion of Mora's ideas and their relationships to her poetry, see my essay "Conserving Natural and Cultural Diversity," upon which the remarks here are based.

2. I use *ecoregional* here as the adjective form of *ecoregion,* as defined by such geographers as Robert G. Bailey, emphasizing climate and vegetation, in his *Description of the Ecoregions of the United States.* The use of *ecoregional* rather than *bioregional* is meant to distinguish a physical phenomenon of existence, the experience of a community or people living in and across ecoregions, from the various and conflictive programs associated with bioregionalism as a political movement.

3. Mora derives her definition of *la mestiza* from Gloria Anzaldúa.

4. This discussion of *Green Fires* is based on a somewhat different and lengthier presentation in my essay "Anotherness and Inhabitation in Recent Multicultural American Literature."

5. For a theoretical discussion of the relationship of the concepts of "other" and "another," and the distinction between "objects of attention" and "mutually speaking subjects," see my first two chapters in *Literature, Nature, and Other.*

6. For overview discussions of taxonomy and orientation in criticism, see, for example, Gifford, Hay, and Lyon. For a specific example of criticism of a poet for breaking out of the meditative, observational mode, see Altieri.

7. The following interpretation of "Fish in Air" is the result of a collaboration with Greta Gaard and is in part based on the ideas represented in her "Toward a Queer Ecofeminism."

8. *Towa* is the word for "people" in the Tewa language. The Tewa is a tribe of the Santa Clara Pueblo. Naranjo-Morse's use of *Towa* emphasizes a sense of community, while her use of *Tewa* emphasizes formal tribal affiliation and lineage.

Works Cited

Adams, Carol J. *The Sexual Politics of Meat: A Feminist-Vegetarian Critical Thoery.* New York: Continuum, 1990.

Altieri, Charles. "Gary Snyder's *Turtle Island:* The Problem of Reconciling the Roles of Seer and Prophet." *boundary 2* 4.3 (1976): 761–77.

Anderson, Lori. *Cultivating Excess.* Portland: Eighth Mountain Press, 1992.

Anzaldúa, Gloria. *Borderlands/La Frontera: The New Mestiza.* San Francisco: Spinsters/Aunt Lute Books, 1987.

Bailey, Robert G. *Description of the Ecoregions of the United States.* 2d ed. Misc. Pub. 1391. Washington, D.C.: USDA, 1995.

Brox, Jane. *Here and Nowhere Else: Late Seasons of a Farm and Its Family.* Boston: Beacon Press, 1995.

Cajete, Gregory. *Look to the Mountain: An Ecology of Indigenous Education.* Durango: Kivakí Press, 1994.

Escamill, Edna. *Daughter of the Mountain: Un Cuento.* San Francisco: Aunt Lute Books, 1991.

Gaard, Greta. "Ecofeminism and Native American Cultures: Pushing the Limits of Cultural Imperialism?" *Ecofeminism: Women, Animals, Nature.* Ed. Greta Gaard. Philadelphia: Temple University Press, 1993. 295–314.

———. "Toward a Queer Ecofeminism." *Hypatia* 12.1 (Winter 1997): 114–37.

Gifford, Terry. "The Social Construction of Nature." *Green Voices.* London: Manchester University Press, 1995. 1–25.

Hasselstrom, Linda. *Going over East: Reflections of a Woman Rancher.* Golden: Fulcrum Publishing, 1987.

Hay, John. "The Nature Writer's Dilemma." *On Nature.* Ed. Daniel Halpern. San Francisco: North Point, 1987. 7–10.

Hogan, Linda. "The Women Are Speaking." *That's What She Said: Contemporary Poetry and Fiction by Native American Women.* Ed. Rayna Green. Bloomington: Indiana University Press, 1984. 172.

King, Ynestra. "Toward an Ecological Feminism and a Feminist Ecology." *Machina Ex Dea: Feminist Perspectives on Technology.* Ed. Joan Rothschild. New York: Pergamon Press, 1983. 118–29.

Legler, Gretchen. Rev. of *Cultivating Excess,* by Lori Anderson. *ISLE: Interdisciplinary Studies in Literature and Environment* 1.1 (1993): 190–92.

Le Guin, Ursula K. *Dancing at the Edge of the World: Thoughts on Words, Women, Places.* 1989. New York: Harper Perennial, 1990.

Lyon, Thomas J. "A History." *This Incomperable Lande: A Book of American Nature Writing.* Ed. Thomas J. Lyon. New York: Penguin, 1991. 3–91.

Mora, Pat. *Nepantla: Essays from the Land in the Middle.* Albuquerque: University of New Mexico Press, 1993.

Mueller, Marnie. *Green Fires: Assault on Eden: A Novel of the Ecuadorian Rainforest.* Willimantic: Curbstone Press, 1994.

Murphy, Patrick D. "Anotherness and Inhabitation in Recent Multicultural American Literature." *Writing the Environment: Ecocriticism and Literature.* Ed. Richard Kerridge and Neil Sammels. London: Zed Books, 1998. 40–52.

———. "Conserving Natural and Cultural Diversity: The Prose and Poetry of Pat Mora." *MELUS* 21.1 (1996): 59–69.

———. *Literature, Nature, and Other: Ecofeminist Critiques.* Albany: State University of New York Press, 1995.

Naranjo-Morse, Nora. *Mud Woman: Poems from the Clay.* Tucson: University of Arizona Press, 1992.

Owens, Louis. "'The Song Is Very Short': Native American Literature and Literary Theory." *Weber Studies* 12.3 (1995): 51–62.

Salleh, Ariel. "Second Thoughts on *Rethinking Ecofeminist Politics:* A Dialectical Critique." *ISLE: Interdisciplinary Studies in Literature and Environment* 1.2 (1993): 93–106.

Tisdale, Sallie. *Stepping Westward: The Long Search for Home in the Pacific Northwest.* New York: Henry Holt, 1991.

Vance, Linda. "Ecofeminism and the Politics of Reality." *Ecofeminism: Women, Animals, Nature.* Ed. Greta Gaard. Philadelphia: Temple University Press, 1993. 118–45.

Walker, Alice. *In Search of Our Mother's Gardens.* New York: Harcourt Brace Jovanovich, 1983.

Warren, Karen J. "Feminism and Ecology: Making Connections." *Environmental Ethics* 9.1 (1987): 3–20.

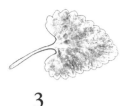

3

Toward an Ecofeminist Standpoint Theory: Bodies as Grounds

Deborah Slicer

IN THIS ESSAY I want to give some sustained attention to the related notions that "women are closer to nature than men" and that, by virtue of that alleged special relationship, women have some privileged insights into our environmental morass or at least sensibilities that are more respectful of nonhuman life. Ecofeminism is identified with these ideas more than with any others; ecofeminism is condemned more often for allegedly holding these ideas than for anything else. Yes, I know, they are a little problematic. But what do these claims mean? Are they in the least plausible? What are the implications of these claims for ecofeminism, for feminism, for environmentalism?

In their most lucid formulations I think these statements mean that it is possible for some women to achieve a certain epistemological *standpoint* vis-à-vis nonhuman life and our environmental crisis. This is still a mouthful, I realize. What women? Is the idea of a standpoint coherent? "A" standpoint? Is the idea of an ecofeminist standpoint politically useful to feminism? Which environmental crisis? Why women and not men (*no* men?)? These are some of the issues that need sorting out to transform this assertion into a working thesis. In the interest of space and my readers' endurance, I will work in more depth with some of these topics than with others.

First, I want to review some recent scholarly debates around feminist standpoint theory, a highly contentious idea in itself. I think that the ecofeminist claim acquires more content, and, in my view, plausibility, once informed by this enormously rich literature, which spans fifteen years of feminist scholarship.[1] Then, I will look at what various ecofeminists have said about women's association with nature and about standpoint. I devote some considerable space to quoting these writers because I want ecofeminists credited or faulted for what they have actually said rather than for what the unread have said about them. In this section, I will look critically at the idea of an ecofeminist standpoint and give some qualified support to the idea. And, last, I will try to articulate a position that I think some Western women in industrialized countries can occupy, and to a significant extent have occupied, that is epistemologically rich, as well as controversial. I argue that bodies may serve as epistemologically privileged sites vis-à-vis nature. And I refer to Judith Butler's work to structure this section theoretically. Jane Smiley's novel *A Thousand Acres* grounds my theses in particular because it is situated in women's experiences and in the sort of politically reflexive context that standpoint theorists and contemporary postmodernists alike endorse.

Standpoint

Standpoint theory is not a new or even a feminist invention. Both Hegel and Marx developed standpoint theories of human consciousness.[2]

Sandra Harding, bell hooks, Uma Narayan (guardedly), Donna Haraway, and Patricia Hill Collins have published defenses of standpoint theories.[3] As Uma Narayan puts it: "The claim of 'epistemic privilege' amounts to claiming that members of an oppressed group have a more immediate, subtle and critical knowledge about the nature of their oppressions than people who are nonmembers of the oppressed group" (35). Sometimes a standpoint theorist will claim that marginalized individuals have a more subtle and critical insight into not only their own immediate situation but also the marginalization of members of other "out" groups and the power dynamics of politics more generally. Some standpoint theorists, such as Sandra Harding and Uma Narayan, point out a difference between an individual knowing that she is oppressed and understanding the daily dynamics of such oppression and having a critical understanding of the causes and institutional dynamics of that oppression. Narayan and Collins will say that knowledge of the former type constitutes a standpoint, while Harding may restrict the definition to the latter type. Narayan also says that epistemic privilege does not mean such knowledge is incommensurable. Outsiders, with sincere and sustained effort, can come to understand the experiences of the epistemologically privileged individual. And privileged knowledge is not incorrigible, she says ("Working Together" 37).

Various standpoint theorists have argued different grounds, starting places, for standpoint theory. Harding summarizes these nicely in *Whose Science? Whose Knowledge?* while Collins uses several of them to articulate an African-American woman's standpoint. Several of these grounds or starting places are by now familiar to anyone at all read in feminist philosophy of science or feminist epistemology more generally, in feminist ethics, and in literature by many marginalized women. Some of these grounds are specific to gender, as in grounds put forward by object-relations theory, for example. Other grounds may be occupied by individuals who stand in other or in multiple positions at once, e.g., race, class, gender, sexuality. Grounds most frequently cited by feminist standpoint theorists and by ecofeminists include positions as "outsiders within" dominant institutions; positions that mediate nature-culture dualisms, usually through work; positions in the "fault-line," which result in a discrepancy between an individual's experiences and the dominant accounts of those experiences; positions as keepers of bodies, a particularly Marxist view that argues causal connections between work and consciousness; and positions that require subordinated individuals to invest in learning the dominant culture to survive and, it is to be hoped, to resist.[4]

For some critics, standpoint theory is unacceptably enmeshed in the essentialist and idealizing tendencies of cultural feminism. Other critics say that standpoint theory substitutes one authoritative vantage point or "Truth" with another equally hegemonic "Truth" that is "Woman's." And others find the theory too chummy with varieties of postmodernism and antifoundationalism that are politically paralyzing. It is a strange hybrid that provokes all of these responses at once.

Feminist resistance to standpoint theory seems inconsistent when feminist theory offers itself, to a significant degree, as an alternative to dominant theories of ontology, epistemology, social relations, and values, as an alternative that is more compelling because it originates in the experiences of those who are often mistheorized about and have been traditionally barred from authorial cites of theorizing.[5] And most white, heterosexual feminists in academic positions of power have at least acknowledged, if not acted on, the necessity of marginalized women generating theory from their own standpoints and the critical insights that these women have brought to bear on the feminist misuse of power inside and outside the academy. While the scope of theorizing gender has become restricted and gender theorizing has been greatly enriched by race, class, sexuality, and other variables, many feminists do continue to do theory, or at least to seek strategies for doing theory, because we believe that our theories address glaring blind spots in the dominant ontological, epistemological, and normative frameworks. Sandra Harding's idea of "strong objectivity" addresses some criticisms that standpoint theory is another totalizing, Enlightenment project *and* addresses concerns that standpoint theory lacks legitimizing criteria to decide between competing judgments or standpoints themselves.[6] The idea of "strong objectivity" is reflexive and indebted to postmodernism. Reflexivity requires the knower to put herself on the same plane as her subject matter in examining her social location as a knower and to do so at all stages of her investigation, not just at the justification stage, which is where most traditional empiricists weed out biases. A significant feature of the reflexive process is a radical critique of race, class, sexuality, and gender biases and a check on colonialist impulses. Conventional, "weak" objectivists are not properly reflexive. In particular, they do not employ radical social critiques in their investigations and they do not imaginatively critique their projects from the perspectives of various excluded others. Nor do they usually start their inquiries from the experiences of these outsiders, as standpoint theorists do. Thus, their results suffer from undetected biases that distort due to overly subjective influences. Harding argues throughout the book that we can sort false from "less false" beliefs. We do this not by using transcendental, ahistorical criteria but by being reflexive (strongly objective) and by starting from the lives of outsiders to generate knowledge that is, if nothing else, less partial and distorted than the experiences of those insiders who have little incentive to construct a bigger picture and very limited experience from which to draw, to cite just one example (Harding, *Whose Science?* 157, 159, 185).

The authorizing communities that Harding proposes are politically self-critical, collaboratively and compassionately in dialogue with each other, and, unlike empiricist authorizing projects, even feminist ones, these communities view reflexivity as a permanent resource, and not a "perpetual problem," in the process of values identification, as distinct from pursuing value neutrality, which is a myth, according to Harding ("Rethinking").

Ecofeminist Standpoints

Not every ecofeminist has had something to say about standpoint; in fact, contrary to many accounts of ecofeminism, many ecofeminists have had nothing to say about it. Some ecofeminists are even quite clear in their aversion to such an idea (Griscom; Roach; Davion). In the following, I work selectively from materials that are well known, that are fairly recent, and that make some claims relevant to standpoint theory. I do not want to imply that each of the ecofeminists I cite considered what they wrote a fully developed thesis.

Some of this ecofeminist work is overtly essentialist and biologistic, most is not.[7] Recently, ecofeminists have become considerably more self-conscious and careful about the standpoint claims they make. For example, Ariel Salleh, who, in 1984, wrote a distinctively biologistic sounding piece, wrote in 1992:

> It is nonsense to assume that women are any closer to nature than men. The point
> is that women's reproductive labor and such patriarchically assigned work roles as

cooking and cleaning bridge men and nature in a very obvious way, and one that is denigrated by patriarchal culture. Mining or engineering work similarly is a transaction with nature. The difference is that this work comes to be mediated by a language of domination that ideologically reinforces masculine identity as powerful, aggressive, and separate over and above nature. The language that typifies a woman's experience, in contrast, situates her along with nature itself. She is seen, and accordingly sees herself, as somehow part of it. Although men and women both wear historically manufactured identities, in times of ecological devastation, the feminine one is clearly the more wholesome human attitude. ("Debate" 208–9)[8]

In this passage Salleh claims that the work a person does significantly shapes the way she thinks, her "orientation to the world" and to self, as Salleh puts it, and that this orientation may be more or less materially aware, dualistic, use-oriented. Salleh also says that it is the "feminine" social identity that is more eco-friendly and the "masculine" identity that is less friendly. This is not to essentialize biological men or women, although she may romanticize the feminine. Harding and Collins discuss this materialist view, a Marxist hybrid, as grounds for a standpoint.

The philosophers Karen J. Warren and Jim Cheney have written: "As a methodological and epistemological stance, all ecofeminists centralize, in one way or another, the 'voices' and experiences of women (and others) with regard to an understanding of the nonhuman world. . . . Centralizing women's voices is important methodologically and epistemologically to the overall critique and revisioning of the concept of nature and the moral dimensions of human-nature relationships" (186). Warren and Cheney are not specific on why we should privilege women's voices as we do environmental philosophy. Cheney implies in other essays that he believes women's and other outsiders' ontological orientations mediate dualisms, are "care" oriented, and thus stand in unique critical positions vis-à-vis our dominant conceptual frameworks ("Eco-feminism"). And elsewhere Warren seems particularly concerned that outsiders, whose perspectives have been neglected in theory-making, be heard ("Power").

Val Plumwood, an Australian philosopher with a long-standing history in environmental philosophy, says that "the argument that women have a different relation to nature need not rest on either reversal [idealization] or 'essentialism', the appeal to a quality of empathy or mysterious power shared by all women and inherent in women's biology. Such differences may instead be seen as due to women's different social and historical position . . . . To the extent that women's lives have been lived in ways which are less directly oppositional to nature than those of men, and have involved different, and less oppositional practices, qualities of care and kinds of selfhood, an ecological feminist position could and should privilege some of the experiences and practices of women over those of men as a source of change without being committed to any form of naturalism" (35). Later she says that "because of their [women's] placement in the sphere of nature and exclusion from an oppositional culture, what women have to contribute to this process [breaking down dualistic culture] may be especially significant. Their life-choices and historical positioning often compel a deeper discomfort with dualistic structures and foster a deeper questioning of dualised culture" (36–37). Plumwood may imply here that because women are identified as part of nature, rather than as discontinuous with nature, and are assigned work that serves and is immersed in material life, women's self-identities and ontological orientations are more continuous with nature and thus serve as helpful starting points in rethinking certain predominant ontological and social assumptions.

In particular, Plumwood is insistent throughout her book that we rethink certain interrelated categories, including and especially "nature," "culture," "man," "woman," and "human," so that men and women are seen as both "continuous with, not alien from, nature" (36). Plumwood's brilliant account of how the "discontinuous" masculine self employs "instrumental" reason, a distinguishing "human" ability, to extract use value from a feminized nature and naturalized feminine human beings advances this argument. The way to untangle this construction is not to deny women's continuity with nature or to embrace it uncritically but to make these categories more permeable— women create culture, too, and culture is not radically discontinuous with nature—and to think carefully about the normative standards that fall out of these radically different socially constructed ontologies. And women, some women anyway, will play a central role as critics and constructionists.

Plumwood's critical analysis is one of the finest pieces of ecofeminist theory around, to my mind. But her accounts of standpoint, while clearer than many, are still underdeveloped. How is it that women have been excluded from oppositional culture? What "life choices" compel a "deeper discomfort with dualistic structures and foster a deeper questioning"? How have women's lives been "less directly oppositional to nature"? What "qualities of care and kinds of selfhood" privilege women's experiences? *What* women is she talking about?

The Indian physicist and social critic Vandana Shiva is quite specific in precisely the areas where Plumwood is vague. Shiva privileges "Third World" women in subsistence economies who are struggling against First World "development/maldevelopment" projects to keep their communities and cultures intact:

> In contemporary times, Third World women, whose minds have not yet been dispossessed or colonized, are in a privileged position to make visible the invisible

oppositional categories that they are the custodians of. It is not only as victims, but also as leaders in creating new intellectual ecological paradigms, that women are central to arresting and overcoming ecological crises. Just as ecological recovery begins from centers of natural diversity which are gene pools, Third World women, and those tribals and peasants who have been left out of the processes of maldevelopment, are today acting as the intellectual gene pools of ecological categories of thought and action. Marginalisation has thus become a source for healing the diseased mainstream of patriarchal development. Those facing the biggest threat offer the best promise for survival because they have two kinds of knowledge that are not accessible to dominant and privileged groups. First, they have the knowledge of what it means to be the victims of progress, to be the ones who bear the costs and burdens. Second, they have the holistic and ecological knowledge of what the production and protection of life is about. (46–47)

Several of Shiva's points are worth highlighting. First, the women she talks about are rural village agriculturalists, the repositories of millennia of agricultural skills and knowledge. Second, although agriculture had traditionally been women's work, men, too, had participated and have had such knowledge of nature. Unfortunately, many rural men have had to take up employment in cities and have thus lost such knowledge. Third, Shiva is talking about women who have not been colonized by Westerners. Western and non-Western women who have been colonized into Western dualistic, reductive, mechanistic conceptual frameworks will not have a privileged standpoint. Fourth, the women she privileges, epistemically, have been economically, socially, and politically victimized by Western attempts to displace them as agricultural experts, but they are not merely victims. Hers is a "post-victimology" study, as Shiva puts it (47). One final critical, and somewhat tricky, point is that the women Shiva privileges embody what she calls the "feminine principle," a nongendered, traditional principle of creative, life-giving power. These women do not essentially or exclusively embody this traditional Hindu force. They are not essentially or exclusively "closer to nature than men." Men may participate in the principle and colonized women may lose touch with it. Shiva's rural women have kept it alive as resisters and as agriculturalists, working cooperatively with the land to sustain ecological, including human, health.

Shiva attributes a standpoint to women who occupy several of the positions that Collins and Harding discuss as "grounds" for standpoint. Shiva's rural women are involved as outsiders and as critics in a struggle against institutions that threaten their traditional social and economic status, against institutions that they cannot afford to be ignorant of if they are to ward off economic imperialization and cultural colonization. They work daily in participation, as they see it, with the land to provide physical sustenance for their families. Their work mediates traditional Western dualisms, and their ontological and normative orientations to the land situate them in "the line of fault" when Western interests introduce dualistic ontologies and technologies in their villages.

Shiva's *Staying Alive* is as local, detailed, and concrete an account of violence against women and nature—of the fields, the forests, the water, the animals—and of resistance as any I know of. Shiva, like Patricia Hill Collins, defends standpoint theory and starts with a local group of marginalized voices in theorizing a standpoint—and in Shiva's case, an ecofeminist standpoint. This standpoint looks critically at both the Western and the Indian associations of women and nature, and it theorizes an alternative that collapses many Western dualisms. It rejects Western ontological conceptions of nature, women, non-European races, and the poor as all "nature." And it proposes a different normative attitude toward women, animals, and the land.

Still, Shiva's analysis is not without its problems. Specifically, gender is not deconstructed or contextualized in Indian culture(s). That is, gender is still a category of some ambiguous but politically suspicious power in this text. And the physically demanding lives of these rural women may be romanticized in some problematic ways. Shiva's account could be more reflexive, in Harding's sense. Despite all of this, I find her standpoint account more compelling than any other in ecofeminist literature. These women may well have a particular critical standpoint on Western ontology, epistemology, and values because of their positions as outsiders and as resisters vis-à-vis Western encroachment. To various degrees some Western women occupy similar positions as outsiders and resisters. But another significant position that Shiva's women occupy is that of members of a non-Western culture with its own nondualized ontological and value framework. They also have intimate knowledge of the land, a knowledge that the vast majority of Western women, living in industrialized societies, do not have. Given that two of these three key positions are currently unoccupied by most Western women, can we still make a case that they have or can achieve a standpoint vis-à-vis nature?

I do not see any widespread tendency among Western women to problematize the interrelated social categories of "woman" and "nature" in any *interesting* ways. Both Harding and Hartsock stress that a standpoint is an "achievement," a critical point of view that is the product of some significant struggle with the dominant, hegemonic conceptual framework. We should be extremely cautious with claims like Salleh's, and perhaps Plumwood's, that women, by virtue of their enforced attention to material life—as mothers, tenders to the sick, cooks, and housekeepers—have some standpoint vis-à-vis nature. Often mothers, nurses, and housekeepers see "nature"—their children's "uncivilized" behaviors and dirty bodies, pathogens and the body's decay, spiders and cobwebs and mud in the kitchen—as the "enemy," as impediments to a "civilized" house. And few Western women appear to regret the slaughter of, or even give thanks to, the animals whose flesh they pull out of the bloody supermarket wrapper and transform into food "fit" for the dinner table.

But, Harding might say, thought that is significantly attentive to material life may be a good place in which to ground a standpoint, or she may say that those who are socially identified as "other," as part of "nature," may have valuable insights into the lives of those, including nonhumans, so designated. Such insights, however, may not have the outcome that most ecofeminists anticipate or desire. In fact, many feminists' critical response to the culture's association of women and nature is, rightly, to reject the essentialist conception of women as "other," outsider, and, more specifically, as body, passive matter, and keeper of bodies but also, unfortunately, to assert other essentialist-sounding claims to the effect that "woman" is ontologically situated in "culture" and is thus fully "human" and entitled to the full spectrum of human privileges, including anthropocentric ones. I agree with Plumwood and Karen Warren, who would say that such critiques have not gone far enough. What we have is a critique of the politics of gender, or genders, but not a thoroughgoing critique of our "dualised conception of human identity," nor have we attempted to "develop an alternative culture which recognizes *human* identity as continuous with, not alien from, nature," as Plumwood puts it (36; see also Warren "Feminism"). We would not have an ecofeminist standpoint, in other words.[9] While it may be fruitful to look at women's perspectives as material caregivers and at our identities as materialized/naturalized "others" to initiate standpoint theorizing, I want to suggest a third starting place, our bodies.

Bodies as Grounds

The "body" is a contested area in both ordinary life and in recent feminist literature: the body as social "text," the body "in the grip," the performative body, the "outlaw" body.

The most recent feminist attempts to de-essentialize and de-naturalize woman as body and the meaning of the "body" have come down emphatically in favor of the social body, in favor of a body that is always mediated by social constructs, that can be read off like other social texts, that is neither more nor less stable than any other site of social inscription and is thus a potential site of disruptive genealogical deconstruction and other destabilizing acts.

I think that such constructionist views, even some of the more radical constructionist views, like Judith Butler's, have something to say to ecofeminism. Certain features of Butler's view are translatable to ecofeminist investigations of a feminized conception of "matter" and of a materially essentialized conception of the "feminine." Butler's genealogical investigations of "sex" and of "gender" in *Gender Trouble* and in *Bodies That Matter* and her deconstruction of Foucault's, Lacan's, Wittig's, and Kristeva's investigations quite effectively destabilize our and their foundationalist—essentialist, static, materially pure—notions of "matter," or at least of "sex."

In *Bodies That Matter*, Butler tells us that she is not a constructionist, or at least not your usual constructionist who insists that everything is discursively constructed. Unlike that variety of constructionist, Butler argues that "there is an 'outside' to what is constructed by discourse, but this is not an absolute 'outside,' an ontological thereness that exceeds or counters the boundaries of discourse; as a constitutive 'outside' it is that which can only be thought—when it can—in relation to that discourse, at and as its most 'tenuous boundaries'" (8). I would still call this a constructionist view, a fairly radical one at that. But Butler is particularly concerned not to articulate a position that is deterministic or to have her position characterized as closing off the possibility for politics. Agency, in a qualified sense of "free," and transgression are possible when the performative body teases the very boundaries of ontological meaning and where such teasing throws those boundaries, both their limits and their possibilities, into a disquieting and disorienting light. Clearly, for Butler, as with Foucault, the body is the primary site of social coercion. For Butler, because gender is an, or possibly the, ontological signifier, and gender is bodily performance, then the body is the site of both ontological reiteration and rupture.

In *Bodies That Matter*, Butler cautions against conceiving of the body as a "site" or "surface," as I have just described the body, vis-à-vis power. Instead, she wants to "return to the notion of matter, not as site or surface, but as *a process of materialization that stabilizes over time to produce the effect of boundary, fixity, and surface we call matter*" (9). "Thus," she says, "the question is no longer, How is gender constituted as and through a certain interpretation of sex? (a question that leaves the 'matter' of sex untheorized), but rather, Through what regulatory norms is sex itself materialized? And how is it that treating the materiality of sex as a given presupposes and consolidates the normative conditions of its own emergence?" (10). I find Butler's antiessentialism, the attention that she gives to the body as both a product of regulatory control and as performatively disruptive, and, especially, her genealogy of "sex" and more recently of "matter" useful for ecofeminism. I will say more about this shortly.

Without a doubt there are aspects of Butler's work in both *Gender Trouble* and *Bodies That Matter* that are incompatible with ecofeminism. Among them, as Susan Bordo notes in her critique of *Gender Trouble*, are Butler's poststructuralist habits of crediting language with the sole power to create "reality"; the implication in some of her work that, to quote Bordo, "'biology' is ipso facto and in all contexts merely the discursive 'product' of heterosexist and sexist regimes"; and Butler's acontextual and overly optimistic treatment of the performative body's potential to subvert (291).[10] I do not see Butler backing off of linguistic foundationalism in *Bodies That Matter,* and I find that problematic. As Bordo says while contrasting Butler with Foucault, for Foucault discourse is not foundational "but is, rather, one of the many interrelated modes by which power is made manifest. Equally, if not more, important for him are the institutional and everyday *practices* by means of which our experience of the body is organized," including "the spatial and temporal organizing of schools and prisons, the 'confessional' mode between physicians and patients, teachers and students, and so forth" (292). In *Bodies That Matter,* Butler does stress that drag, the subversive performance of choice in *Gender Trouble,* is not necessarily subversive, "that drag may well be used in service of both the denaturalization and reidealization of hyperbolic heterosexual gender norms" (125). And in her chapter on the film *Paris Is Burning,* Butler contextualizes and analyzes performances that subvert and that fail to subvert, speaking, in part, to critics like Bordo, who insist on such contextualization.

My biggest concern with and also my greatest interest in Butler are related to what Bordo describes as Butler's characterization of the body as *merely* a discursive product. I find Butler's answer to such concerns intriguing for ecofeminism. Her claim is that the materiality of the body cannot be thought outside of our regulatory norms that constitute "sex": "'Sex' is, thus, not simply what one has, or a static description of what one is: it will be one of the norms by which the 'one' becomes visible at all, that which qualifies a body for life within the domain of cultural intelligibility" (2).

And, further, she says that to reassure the critic of the undeniability of materiality—of the "alleged facts of birth, aging, illness, and death," for example—is only to concede "some version of 'sex,' some formation of 'materiality.'" "Is the discourse in and through which that concession occurs—and, yes, that concession invariably does occur—not itself formative of the very phenomenon that it concedes? To claim that a discourse is formative is not to claim that it originates, causes, or exhaustively composes that which it concedes; rather, it is to claim that there is no reference to a pure body which is not at the same time a further formation of that body" (10).

Later, she repeats that she is not disputing the materiality of the body, that she wants only to "establish the normative conditions under which the materiality of the body is framed and formed, and, in particular, how it is formed through differential categories of sex" (17). To posit some stable, pure ontological status for the body is to obscure the political dynamics that construct matter. Butler is speaking quite literally here in terms of not only how categories construct perception but also how the physical itself is constructed by cultural signifiers. The body's erotically pleasurable and erotic "dead zones" are examples of such material constructions.

What this means, of course, is that there is no pure matter and, by extension, no pure bodies or, Butler states, pure nature, not even a noumenal matter, bodies, or nature in some pure nonconstructed state that underlies a constructed framework. "Sex" is culturally naturalized and so are these other "natural" phenomena. Such radical constructionist views of nature are understandably upsetting to environmentalists, including ecofeminists, who wish to view nature as something materially and epistemologically untrammeled, or else trammeled but rehabilitatable to a "pure" (natural) or near "pure" state. To insist that the body or more generally nature can somehow escape the effects of institutional power seems to me somewhat naive. Even what we call "wilderness," whether legally designated as such or simply roadless lands, is affected and in some areas significantly altered by such phenomena as acid rain, adjacent logging, human extermination of large predators, and horse traffic. And, at least internationally, conceptions of what "wilderness" is and of what it is to be used for vary, are seriously contested, and, of course, ultimately affect the physical constitution of these places.[11] To concede a constructionist view is not to give over to a radical idealism or to skepticism about the existence of physical stuff; nor does constructionism necessarily result in political nihilism. As Butler says with regard to constructionist views of the body specifically: "This unsettling of 'matter' can be understood as initiating new possibilities, new ways for bodies to matter" (*Bodies That Matter* 30).

Both deep ecologists and ecofeminists have urged that we reconceive our Western metaphysics of nature (as inert, passive matter), of what it is to be human (as ontologically distinct from nature/matter), and of the relationship between humans and nature. Butler's attempt to politicize the metaphysics of matter, in her case of the naturalized category of "sex," seems consistent with and potentially helpful to the projects of deep ecology and ecofeminism.

I do want to accentuate an underdeveloped feature of Butler's work, at least as I read it. I do not think that the physical is entirely malleable or that it has been entirely constituted by culture. More specifically, I would argue that the physical imposes certain limits to malleability *and* that the physical is a "player," has its own agency, in relation to social construction. For example, I can imagine a woman's second toe being socially fetishized as a highly erotic and thus pleasurable site. But she cannot produce sperm. And any constructionist view that says she does produce sperm has got it wrong, as we would discover if we asked her for a sample. The problem is not that the concept of a sperm-producing biological female (a mammal with ovaries, not testes) is outside the boundaries of discursive intelligibility (in fact such a person may not be so outside such boundaries, as Kessler and McKenna's research has shown). The problem is that another sort of limit, a lack, and not *necessarily* a politicized one—or, if a constructionist insists, then a conceivably, differently politicized lack—of a crude anatomical sort.

With regard to my point about agency, a student of geologic time can look at a rock and tell astounding stories of immense forces that shaped and consolidated and placed that rock where she found it, forces that both predate human existence and are beyond human control. Granted the stories that the geologist tells are human constructions; she could tell other stories, and she will readily admit as much. But these stories will almost inevitably be about certain forces that are older and bigger than human beings, that acknowledge limits, and that are properly and importantly humbling. Stories of both scientific and religious "myth" have consistently acknowledged this much. To engage in a hubris that forgets the material as player, whether we are talking about a human body or a watershed, is self-destructive, as environmentalists have been saying all along.

The yearling brown bear who pounded on my front door and then stuck her face up against my kitchen window to get a better look yesterday morning was already, and in an unfortunate way, enmeshed in human practices. She was attracted by my compost. But she was also presenting herself in clear enough terms: "I am I," curious, wanting.[12] The baseball-sized tumor that I grew on my right ovary three years ago was the product of overwork and externally generated stress, but it was also my body warning me: "Slow your butt down!" To ignore or overly enculturate the black bear in my compost, as my neighbors who are feeding her sunflower seeds are now doing, is to place the bear, and perhaps my household, in great danger. To ignore my body's speech is similarly dangerous, even deadly. We are a culture generally deaf to both our bodies and the rest of material life, deaf at an increasing cost.

Recent work by N. Katherine Hayles sharpens this point somewhat. Hayles argues what she calls a "constrained constructivism," a view that acknowledges the respective roles of bodies, social forces, and the "constraints" physical matter imposes on any epistemological effort. In addition to the social forces that constructionists usually say structure knowledge, Hayles mentions the organizing roles of the human body—"our physiology, including binocular vision, vertical posture, bilateral symmetry, apprehension of the electromagnetic spectrum we call light, and so forth"—as playing a significant role in knowledge construction (49). Frogs, hawks, cetaceans, elk, and human beings, for example, are going to bring some very different bodily orientations to what Hayles calls (sounding quite Kantian) the "flux" of the preconstructed world. In addition, certain "constraints," regularities in the preconstructed world, "enable scientific inquiry to tell us something about reality and not only about ourselves" (49).

Hayles's constructivism involves interplay, "active engagement," between the flux—the preconstructed world—and perceiving beings. The product— knowledge, reality, truth—will consist of various worlds—products of these complex interplays—that share certain consistent features that mark constraints. Hayles attributes certain limits to the epistemological malleability of nature. And these limits seem to be a function of the ontological givens of physical things that are the presorted flux. This is roughly the sort of concession I want from social constructivism—constraints that make significant sense of freedom, a bear with significant free will. With regard to the body, I would argue that the "body" is a socially and physiologically constructed ontological category through and through. But I would also argue that bodies while, partly and significantly, socially constructed ontological categories and (unlike gravity, perhaps) partly materially constructed by culture (per Butler), these constructions are also grounded in and constrained by nonconstructed physical stuff.

Butler talks about "rematerialized" bodies, the coextensiveness of materialization and power, about how "language and materiality are fully embedded in each other, chiasmic in their interdependency, but never fully collapsed into one another" (*Bodies That Matter* 69). A body comes to "be," matter, ontologically, within a discursive framework insomuch as it becomes coextensive with the framework's mechanism of power, *and* a body literally materializes under such regimes of power. And in all of this there is always physical actuality, not wholly malleable, certainly not passive. Still, as Butler says, the "irrefutability" of the physical "in no way implies what it might mean to affirm [it] and through what discursive means" (xi).

The women in the following story are attentive to bodies as both social texts and as players, interacting with and sometimes rupturing those texts. Sometimes the bodies they create and attend to are what Butler has called "abject bodies," bodies that do not "matter," that in various ways are deformed according to our ontological, qualifying standards. I think that such attention to and creativity around our bodies may constitute starting points for articulating ecofeminist standpoints, points from which we can critically and constructively theorize various of our social and environmental locations.

A Thousand Acres

Jane Smiley's *A Thousand Acres* won both the Pulitzer Prize and the National Book Award in 1991. The novel is a retelling of Shakespeare's *King Lear*. Smiley wanted to understand the story from the perspective of the patriarch's two eldest daughters, the women who seem to betray him out of some kind of unexplained, essential malice. In an interview in *Iowa Woman*, Smiley says that "in my experience, the only women I know who are as angry as these daughters are women who have suffered abuse of some kind from their parents, particularly their fathers" ("Q and A" 16). Every character in this story is economically secure, not particularly well educated, heterosexual, rural, and white, in fact painfully white in their flatness at times. Smiley does not pretend or try to tell any other story. Her focus, like Collins's and Shiva's, is limited and utterly convincing.

Smiley opens with an epigraph from Meridel Le Sueur: "The body repeats the landscape. They are the source of each other and create each other." Smiley's association of women's bodies, animals' bodies, and the land—"matter"—all similarly inscribed by a masculine gaze and by the literal force of male bodies, is deliberate and obvious. That these bodies carry their own agency is obvious, too.

Larry Cook, patriarch of a thousand acres of productive Iowa farmland, has three daughters. Ginny and Rose, the oldest two, are married and living in different houses on the family farm. Caroline, her father's favorite, practices law in Des Moines. Larry lost his wife to breast cancer some twenty-five years prior to the beginning of the novel. Rose is less than a year postmastectomy.

The first and final consolidations of the Cook family's one thousand acres involved the exchange of women's bodies. Ginny, the narrator, tells the story of how her English great-grandparents, the original homesteaders, gave their sixteen-year-old daughter, Edith, in marriage to another Englishman, John Cook, so that the two families could formally merge as co-owners of the 30-acre farm that they had been co-working. Ninety years later, Larry Cook secures the last few acres of his 1000-acre kingdom when Ginny marries Ty, a neighboring farmer with a productive 160 acres. When Larry, like Lear, suddenly decides to divide his kingdom among his appropriately obedient daughters, it becomes painfully obvious that Ty had been dreaming of this sort of inheritance all along. The women's bodies, like the body of the land, come to matter—come to meaning—in this ancient patriarchal system of exchange. Ginny first comes to realize this as she and Ty talk about her father's growing irritability and irrationality. Significantly, they have this conversation at bedtime as Ginny undresses and as Ty stands watching her, as she exposes her body to his gaze. She suggests they give the land back to her father and then notes: "The freight of his look was seventeen years of unspoken knowledge that he had married up and been obliged to prove his skills worthy of, not a hundred and sixty acres, but a thousand acres" (104). He then implies that the women are responsible for Larry's advancing madness: "But you women could handle it better. You could handle him better. You don't always have to take issue. You ought to let a lot of things slide" (104). In fact, both Larry and Ty owe what they have to a system that barters women's bodies, including Ginny's body. Ginny is just beginning to recognize this at this early point in the novel. By undressing Ginny's body in this episode, Smiley seems to invite us to read her body as a historical and cultural record, as a standpoint, for deciphering the narrative's dramatic tensions.

The Iowa land that Ginny's homesteading great-grandparents settled in was originally covered in water and inhabited by aquatic wildlife. They drained the land, completely altering its natural state, and installed a permanent drainage system of tiles that drew the water, warmed the soil, and made it fertile and easy to work. Early in the novel Ginny walks along the Scenic River and notices a small flock of pelicans: "Maybe twenty-five birds, cloud white against the shine of the water. Ninety years ago, when my great-grandparents settled in Zebulon County and the whole county was wet, marshy, glistening like this, hundreds of thousands of pelicans nested in the cattails, but I hadn't seen even one since the early sixties. I watched them. The view along the Scenic, I thought, taught me a lesson about what is below the level of the visible" (9). The land is literally and metaphorically not what it appears to be. But the birds remember and continue to seek out the water.

The women, too, in this story are drawn to water, the original element that continues to run beneath and onto the fields, to push up continually against the tiles, to rupture and remind at the boundaries. It is as though there is a discrepancy between the women's experiences of water and the dominant men's account of water. Women exchange secrets around swimming pools. Ginny remembers how her father kept the girls from looking into the field drains and the dangerous waters below them. And she notes how he filled in the girls' favorite swimming hole, Mel's pond, destroying their meeting place. Not only does he cut off the girls' access to this original and resisting element but he also poisons it with agricultural chemicals, including the nitrates that cause Ginny's five miscarriages. The women's bodies and the land literally merge as poisoned under the same institutions of power. But they also continue to assert themselves against the literal constraints that Larry Cook imposes on them.

Men in this story have tragic relationships with water. Their destructive uses of this element eventually destroy them. For example, when one of the Cooks' neighbors and local competitors is sprayed in the face with anhydrous ammonia, he runs to a nearby water tank to rinse his eyes. There, he finds the tank empty and is permanently blinded. Later, we find out that Pete, Rose's husband, had emptied the tank, hoping to hurt Larry. Pete himself later dies by drowning, a possible suicide, in a local water-filled quarry. The reader gets the impression that a certain hubris, a refusal to acknowledge certain limits, is punished, or, put in more neutral terms, is consequential. A reader could take either the patriarchal "materialization" of water *or* women's bodies as epistemological standpoints for ecofeminist theorizing. Both women's bodies and water have been similarly inscribed—literally and in their meanings—by the men in this story.

Smiley makes amply clear the grip of the male gaze on the land and on the women's bodies. For example, Ginny says: "Perhaps there is a distance that is the optimum distance for seeing one's father, farther than across the supper table or across the room, somewhere in the middle distance: he is dwarfed by trees or the sweep of a hill, but his features are still visible, his body language still distinct. Well, that is a distance I never found. He was never dwarfed by the landscape—the fields, the buildings, the white pine windbreak were as much my father as if he had grown them and shed them like a husk" (20).

"There he stood, the living source of it all, of us all," she says. "Of course it was silly to talk about 'my point of view.' When my father asserted his point of view, mine vanished. Not even I could remember it" (176). And in a passage that explicitly shows the power of Larry Cook's grip on his daughter's body, Ginny, who is walking to her house to fetch eggs after her father demands them for breakfast, says: "The whole way I was conscious of my body—graceless and hurrying, unfit, panting, ridiculous in its very femininity. It seemed like my father could just look out of his big front window and see me naked, chest heaving, breasts, thighs, and buttocks jiggling, dignity irretrievable" (114–15). And her "ridiculous femininity" materializes her body as, when she returns to fry his eggs, she covers her body with an apron, hurries to serve up his food, hovers by his chair waiting for further orders as he eats.

Rose puts the situation accurately: "We were just his, to do with as he pleased, like the pond or the houses or the hogs or the crops" (191). Throughout the book Rose makes repeated references to a worldview and to practices that have similarly violated the integrity of the land, the animals, and the women in the story, and she insists that Ginny recognize these associations and consequences. But Ginny comes very slowly and reluctantly to this standpoint; it is a hard-earned achievement, as Harding might put it. And, for both Rose and Ginny, this perspective is achieved as they critically attend to material life as a site of materialized power and resistance. And the first sites that they attend to are their own bodies.

Larry Cook's gaze as well as his body asserted itself over his young daughters. Ginny, reluctantly, remembers their father's assaults. The first time she remembers is in her father's house, after, like Lear, Larry has gone mad and leaves the farm. She goes to change sheets on her old bed and says: "I experienced a kind of self-conscious distance from my body as it rose up the staircase" (227). And when she lies down in her childhood bed, she remembers "that he had been in there to me," and, using language very similar to a previous description of her father as "spreading himself more widely over the landscape," she recalls what he did to her (228). Her next memory is of her mother's clothing—the cloth that took the shape and smell of her mother's body, that presented the public body—distributed to and appropriated by the bodies of numerous strangers. The image is one of physical dismemberment, appropriation, consumption, mirroring the eventual fate of Ty's hogs. The meaning and fate of both the hogs and the Cook women is made graphic in this image. "So I screamed. I screamed in a way that I had never screamed before, full out, throat-wrenching, unafraid-of-making-a-fuss-and-drawing-attention-to-myself sorts of screams that I made myself concentrate on, becoming all mouth, all tongue, all vibration" (229). And from then on she inhabits her body as she could not inhabit it when Larry Cook came for her those nights twenty years before.

Ginny says "one thing that Daddy took from me when he came to me in my room at night was the memory of my body" (280). Here she is referring to certain childhood memories—of the cool and reassuring feeling of water on her skin as she floats in Mel's pond, the graceful curve of her ankle that she notes and then turns away from in self-conscious shame as a young teen.

But these women's bodies are not entirely lost to them. The gaze is not omnipotent. The narrative may be heterosexist, but those terms can be scrambled, parodied, ruptured in politically significant ways. I think this is possible because, in this case, Ginny exists in what standpoint theorists call a "fault line." In attending to her body, she experiences discrepancies between the shame and loathing her father has made her feel about her body and her own desire, a presence that she is often aware of and that at times takes her by surprise. For example, in the following, Ginny's body, while certainly not out of the heterosexist matrix, desires in ways not entirely conforming to it. After spending a long afternoon with Ty docking and castrating baby pigs, Ginny briefly dreams, erotically, that night that she is a sow and then wakes as Ty presses an erection against her leg. She had been previously fantasizing about sex with Jess Clark, a neighbor's son and friend, and says: "Normally I hated waking in the night with him so close to me, but my earlier fantasies must have primed me. . . . Instantly I was breathless. . . . I put my hand around it and turned toward it, then took my hand off it and pulled the curve of his ass toward me" (161). The "sow" objectifies and sexually "consumes" the man.

And a few hours later she chooses to have sex with Jess in the "dump," a place where native plants still grow in the watery ooze somewhere in a forgotten field on the farm. After Jess removes himself from her, she says, "I began all at once to shiver. . . . Now the shaking was pure desire. As I realized what we had done, my body responded as it hadn't while we were doing it—hadn't ever done, I thought. I felt blasted with the desire, irradiated, rendered transparent . . . and I came in a drumming rush from toes to head" (163). Interestingly, Ginny's body responds to the *thought* of what she has done, after it is done, not to the man as he is inside of her. She has committed adultery. Her body defies the heterosexist order that consolidated the Cook's one thousand acres when first Edith and then Ginny were bartered in marriage. Her desire is abject, an ontological corruption, but for Ginny, it is a desire like nothing that she had ever before experienced. Her desire, a bodily wanting, may well serve as another starting place, a standpoint, for theorizing. And this standpoint is only available to those desiring abjectly. Readers might also note how Ginny attributes agency to the body—"I began all at once to shiver"; "my body responded as it hadn't while we were doing it"—showing, in my view, the body pushing back at other more predominant, patriarchal materializations.

Slightly later in the novel her father, as if knowing and naming what she has done, says to her, in his rage and in front of the entire assembled Cook family: "You barren whore! I know all about you, you slut. You've been creeping here and there all your life, making up to this one and that one. But you're not really a woman, are you? I don't know what you are, just a bitch, is all, just a dried-up whore bitch" (181). Larry names her "unnatural" act, her ontologically corrupt body, her position on the edge of the conceivable. None of the male family members, not even Ty, comes to her defense during this encounter. Only Rose confronts her father, confronts him with veiled threats to reveal his own transgression. "You say you know all about Ginny, well, Daddy, I know all about you, and you know I know" (182). Much later, when Rose does talk openly about her father's incest, no one will believe her, or maybe no one cares.

Jess Clark, who returns after several years off the farm, comes home in the role of what standpoint theorists call an outsider within. He has traveled extensively, avoiding the draft. He preaches organic farming, warns Ginny of the health effects of agricultural chemicals, including those that likely caused Ginny's five miscarriages and Rose's cancer. He's a vegetarian. As a result, he has some critical distance on what he rediscovers at home. Jess helps Ginny and Rose achieve some critical perspective on their marginalized status, a perspective grounded largely on the materializations of their bodies and on their bodies as signs that could stand for other bodies, for the land, for animals, and for other farm women's bodies, including their—Rose and Ginny's and Jess's— mother's body.

Ginny, Rose, and sometimes Jess constitute what Harding calls an authorizing or reflexive community, albeit a very small and homogenous one. These characters are not theorizing, but they are desperately seeking starting places or standpoints that they can use as they begin to piece together a more comprehensive and encompassing story of their families, community, moral life. Like Harding's communities, they are in collaborative, compassionate, and often contentious dialogue with each other, and they try, and sometimes fail, to bracket political biases—their middle-class inertia, rural isolation, and gender viewpoints—that might distort the stories they piece together. In seeking a "best" story, Ginny and Rose repeatedly refer to and employ their bodies as histories, as paradigms of the materialized body more generally, as resisters. They do not use ahistorical, transcendental criteria in evaluating the epistemological status of their discoveries. They trust the corporeal and their dialogue about it.

This novel is painful; it never lets up and does not have a happy ending. Rose, in some egocentric ways her father's daughter, initiates an affair with Ginny's lover, Jess, and Ginny realizes that Rose's "body wasn't mine after all," despite her lifelong identification with Rose (307). When Rose's body goes its own way, Ginny, in some ways her father's daughter, too, tries to poison Rose, to destroy the body that had succeeded in pregnancy, in pleasing Jess, and, Ginny says, in a "bizarre way" pleasing her father in ways Ginny could not (307). Rose dies of cancer, although many of my students say that Rose's anger, always bent on accountability and retribution, destroyed her body, an especially grim thought, indicating that her father literally gripped her body to death.

The farm is auctioned and Ginny, separated from Ty, takes Rose's two daughters to St. Paul, Minnesota, to raise them. Throughout the story Ty remains an invested "insider" who never quite gets it. When Ginny confronts him for the last time, she explains, bluntly, how her father, her father's father, "history," has held the "matter"—the bodies of women, animals, and the land—in its grip: "You see this grand history, but I see blows. . . . Do I think Daddy came up with beating and fucking us on his own? . . . No, I think he had lessons, and those lessons were part of the package, along with the land and the lust to run things exactly the way he wanted to no matter what, poisoning the water and destroying the topsoil and buying bigger and bigger machinery, and then feeling certain that all of it was 'right,' as you say" (343).

In the epilogue the body and the land are one; there is no traditional metaphysical transcendence of them, not for the women *or* the men in this story. Finally Ginny achieves the standpoint that Rose has been trying to explain to her all along. Ginny says:

> My inheritance is with me, sitting in my chair. Lodged in my every cell, along with the DNA, are molecules of topsoil and atrazine and paraquat and anhydrous ammonia and diesel fuel and plant dust, and also molecules of memory: the bracing summer chill of floating on my back in Mel's pond, staring at the sky; the exotic redolence of the dresses in my mother's closet; the sharp odor of wet tomato vines; the stripes of pain my father's belt laid across my skin; the deep chill of waiting for the school bus in the blue of a winter's dawn. All of it is present now, here; each particle weighs some fraction of the hundred and thirty-six pounds that attaches me to the earth, perhaps as much as the print weighs in other sorts of history. (369)

The body is social construction—the print that weighs "as much as other sorts of print"—but it is more than just Larry Cook's construction—"The body repeats the landscape." The physical body and the land are limits, are not entirely malleable, and "engage" with paraquat, atrazine, anhydrous ammonia, and with the grip on our reproductive lives. And we have put ourselves at great risk in ignoring such limits, as Ginny acknowledges in the end.

"The sharp odor of wet tomato vines," "the deep chill . . . in the blue of a winter's dawn," "the shaking that is pure desire," "I come in a drumming rush from toes to head"—I like to think there are some parts of the body that do not belong to Larry Cook, which is not to say that they are untouched by him or inaccessible. They, too, are actors, not inert recipients in this story.

The body is a position, or I should say bodies are positions, from which we can recognize and assess the gaze as it grips, similarly, the female body and culturally feminized other bodies/matter. And in attending to bodies we should also recognize their intentionality, bodies as agents. Beginning with our own bodies, we have positions conducive to ecofeminist standpoint theorizing that may radically challenge traditional Western ontological and normative paradigms that are particularly unfriendly to everything ontologized as material life, including women. One quite viable place to position such theorizing is as locally as possible, with the body. We should not be intimidated from this project by past mistakes, by overly determining theories that are biologically or culturally essentialist.

Conclusion

I hope that my sympathies with standpoint theory in general and with the possibility of ecofeminist standpoint theories more specifically are clear by now. I am particularly interested in looking at political definitions of "matter," of bodies as matter, and of women as bodies. Of course such definitions are significantly qualified by species membership, by class and race, by whether one is sentient or not, and I have hardly begun to explore those and other distinctions here. I do suggest that environmentally concerned women attend to their bodies as *materialized* starting points for theorizing similarly materialized nature and for conceiving of and enacting other material possibilities.

Notes

1. I am dating debates over standpoint to Hartsock's "The Feminist Standpoint," even though other pieces identified as "standpoint" pieces certainly appeared before this one.

2. Lloyd nicely summarizes Hegel's and Marx's standpoint views.

3. Jaggar summarizes standpoint theory, and Sandra Harding (*The Science Question*) summarizes several standpoint positions, most having to do with feminist philosophy of science; see also Harding, *Whose Science?*

4. Harding summarizes these positions in *Whose Science?* 121–33.

5. For more on my point about the necessity of marginalized people, see Lugones and Spelman.

6. On raises concerns about Enlightenment projects and Longino raises concerns about adjudicatory criteria for deciding between conflicting standpoints.

7. See essentialist-sounding pieces by Salleh ("Class") and Doubiago.

8. I think that by *reproductive labor* Salleh means social labor and not biological labor. She explicitly refutes biologism in this essay. And even more recently, she wrote that "it is not only women's socialization, the various belief systems which shape 'the feminine role,' but also the very practical nature of the labor which most women do that gives them a different orientation to the world around them and, therefore, different insights into its problems. In both North and South, this labor may include the physicality of birthing, suckling, and subsequent household chores, but is not restricted to such activities. Even in the public work force, women's employment is more often than not found in maintenance jobs—reflecting cultural attitudes to women as 'carers'" ("Class" 227).

9. Nonetheless, Western ecofeminist standpoints or standpoints verging on ecofeminist standpoints have emerged out of some of the grounds that Harding and Collins discuss. Many women have found themselves on the "fault-line" of authorized accounts of certain health issues and found that they could not afford to remain ignorant of

environmentally caused diseases, birth defects, and spontaneous abortions. A good deal of this focus has been on reproductive health and on children's health. Perhaps this is because women in nearly every culture, if not *every* culture, are still primarily responsible for reproduction and for children. Not all of the literature or agendas that these women have produced is deeply critical of the politics of gender, race, or class, and not all of it is critical of anthropocentrism. In other words, not all of it is ecofeminist. But ecofeminist insights are present in much of this literature, encouragingly.

Women theorists with feminist and environmentalist sympathies have found themselves working as "outsiders within" various authorial sites of theory construction and found the theories lacking. A particularly bothersome and apparent rift has developed between deep ecology and ecofeminism, two "radical" environmental movements and philosophies, as ecofeminists use their vantage points as outsiders within the largely masculine-defined environmental debates to critique their terms and dynamics. Ecofeminist theorists have also contributed constructively to theory that "reinvents" the concepts of nature, culture, humankind, man, and woman. Much, but not all, and not unproblematically, of this theorizing has been influenced by relational ontological frameworks and by permutations on ethics of care. These theorists, including several of those that I have cited in this section, could be more reflexive, particularly in problematizing femininity as a social construction and in localizing their theories in race and class contexts.

10. Bordo is referring exclusively to Butler's *Gender Trouble* in her critique.

11. See Guha; see Soulé and Lease for discussions of environmental postmodernism.

12. This nonhuman *subject* is a prime example of what Butler calls an "abject body," a body that defies cultural constraints on the "thinkable" (*Bodies That Matter* xi).

Works Cited

Bordo, Susan. *Unbearable Weight: Feminism, Western Culture, and the Body.* Berkeley: University of California Press, 1993.

Butler, Judith. *Bodies That Matter: On the Discursive Limits of "Sex."* New York: Routledge, 1993.

———. *Gender Trouble: Feminism and the Subversion of Identity.* New York: Routledge, 1990.

Cheney, Jim. "Eco-feminism and Deep Ecology." *Environmental Ethics* 9.2 (1987): 115–45.

Collins, Patricia Hill. *Black Feminist Thought: Knowledge, Consciousness, and the Politics of Empowerment.* New York: Routledge, 1991.

Davion, Victoria. "Is Ecofeminism Feminist?" *Ecological Feminism.* Ed. Karen J. Warren. New York: Routledge, 1994. 8–28.

Doubiago, Sharon. "Mama Coyote Talks to the Boys." *Healing the Wounds: The Promise of Ecofeminism.* Ed. Judith Plant. Philadelphia: New Society Publishers, 1989. 40–45.

Griscom, Joan L. "On Healing the Nature/History Split in Feminist Thought." *Heresies 13* 4.1 (1981): 4–9.

Guha, Ramachandra. "Radical American Environmentalism and Wilderness Preservation: A Third World Critique." *Environmental Ethics* 11.2 (1989): 71–83.

Haraway, Donna. "Situated Knowledges: The Science Question in Feminism and the Privilege of Partial Perspective." *Feminist Studies* 14.3 (1988): 575–99.

Harding, Sandra. "Rethinking Standpoint Epistemology: What Is Strong Objectivity?" *Feminist Epistemologies.* Ed. Linda Alcoff and Sandra Potter. New York: Routledge, 1993. 49–82.

———. *The Science Question in Feminism.* Ithaca: Cornell University Press, 1986.

———. *Whose Science? Whose Knowledge?: Thinking from Women's Lives.* Ithaca: Cornell University Press, 1991.

Hartsock, Nancy. "The Feminist Standpoint: Developing the Ground for a Specifically Feminist Historical Materialism." *Discovering Reality: Feminist Perspectives on Epistemology, Metaphysics, Methodology, and Philosophy of Science.* Ed. Merrill B. Hintikka and Sandra Harding. Dordrecht: Reidel, 1983. 12–29.

Hayles, N. Katherine. "Searching for Common Ground." *Reinventing Nature? Responses to Postmodern Deconstruction.* Ed. Michael E. Soulé and Gary Lease. Washington, D.C.: Island Press, 1995. 98–104.

hooks, bell. *Feminist Theory: From Margin to Center.* Boston: South End Press, 1983.

Jaggar, Alison. *Feminist Politics and Human Nature.* Totowa, N.J.: Rowman and Littlefield, 1983.

Kessler, Suzanne J., and Wendy McKenna. *Gender: An Ethnomethodological Approach.* Chicago: University of Chicago Press, 1985.

Lloyd, Genevieve. *The Man of Reason.* Minneapolis: University of Minnesota Press, 1984.

Longino, Helen. "Subjects, Power, and Knowledge: Description and Prescription in Feminist Philosophies of Science." *Feminist Epistemologies.* Ed. Linda Alcoff and Elizabeth Potter. New York: Routledge, 1993. 101–20.

Lugones, Maria, and Elizabeth Spelman. "Have We Got a Theory for You!: Feminist Theory, Cultural Imperialism, and the Demand for 'The Woman's Voice.'" *Women's Studies International Forum* 6.6 (1983): 573–81.

Narayan, Uma. "The Project of Feminist Epistemology: Perspectives from a Nonwestern Feminist." *Gender/Body/Knowledge: Feminist Reconstructions of Being and Knowing.* Ed. Alison M. Jaggar and Susan R. Bordo. New Brunswick: Rutgers University Press, 1989. 256–69.

———. "Working Together across Difference: Some Considerations on Emotions and Political Practice." *Hypatia* 3.3 (1988): 11–22.

On, Bat-Ami Bar. "Marginality and Epistemic Privilege." *Feminist Epistemologies.* Ed Linda Alcoff and Elizabeth Potter. New York: Routledge, 1993. 83–100.

Plumwood, Val. *Feminism and the Mastery of Nature.* New York: Routledge, 1993.

Roach, Catherine. "Loving Your Mother: On the Woman-Nature Relationship." *Hypatia* 6.2 (1991): 46–59.

Salleh, Ariel. "Class, Race, and Gender Discourse in the Ecofeminism/Deep Ecology Debate." *Environmental Ethics* 15.3 (1993): 225–44.

———. "Deeper than Deep Ecology: The Eco-Feminist Connection." *Environmental Ethics* 6.2 (Winter 1984): 339–45.

———."The Ecofeminist/Deep Ecology Debate." *Environmental Ethics* 14.3 (1992): 195–216.

Shiva, Vandana. *Staying Alive: Women, Ecology, and Development.* London: Zed Books, 1988.

Smiley, Jane. "Q and A with Jane Smiley." Interview with Asha S. Kanwar. *Iowa Woman* (Spring 1993): 16.

———. *A Thousand Acres.* New York: Fawcett Columbine, 1991.

Soulé, Michael E., and Gary Lease, eds. *Reinventing Nature?: Responses to Postmodern Deconstruction.* Washington, D.C.: Island Press, 1995.

Warren, Karen J. "Feminism and Ecology: Making Connections." *Environmental Ethics* 9.1 (1987): 3–20.

———. "The Power and the Promise of Ecological Feminism." *Environmental Ethics* 12.2 (1990): 125–46.

Warren, Karen J., and Jim Cheney. "Ecological Feminism and Ecosystem Ecology." *Hypatia* 6.1 (1991): 186.

4

Ecofeminist Literary Criticism:
Reading the Orange

Josephine Donovan

There is a time for listening to the vibrations that things produce in detaching themselves [imperceptibly from] the nothing-being to which our blindness relegates them, there is a time for letting things struggling with indifference give themselves to be heard.

Il y a un temps pour écouter les vibrations que produisent les choses en se détachant imperceptiblement de l'être-rien en lequel notre aveuglement les relègue, il y a un temps pour laisser les choses en lutte avec l'indifférence, se donner à entendre.

Hélène Cixous, "Vivre l'Orange" ("To Live the Orange")

ECOFEMINIST THEORY has provided a critique of the ontology of domination, wherein dominators are thought to be of a higher order of being than the dominated. In the modern era this ontology has been enabled by a binary epistemological mode and practice that reduces living beings to the status of objects, thereby dismissing their moral significance and permitting their exploitation, abuse, and destruction (Warren 6; Adams, *Ecofeminism* 1–2).

Dominative modes pervade Western practice, including the institutions of literature and literary criticism. In this essay I will explore the nature of this domination and propose the possibility of an ecofeminist literary and cultural practice whereby texts are reconceived as vehicles for the disclosure of being, rather than as mechanisms for its elision, thereby helping to reconstitute the "objects" of discourse as "subjects." Such a reconception will restore the absent referent as a "thou" to the text.

The absent referent, an idea developed in structuralist and poststructuralist language theory, is a useful concept for analyzing the ontology of domination. It is central to the Freudian linguistics of Jacques Lacan and has been reworked for feminist and ecofeminist critical purposes by Margaret Homans and Carol J. Adams, respectively.

The absent referent refers to the real or material entity signified by the linguistic symbol, the word, which is termed the *signifier*. In classic structuralist theory there is, in effect, a threefold layer of signification: the elided referent, the concept that designates the referent (termed the *signified*), and the word that designates the concept or signified (termed the *signifier*). While structuralist theory originally focused on language itself as a sign system, the concepts *signifier*, *signified*, and *referent* are pertinent to any symbolic discourse, including art forms and cultural ideologies, which may be seen as operating like languages.

Thus, as Carol Adams brilliantly recognized, in the cultural discourse of carnivorism, meat-eating is a text in which "meat" is the signifier and "animal" is the absent referent. The animal is absent from the text; its being as a thou is elided and dominated by the signifier *meat*, which deadens the animal's aliveness, turning her or him into an it (Adams, *Sexual* 40–62). The process thus denigrates the ontological status of the animal, eliding its living subject-hood; in this way the sign (meat) dominates the referent (animal), reflecting the ontology of domination that supports carnivorism.

To further develop Adams's theory and to further refine our analysis of language as a dominative practice, let us consider the question of whether the concept *animal* (the *signified*) itself necessarily dominates the actual animal (the *referent*). My answer is no. The signified, that is, the concept animal, need not be dominative if respect and careful attention are paid to the actual realities of the entity being designated. Nor need the signifier *animal* be dominative if the referent remains present in the signified as an active presence. It is only when the signifier *animal* is transformed into the signifier *meat* that an ontology of domination is enacted. It is the signifier *meat* that as an interpretant transforms the concept (animal) and the referent (real animal) into objects for use or exchange in a human chain of signifiers. The living being of the actual cow is thus repressed as the signifier *meat* takes over, inscribing the referent as an exchange object within a symbolic commerce, which legitimizes the actual commerce of the meat market exchange.

Similarly, in other symbolic systems the text, a chain of signifiers, tends to dominate, distort, and deaden what is signified—the absent referent—commodifying it for cultural and economic exchange. An important vein in postmodernist theory—which includes ecofeminism—has critiqued the Western texts of modernism on precisely this point.[1] Thus, feminist/postmodernist critiques of science have focused on the way in which the mathematizing, universalizing texts of science and medicine have elided the anomalous, the marginal, the local, the particular, erasing them, absenting them, dominating them with a generalized signifier. Some theorists have called for a revaluation of narrative, telling the history of a particular individual, as a means of restoring the absent referent, the thou, to the texts of medicine, science, and social science (Hunter).

Such epistemological reorientations would seem to invite a reappraisal of narrative fiction as an important form of knowledge, validating, as it does, the individual stories of particular beings who are embedded in contingent social and historical contexts (I am thinking here particularly of the novel). But much literature does not remain faithful to the absent referent and its story, its reality; rather literature—like other ideological discourses—twists, cuts, distorts, and reshapes the referent to fit the requirements of the signifier, whose identity itself is determined largely by its interrelation with other signifiers in the signifying text, its exchange value. Even literary texts thus reshape, obscure, and dominate the "literal," subduing it to the claims of the "figurative."

In the nineteenth century Sarah Orne Jewett repeated this advice to aspiring writers: "*Tell the thing!*" (*SOJ Letters* 120). In the twentieth century several women writers have used strikingly similar language to similarly urge that writers circumvent figurative domination by remaining faithful to the literal in their writing. In an early poem Adrienne Rich explained "the thing I came for: the wreck itself and not the story of the wreck / the thing itself and not the myth" (23). Brazilian writer Clarice Lispector also claimed, "I want the thing itself" (qtd. in Cixous, *Reading* 14). And Virginia Woolf in critiquing Kantian ontology maintained, "We are the thing itself" (*Moments* 72). All these statements suggest, I propose, a proto-ecofeminist desire to liberate the "thing," the literal, the natural, the absent referent—which is conceived as a presence, a thou—from domination by falsifying, destructive signifiers.

It is important to stress that the women writers treated here clearly conceive of "reality" or physical nature as animated by a spiritual presence. "Telling the thing" means expressing the thou-character of the "objective" world. It means restoring the absent referent to the text as a living being. Instead of seeing the referent as absent, these writers posit that the referent informs the *signified* as a living presence, such that it holds equal ontological status with the *signifier*.

Conventional idealist literary criticism (whether formalist, structuralist, or poststructuralist) replicates the ontology of domination seen in conventional literary practice.[2] Formalists, such as the New Critics, viewed the text as an "it," a dead body available to the vivisectionist/critic for dissection/consumption/exchange. Like dead animals in the cultural text of carnivorism, literary works are deemed significant insofar as they fit into or can circulate (as commodified "meat") within the discourse of literary criticism. Virginia Woolf's famous Professor von X.—who "jab[s] his pen on the paper as if he were killing some noxious insect as he wrote"—suggests the dominative mentality involved in this critical practice (*Room* 31).

Western symbolic discourses, then, often operate in this way as dominative practices. Their signifying texts take over and reshape the literal, the material, expunging in the process the living being, the thou, the subject, casting it in the passive form as a signified, while retaining agency for the dominative signifier.[3] Such a mentality has enabled destructive Western dominative practices toward nature.

Ecofeminism has already provided a critique of such practices; in this essay I propose to further this critique through an analysis of the mentality of domination enacted in literature and literary criticism. First I will examine several women writers' articulation of their desire for a nondominative literary practice and then I will develop a theoretical basis for alternative, ecofeminist modes of critical response.

I begin with Margaret Homans's presentation of Dorothy Wordsworth as an exemplar of the inclination (Homans finds) of many women writers toward a "presymbolic or literal language, with its lack of gaps between signifier and referent" (14). Homans notes, "Women's place in language . . . is with the literal, the silent object of representation, the dead mother, the absent referent, so that within a literary text the shift from figurative to literal connotes a shift from the place of the signifier, the place of the speaking subject, to the place of the absent object" (32).

Dorothy Wordsworth, sister of the more famous William, was an early nineteenth-century journal keeper. Unlike her brother, whose figurative language requires the "death of [the] nature" it is representing (Homans 49), Dorothy "invents a mode of figuration . . . that does not demand the distance or absence of the referent . . . a nonsymbolic discourse" (53). Even for her brother, Dorothy's writing came to signify a mode where "images [are] not killed into meaning" (51). In other words, Dorothy managed to write "in a language that is as literal as possible and that literalizes" (39). Her brother, on the contrary, although desirous of retaining an unmediated connection with nature, with the natural entities he treated in his poetry, nevertheless ended by imposing his own autobiomythography upon them, transforming them into signs that are significant within that myth, but which erase the literal referents, absenting them from his field of significance. Dorothy in her journals "speaks for the literal nature that is often silent within his texts" (56).

Homans provides a comparative example of the way the two treat a common subject—a journey taken by William through the Alps in 1790, treated in *The Prelude* (written circa 1805), and retraced in 1820; the latter trip is covered in Dorothy's *Journal of a Tour of the Continent*:

Skeletons of tall pine-trees beneath us in the dell, and above our heads—their stems and shattered branches as grey as the stream of the Vedro, or the crags strewn at their feet. . . . We sate upon the summit of a huge precipice of stone to the left of the road—the river raging below after having tumbled in a tremendous cataract down the crags in front of our station. On entering the Gallery we cross a clear torrent pent up by crags. (Dorothy Wordsworth qtd. in Homans 61)

> The immeasurable height
> Of woods decaying, never to be decayed,
> The stationary blasts of waterfalls,
> And in the narrow rent at every turn
> Winds thwarting winds, bewildered and forlorn,
> The torrents shooting from the clear blue sky,
> The rocks that muttered close upon our ears,
> Black drizzling crags that spake by the way-side
> . . . .
> Were all like workings of one mind, the features
> Of the same face, blossoms upon one tree;
> Characters of the Apocalypse,
> The types and symbols of Eternity.
> (William Wordsworth, *Prelude* 6, ll. 624–39, qtd. in Homans 48–49)

The contrast is evident. Dorothy is clearly concerned with transcribing the reality of the gorge as faithfully as possible, remaining in touch with the literal specifics of nature, whereas William first hyperbolizes the scene with a melodramatic violence that is imposed by his own imagination and then interprets the natural world symbolically; its significance lies not on the literal level but rather as a reference for his symbolizing theory, that of transcendental idealism, where natural elements become "types and symbols of Eternity."

Homans gives another pertinent example of Dorothy's ability to resist figuration of the literal. In her journal of 1802 she follows for several days the fates of a pair of swallows who have built a nest by her window. Instead of turning their story into a metaphor for events in her own life (which would have been easy because the episode occurred just prior to her brother's marriage, a traumatic event in her life), she is concerned only with the swallows as swallows: "she convinces us by her long and minute observations of their behavior that the swallows have their own life quite apart from hers" (55). In short, unlike her brother, Dorothy "sees before she reads" and in this way corrects his tendency (and indeed the tendency of much Western literature) "to obliterate the image in favor of meaning" (63)—to impose a symbolic order upon the literal, the natural, denying its "thouness," killing it in order to exploit it for the signifying purposes of the author. To be interested in the swallows as swallows

suggests that the swallows have a being that is valuable and worthy of attention. Such attention indicates respect; it validates the ontological status of the
swallow. It acknowledges the swallow as "thou."

In a brilliant passage in *A Room of One's Own* Virginia Woolf envisages the
writer as a seer who discloses that the "things" of ordinary life are informed
with intense being, with a spiritual presence. It is the writer's job, she feels, to
transmit this reality, these "moments of being," without occluding, distorting, or dominating them with figurative interpositions:

> What is meant by "reality"? It would seem to be something very erratic, very unde-
> pendable—now to be found in a dusty road, now in a scrap of newspaper in the street,
> now in a daffodil in the sun. . . . It overwhelms one walking home beneath the stars
> and makes the silent world more real than the world of speech—and there it is again
> in an omnibus in the uproar of Piccadilly. . . . Now the writer . . . has the chance to
> live more than other people in the presence of this reality. It is [her] business to find
> it and disclose it and collect it and communicate it to the rest of us. (113–14)

Woolf's use of the narrative form here enables her, as elsewhere in *A Room*, to
explicate her ideas through concrete examples— "a daffodil in the sun"—existential details in context. As I have argued elsewhere ("Everyday Use"), Woolf
uses this method throughout *A Room* to provide an implicit critique of the
epistemology of Western science and its dominative methodology of distorting the literal through mathematizing manipulation, which, I contend here,
is analogous to Wordsworth's figurative manipulation of nature.

Instead, Woolf follows a procedure that does not force reality into preconceived
patterns; rather she remains faithful to the literal event, allowing it to exist in its
contingent context and as a random occurrence. In *A Room* Woolf focuses her
attention on a succession of chance events: a manx cat who *happens* to wander
by her window and a newspaper that *happens* to have been left behind, for example. "I take," she says, "only what chance has floated to my feet" (78).

Elsewhere, Woolf urges similarly that the writer should remain faithful to the
literal order of occurrences. "Let us record," she proposes, "the atoms as they
fall upon the mind in the order in which they fall, let us trace the pattern, however disconnected and incoherent in appearance, which each sight or incident
scores upon the consciousness" ("Modern" 107). Clearly, Woolf is concerned,
as was apparently Dorothy Wordsworth, to capture reality before it is transformed into an object by signifying texts. She is concerned to render it as a living, real entity, as a thou. Literature in this view is an attempt to achieve what
Homans termed a "nonsymbolic language," or indeed a "pre-symbolic or literal language, with its lack of gaps between signifier and referent" (225, 14).

A similar attempt is evident in the writings of the nineteenth-century U.S.

writer Sarah Orne Jewett and the twentieth-century Brazilian writer Clarice Lispector (as mediated by French theorist Hélène Cixous). Jewett came to express a kind of existentialist mysticism via the influence of the Swedish theosophist Emmanuel Swedenborg and his U.S. disciple Sampson Reed (Donovan "Jewett").

Reed postulated an intriguing prelapsarian, preverbal world of "presymbolic language" (to use Homans's term), where "there is a language, not of words but of things": "Everything which is, whether animal or vegetable, is full of the expression of that use for which it is designed, as of its own existence. If we did but understand its language. . . . [But] we are unwilling to hear . . . and drown the voice of nature." Instead, he urges, "Let [us] respect the smallest blade which grows and permit it to speak for itself. Then may there be poetry which may not be written perhaps, but which may be felt as part of our being" (qtd. in Cameron 266–67).

While Swedenborgians in general did not permit nature "to speak for itself," as Reed enjoins, but rather cast upon it heavy allegorization (their influence is seen in the Romantic poets, such as Wordsworth), Jewett did seek a language and a literary style that would remain faithful to the literal. She was, not surprisingly, an admirer of Dorothy Wordsworth. For Jewett, figuration should not be imposed upon nature by the artist to explicate his or her own inner spirit nor is it a "pasteboard mask" (Herman Melville's term) that the poet strips away or deciphers to reveal a transcendent signified. Rather, the literal or the natural is itself significative; it speaks in its own language, which humans must seek to hear—not erase through their symbolic code.

In the little-known essay "A Winter Drive" Jewett explains her animist theory in connection with trees. There is, she notes approvingly, "an old doctrine called Hylozoism . . . the theory of the soul of the world, of a life residing in nature, and that all matter lives; the doctrine that life and matter are inseparable." Thus, while "trees are to most people as inanimate and unconscious as rocks," she contends that "it is impossible for one who has been a great deal among trees to resist the instinctive certainty that they have thought and purpose." But she rejects dryadic theories that the trees' "thouness" can be explained as human spirits encased within them; she sees that as distorting the trees' reality as trees, making them "too much like people." On the contrary, "the true nature and life of a tree [can] never be . . . personified" (168–70). Thus, Jewett espouses a theory of nature as a subject, a thou, which must not be distorted through personification, allegorization, or other exploitative figuration.

Jewett's theory is exemplified in her fiction. In her celebrated story "A White Heron" a tree and a bird are "persons," or "thous," whose moral significance weighs as greatly as those of the human characters and who are therefore important players in the unfolding of the plot, which indeed hinges on the issue of whether the white heron will be treated as an object to be used for scientific purposes or as a "thou" with rights of its own. The protagonist, a young girl named Sylvia (from the Latin for *woods*), aided by an old pine tree, comes to the determination to save the bird's life, to defy the ornithologist who has asked her to reveal the bird's whereabouts. Speaking of the tree, Jewett notes, "it must truly have been amazed that morning through all its ponderous frame as it felt this determined spark of human spirit creeping and climbing from higher branch to branch. Who knows how steadily the least twigs held themselves to advantage this light, weak creature on her way! The old pine must have loved his new dependent. More than all the hawks, and bats, and moths, and even the sweet-voiced thrushes, was the brave, beating heart of the solitary gray-eyed child. And the tree stood still and held away the winds" (169).

Significantly, in her critical decision whether to disclose the bird's location to the ornithologist, Sylvia recalls the pine tree's presence: "The murmur of the pine's green branches is in her ears, she remembers how the white heron came flying through the golden air and how they watched the sea and the morning together, and Sylvia cannot speak; she cannot tell the heron's secret and give its life away" (171). Thus Sylvia, a nonliterate rural child, resists the dominative intrusions of scientific discourse, which would colonize her natural environment, erasing it as a subject, objectifying it for exploitative purposes.

"She must keep silence!" (170) because the language of scientific discourse cannot hear the "presymbolic language" she shares with the tree, the bird, and other creatures of the wood. They and she are constituted as subjects in a "bioregional narrative" (Cheney "Postmodern") that the Western discourses of domination cannot hear.

In an early work, *Deephaven* (1877), Jewett suggested that uneducated country people, because they "are so instinctive and unreasoning . . . may have a more complete sympathy with Nature, and may hear voices when wiser ears are deaf" (186). Jewett does not intend "instinctive" and "unreasoning" pejoratively but rather as alternatives to the hegemonic discourses of Western "reason." The "voices" they hear are those of nature as a subject: "the more one lives out of doors the more personality there seems to be in what we call inanimate things. The strength of the hills and the voice of the waves are no longer only grand poetical sentences, but an expression of something real" (186–87).

Jewett's literary theory, which was expressed in informal advice she gave to younger writers over the years—including Willa Cather—reflects her belief that the "inanimate" world of nature is indeed animate. "Don't write a 'story,'" she told them, "just *tell the thing!*" (*SOJ Letters* 120). In other words, do not impose a prefabricated script upon the literal; instead remain faithful to "the atoms as they fall." For the "thing" is itself animated with a spiritual presence; do not allow this "thou" to be silenced as an absent referent. In an early letter to a mentor Jewett said she needed "new words," which I interpret as a "presymbolic language," to express her sense of nature (Letter to Parsons). And in a late letter to a friend she commented on how "it is those unwritable things that [a] story holds in its heart . . . that makes the true soul of it" (*Letters of SOJ* 112).

In suggesting a hermeneutic appropriate to reading Clarice Lispector, Hélène Cixous suggests a similar idea: "one has to listen to what is said between the lines, to the silences, the breathing . . . to the living reality of the text. . . . A text has to be treated like a person" (*Reading* 99). Cixous sees Lispector as a writer who attempted to remain faithful to the literal by capturing immediate, unmediated, and sacramental encounters with the world—"moments of being." This Cixous sees as a particularly feminine mode of writing (*écriture féminine*).

In a worshipful essay on Lispector, Cixous reveals that the Brazilian writer helped her overcome an apparent writer's block by showing her the possibilities of this kind of writing, where the writer enables the being of the signified to come alive, to be seen, to be attended to. In "To Live the Orange" Cixous notes that her own writing had apparently grown too abstract, too distant from the literal, when "from Brazil a voice came to return the lost orange to me" (*Reading* 16). Before Lispector's influence

> Mute I [had] fled the orange, my writing fled the secret voice of the orange, I withdrew from the shame of being unable to receive the benediction of the fruit giving itself peacefully, for my hand was too lonely, and in such loneliness, my hand no longer had the strength to believe in the orange, I had in common with myself only the shame and discouragement, my hand had no more the goodness of knowing the orange's goodness, the fruit's fullness, my writing was separated from the orange, didn't write the orange, didn't go to it, didn't call it, didn't carry the juice to my lips. (14)

But "from far away, from outside of my history, a voice came. . . . To save the orange" (14).

Cixous was able to reconnect with the orange by means of childhood—perhaps preverbal—experiences: "And it was a childhood that came running back to pick up the live orange and immediately celebrate it. . . . There was originally an intimacy between the orange and the little girl, almost a kinship" (14).

Like Dorothy Wordsworth and Jewett, Lispector attempts to reduce "the gap between . . . the living and the saying of the living" (118). In analyzing a meditation on rain that occurs in Lispector's story "Tanta Mansidão" ("Such Mansuetude" 1974), Cixous reflects on the following passage: "Hardly this: it rains and I am watching the rain. How simple. . . . The rain falls not because she needs me, and I watch the rain not because I need her. But we are as close as the water of the rain is to the rain. . . . I am a woman, I am a person, I am an attention, I am a body looking out the window. Thus the rain is not cognizant of not being a stone. She is a rain. Perhaps that is what one could call living being" (Lispector qtd. in *L'Heure* 154; my translation).

This passage is characteristic of Lispector in that it reveals the author attempting to give voice to what we generally consider an inanimate object, rainwater. The rain becomes a subject with its unique living being; the woman is also a living being, and the two "thous" are very close, but they are not the same. Cixous suggests that the writer is allowing the being of the rain to be expressed: "Maybe the text is the very writing of the rain itself" (*Reading* 78). She further claims that this kind of writing, which gives voice to a referent that would ordinarily be signified an "it," is "feminine": "It is this barely writing the rainy aspect of rain that one could call . . . an emanation of femininity. It is a capacity to make a nonviolent, nonexclusive difference. . . . The rain is so much rain that it suffices to itself as rain" (78). Of another text she remarks, "it is difficult to think, to write, to read rain" (79).

Lispector, according to Cixous, is able through a kind of meditation (*L'Heure* 18) to unveil, to see the "living orange before she is reveiled" (*Reading* 74) and to transcribe it in a mode that is "prelogical, prediscursive" (23), or what Homans termed "presymbolic." Cixous calls this epistemological mode *clariceant,* or "clariseeing" (*L'Heure* 74–75). Lispector urges us "to call each thing 'tu'"—the French form for *thou* (*L'Heure* 102). For Lispector "the quotidian is supernatural" (*Reading* 99); she asks us to "go to find the thing" (*L'Heure* 104).

Cixous notes that Lispector is able to operate outside the law of the symbolic, which requires that "when we name . . . we attribute an identity to the thing or being in such a way that it takes its place in a general classification and falls under the *coup* of all the laws." But Lispector manages to name without imprisoning the designated object in a prescripted system, without dominating it by a signifying text. "Clarice names through love" (*Reading* 12).

"She says that God does not belong to any language" (12), meaning that God or Being exists in a prediscursive, presymbolic space. "Clarice does not imprison [God]. She gives [her] a name, but she does not take [her] by the name. She does not give [her] a name in order to take [her]. She gives [her] . . . a name that does not belong to any language, and . . . is not going to capture [her]" (12).

Lispector sees animals as providing a model for the kind of seeing and writing outside the law that she is attempting. "'An animal never substitutes one thing for another,' says Clarice" (12). For, "substitution, the foundation of the symbolic order, also functions as repression" (12). Thus, animals' immediate, nondominative, presymbolic awareness is what Lispector is striving for. According to Cixous, Lispector "regrets not having been born an animal" (12). Indeed, Lispector is noted for her respectful portrayal of animals in her fiction as thous (Scholtmeijer). Thus Lispector, like the other writers treated here, seems to express a desire for the restoration of the absent referent to the text, its restoration as a living being, a thou.

In this part of the essay I will attempt to provide a theoretical basis for an ecofeminist literary and cultural practice that would honor the intuitions of these writers, suggesting ways in which literary criticism may become less dominative. Several concepts help explain further the explorations initiated above. First is the concept of the I-thou relationship developed by Martin Buber. Since this idea is fairly familiar, I will concentrate mainly on Steven Kepnes's application of it to literary criticism and on Bakhtin's extension of the idea in his theorizing about dialogics (appropriated for ecofeminist critical purposes by Patrick D. Murphy). Second is the idea of attention expounded principally by Iris Murdoch. And third is what I see as an extension of this idea explored (principally) by Carol Bigwood, the notion of a critical erotics.

The idea of grounding ethical and aesthetic judgments in the I-thou relationship was first fully developed by the theologian Martin Buber. One of the most compelling examples Buber uses to illustrate the dialogical I-thou relationship is an experience he had as a boy with a horse. "When I was eleven years of age, spending the summer on my grandparents' estate, I used . . . to steal into the stable and gently stroke the neck of my darling, a broad dapple-grey horse. It was not a casual delight but a great, certainly friendly, but also deeply stirring happening. . . . What I experienced in touch with the animal was the Other, the immense otherness of the Other, which, however, did not remain strange . . . but rather let me draw near and touch it" (*Between* 22–23).

Buber recalls that in stroking "the mighty mane" and feeling "the life beneath my hand, it was as though the element of vitality itself bordered on my skin, something that was not I . . . and yet let me approach, confided itself to me, placed itself elementally in the relation of *Thou* and *Thou* with me" (23).

In his important study of Buber's aesthetics, *The Text as Thou* (1992), Steven Kepnes notes that Buber felt that narrative was the most effective means of revealing the I-thou relationship. This is because narrative not only focuses on specific details (and the I-thou encounter is always a specific existential event between two individuals), it also shows those details in relation. In the example cited of the boy's relationship with the horse, as Kepnes notes, the details of his touching the horse's "mighty mane"—that it was "sometimes marvellously smooth-combed, at other times just as astonishingly wild" (Buber, *Between* 23)—are essential to comprehending the nature of the relationship (Kepnes 86). Narratives, in short, are able to "say things that concepts cannot.

Narratives capture, express, 'hold' the complex mix of I and thou and world that cannot be clearly summed up in a philosophical concept. . . . Only story can hold within it the web of relationships within which the I-thou occurs" (87).

Literature and other forms of art can be a primary means of expressing or disclosing the thou, which is always revealed in concrete embodiments. Buber, indeed, presents an incarnational theory of art. The artist embodies the thou, which he or she experiences in the creative process, in form; the viewer or reader brings the thou to life in the encounter with the work of art. Buber uses the term *geistige Wesenheiten* to encompass creative works; while variously translated as "spiritual beings" or "forms of the spirit," Buber suggested "spirit in phenomenal forms" as an appropriate English translation (Kepnes 23). Thus, the work of art, though an object in concrete form, becomes alive as a thou in the encounter with the viewer: "a *geistige Wesenheit,* a work of art or form of spirit, although an It, can 'blaze up into presentness,' into the status of a Thou, again" (Kepnes 24).

For this to happen, however, the reader (in the case of literature) must approach the text in a nondominative, nonviolent way. "What Buber's hermeneutic method . . . requires is that the integrity, the otherness, the wholeness of the text be respected and not violated by radical refashioning" (Kepnes 22). It requires special receptivity—one might say an erotic responsiveness—whereby the "interpreter must take the attitude of a 'receptive beholder' (*empfangend Schauender*) who finds himself or herself 'bodily confronted' by the work" (24). In short, "interpreting a form of spirit requires us to face the work as we face another being. We open our senses to it, to its particularities, to its total gestalt. We allow it to move us, to confront us, to speak to us. We try to perceive its special message and disclosure of reality" (25). Thus, unlike the I-it relationship, which Buber sees as a means of "'conquering' the world" (*I and Thou* 91), the I-thou relationship is dialogical: both terms of the relation are seen as spiritual presences that have a reality of their own to communicate, which must be respected and attended to.

Buber's dialogical theory thus provides an important base for the development of alternative nondominative ecofeminist critical practice. Elaborations by the Russian critic Mikhail Bakhtin contribute further to the ecofeminist project. Bakhtin was in fact significantly influenced by Martin Buber—indeed the commonalities in their thought are striking (see Perlina). Bakhtin was also clearly influenced by Marx in his resistance to *reification* or the objectification of persons by signifying systems/ideologies.

In his early work *Problems of Dostoievsky's Poetics* (1929) Bakhtin valorized the Russian writer for his "struggle against the *materialization* of [people], and of all human values under the conditions of capitalism" (51). "In Dostoievsky's works [humans] overcome . . . [their] 'thingness'" (70). Dostoievsky's work is in this way "dialogical. It is not constructed as the entirety of a single consciousness which absorbs other consciousnesses as object, but rather as the entirety of the interaction of several consciousnesses, of which no one fully becomes the object of any other one" (14).

Bakhtin analyzes, as an example, the character Devushkin in Dostoievsky's early novel *Poor Folk*. This character, himself a poor man, resents all attempts to fix him, to stereotype him, to objectify him as a poor person. "Already in his first work Dostoievsky shows how the hero himself revolts against literature in which the 'little man' is externalized and finalized without being consulted." Devushkin is "*personally* deeply insulted . . . and outraged" by the characterization of poverty in Gogol's *Overcoat;* he felt that "he had been defined totally once and for all" (47). In short, Devushkin had been erased as a person, as a thou, by being designated or signified a "poor person" in someone else's text. He is thus rendered an absent referent.

Throughout his work Bakhtin resisted what he called "theoretism" or what Gary Saul Morson and Caryl Emerson term "semiotic totalitarianism" (28), namely, generic linguistic systems that eradicate the living particularized subject, who must be understood, according to Bakhtin, in a chronotopic context, that is, a specific spatiotemporal environment (Morson and Emerson 366–69). In opposition to theoretism Bakhtin proposed an ethical and aesthetic focus he terms a *prosaics*, which concerns itself with "quotidian events that . . . elude reduction to . . . laws or systems" (Morson and Emerson 33). Like Iris Murdoch, Bakhtin saw the novel as "the richest form of ethical thought" because it deals with "particular, concrete cases, and not rules to be instantiated" (Morson and Emerson 366). In the novel one finds "a non-monologic, antisystemic conception of truth" (234) that provides an alternative to the dominative conceptions that have characterized, according to Bakhtin, Western philosophy and literature for centuries (234).

Historically, Bakhtin recognized, the emergence of Western nation-states had as a by-product the eradication or domination of regional dialects by official "standard" national languages. The imposition of standard English versus the affirmation of regional dialects was a central literary issue in the United States in the nineteenth century. The so-called local color schools, of which Sarah Orne Jewett was a member, were a point of resistance to the colonization of regional discourse by the centralized "standard" language. Jewett's "A White Heron" reflects this regional resistance to cultural imperialism, or, to use Morson and Emerson's term, semiotic totalitarianism: the girl Sylvia refuses to be co-opted by the ornithologist, who is a synecdoche for all homogenizing modernist discourses that disregard the anomalous, the particular, the local (see Donovan, "Breaking" 229–30). As John B. Thompson has noted, "the most striking feature [of this historical process] is the silence to which those dispossessed of the official language are condemned. . . . Lacking the means of legitimate expression, they do not speak but are spoken to" (46).

In pioneering articles ("Ground," "Prolegomenon") Patrick D. Murphy shows the potential that Bakhtin's theories have for the development of an ecofeminist literary criticism.[4] Murphy suggests that Bakhtin's attempt to valorize deviant dialects (or idiolects) should be extended to include nonhuman "languages," i.e., the dialects of animals and nature. While Bakhtin saw Dostoievsky as rendering human "others" as "speaking subjects," Murphy suggests that we extend the idea of the speaking "other" to nonhuman entities such as animals, suggesting that their "language" be considered a form of dialect that must be revalidated and heard, not erased by "theoretistic" discourses that elide their subjectivity. "The point is not to speak for nature but to work to render the signification presented us by nature into a verbal depiction by means of speaking subjects" (Murphy, "Ground" 152).

Such understanding can best come through narrative, which is localized and particularized, a chronotopic narrative (such as seen in the novel), or, to use Jim Cheney's term, a bioregional narrative ("Postmodern"). As Carol Bigwood notes, "To really encounter difference on its own terms rather than on terms of the dominant faction there is a need for theories and stories that emerge from localized places and continually bend back to it so as never to fly off into fleshless abstractions and subjugating universals. Such bioregional theories and stories that relinquish their supposed timeless authority for the sake of the gifts of localities, particularities, and uncertainties would bring about profound change in our modes of being" (270).

Cheney proposes the concept of "contextual discourse" as an epistemological mode that enables a genuine reciprocity of information sharing, where the "thing" is not elided but attended to, where, in short, one sees the orange. Unlike what he calls "totalizing language," which "assimilate[s] the world to it," contextual language "assimilates language to the situation, bends it, shapes it to fit" ("Postmodern" 120). Such a mode enables a kind of consensual praxis of reaching the truth of a situation, where no one's realities are ignored, where all are consulted, where all have their place in the story of the moment (see Cheney, "Eco-feminism" 132; Bigwood 286). Again it appears that literature is best suited for the conveyance of this nondominative epistemology. Knowing the thou means hearing her story.

The epistemological practice involved in hearing her story is that characterized by Iris Murdoch (following Simone Weil) as "attentive love." As extended by Sara Ruddick, attentive love is a central theoretical component of the contemporary feminist ethic of care (119–23; Donovan, *Feminist* 173–78). Weil in 1942 explained it thus:

> The love of our neighbor in all its fullness simply means being able to say to [her]: "What are you going through?" It is a recognition that the sufferer exists, not only as a unit in a collection, or a specimen . . . but as [an individual]. . . . For this reason it is . . . indispensable to know how to look at [her] in a certain way.
> This way of looking is first of all attentive. (51)

Murdoch developed Weil's idea as a basis for the ethic that undergirds her moral theory of literature. Attentive love, which Murdoch defines as "a just and loving gaze upon an individual reality," is "the characteristic and proper mark of the active moral agent" (*Sovereignty* 34). Murdoch sees attentive love as a discipline similar to that practiced by great artists and scholars (Weil originated the idea in an essay on the discipline of scholarly study); it focuses the attention without, toward others who are different, "toward the great surprising variety of the world" (66). The "ability to so direct attention is love" (66). Such a focus makes one realize that the "other" has a being with "needs and wishes" of her or his own; this awareness makes it "harder . . . to treat a person as a thing" (66).

Great literature, Murdoch maintains, can lead one to this kind of awareness, because great novelists are not "afraid of the contingent" ("Sublime Revisited" 257). They are able to achieve "the extremely difficult realization that something other than oneself is real" ("Sublime" 51), expressing thereby a "nonviolent apprehension of difference" (54). "Love, and so art and morals, is the discovery of reality" (51).

In *The Souls of Animals* (1991) Gary Kowalski proposes an "interspecies meditation" derived from Buddhist meditative practice via Joanna Macy. It is designed to enhance one's awareness of animals as thous, and thus one's "attentive love" for them.

> Look into the eyes of an animal. It might be your dog or cat. . . .
> Pay attention to what you see: the years of living present within those eyes. . . .
> Contemplate their shape. Notice the angles and curves of individuality that make the face of this creature a unique work of art, crafted by time and desire.
> And as you look into this being's eyes, pay attention also to what you cannot see, the inwardness, the selfhood, the "I" that is as singular as its outward expression.
> What you look upon is a living spirit. Greet and respect it. Appreciate it for what it is. . . .
> Sense a solitude you can never fully enter into or understand. (91)

Ecofeminist literary and cultural criticism can and should, I believe, encourage the development of the kind of *meditative attentiveness* seen in these examples and in the literary practice of writers such as Dorothy Wordsworth, Sarah Orne Jewett, and Clarice Lispector in the hopes that such a reawakening to the reality of the literal, construed as a spiritual presence, will motivate people to treat the natural world, including animals, as a "biospiritual" reality (Kowalski 111) that merits sacramental respect. Ecofeminist criticism might also consider literature, in the fashion of Murdoch, as a means of fostering this reawakening and, with Woolf and Buber, as a vehicle for the revelation of being, not a mechanism for its domination.

In the remainder of this essay I would like to propose the idea of a critical erotics, a mode of appreciation and understanding that is radically at odds with traditional analytical critical practice, seen in Professor von X., which reduces the text to an "it" for dissection, to meat for carving.[5] This new emotional hermeneutic engages in "contextual discourse" (Cheney, "Postmodern" 120) in which dialogue, conversation, and consensus are utilized, fostering a nonviolent apprehension of difference and a receptiveness to the living being of the "other."

In the now-classic essay "Against Interpretation" (1964) Susan Sontag argued that "in place of a hermeneutics we need an erotics of art" (14), which will enable us to experience an artwork directly instead of obscuring its vitality by locating it within an interpretive, signifying network. Here also it is a question of allowing the being of the signified to be, rather than erasing it by the signifier. The way to do this, according to Sontag, is to allow our senses to respond fully and immediately to the work—hence the idea of a critical erotics.

Carol Bigwood's *Earth Muse* (1993) is probably the most important theorizing about ecofeminist aesthetics yet to appear. In it Bigwood calls for what is essentially a critical erotics. Like Audre Lorde in her classic essay "Uses of the Erotic: The Erotic as Power" (1978), Bigwood protests against falsely dichotomizing the erotic and the spiritual. And following the existentialist phenomenology of Maurice Merleau-Ponty, she argues for an epistemology and an aesthetic rooted in the living body: "This body that is sensitive and in deep communion with its environment is not the biological object body that science describes but is the 'living body' or the 'phenomenological body'" (50)— the body that is experienced from within as a living presence, a thou.

Bigwood thereby rejects the poststructuralist view that the world is a text, seeing that as just another Western theory that obliterates the living signified with a network of signifiers. In particular, she singles out Judith Butler's recent work, in which nature and the body are seen as a cultural construction, "a play of signifying practices inscribed on the surface of bodies" (41); for Butler "the body is not an abiding natural ground but is always a 'cultural sign'" (42). Bigwood maintains that "if we reduce the body . . . to a purely cultural phenomenon . . . then we perpetuate the deep modern alienation of our human body from nature. . . . The way to deconstruct the nature/culture dichotomy is not to make everything cultural" (44).

Bigwood emphasizes that it is as a living body that we are embedded in the physical, natural world. And it is through the senses of that body that we respond to it. As an example of this "sensuous contact" Bigwood describes what is essentially a thou-encounter with the sky: "My living situation becomes one of blue. I can feel the blue profundity and become immersed in it because of a bodily openness that lets the sky pulse through me and, in the same trembling stroke, lets my sensing breathe life into the blue sky" (50).

Such an encounter forms the basis for a knowledge that is real and has validity, even though it is "nonlinguistic, noncognitive" (52). The reality of such knowledge is greeted with skepticism in feminist poststructuralist theory, but Bigwood faults the latter's notion of a "culturally inscribed body" as "disembodied"; it denies the reality of "the body's incarnate situation" (52).

In a series of extraordinary meditations on specific works of art, Bigwood reveals a nondominative aesthetic in which the boundaries between art and "the world" are fluid—even dialogical—like the relationship between the living human body and the sky described above.[6] Again, such fluidity is possible only if one recognizes the existence of spiritual presence in the "object" world. Bigwood's reflections on Brancusi's sculpture "The Seal" exemplify her approach. Noting its exquisitely "balanced bodily composure," which she labels its "ecosystem," Bigwood observes that "an appropriate balanced ordering would let in contingency and not work to secure itself against what appears to be disorder in this relation of opposition. The Seal's balance is so beautiful precisely because it is laced with contingency" (66). Bigwood responds to The Seal through an erotics of touch, noting, "perhaps, before all rationality, compassionate touch is the distinctive mark of being human. We are gentle flesh" (121).

Following Heidegger, Bigwood suggests that today the primary mode through which being is brought to life, or revealed, is through technology, the mode of Gestell. But through Gestell, "entities can only appear as products, either as manufactured or as raw materials for them in the service of technology." In such a process "beings are revealed, not by letting them come forth freely from concealment into unconcealment, but by aggressively challenging them . . . wrenching them from concealment" (149). Thus, a tree is "challenged out by technology to serve as a raw product for the making of paper products" but it "does not stand in itself, shining forth from concealment" (148).

Bigwood is looking for alternative, respectful, and nonviolent modes for the unconcealment of being, such modes as "have been ontologically exiled, devalued, suppressed or lost in the Western tradition" (161). The primary victim of such ontological exile has been the feminine (4, 75). Like Cixous, Bigwood sees the mode of attentive sensitivity, the responsiveness to the thouness of the "other," as feminine. It is rooted in a kind of special empathy that enables a dialogical relationship between "subjects" and "objects."[7]

"There is a need to let our thinking be first moved by empathy rather than functioning according to the systems of power that are currently in place and dictate what counts as reason" (204). We should "fluidly release our thinking from the institutionalized constraints of *ratio*." It means "thinking for lepers and nomads, for bats and nettles." It is a matter of entering "feelingly into the life of the other, the life of all that has been assaulted by phallocratic western reason" (206). In short, "it is through a new human love and respect for oceans of difference, not through western indifference, that we are woven into the neighborhoods of the earth" (207).

In *Metaphysics as a Guide to Morals* Iris Murdoch sees the epistemological and aesthetic reorientation that I treat here—that is, developing a "reverent sympathy" that entails "a tender and respectful interest in the diversity of the world"—as engendering a needed spiritual transformation or conversion, a *metanoia* (72, 383, 54). What is required for people to achieve this "new state of being" (165) is to learn the practices of "morally disciplined attention" (23), that is, "serious contemplative perception, as when we *attend* to a human face, music, a flower, a visual work of art." Murdoch notes that "such close mental attention involves the conception of 'presence'" (425), a recognition that "spiritual reality is the same as ordinary reality" (297).

Murdoch thus sees epistemology and ethics as integral: *seeing* the world in all its diversity is a moral activity; it engenders ethical consciousness. "The daily momently quality of our consciousness, our ability to *look at particulars,* must be thought of as an organic part of our morals. . . . Consciousness is a form of moral activity: what we attend to, how we attend, whether we attend" (167). "Knowledge," in short, "informs the moral quality of the world, the selfish self-interestedly casual or callous man *sees* a different world from that which the careful scrupulous benevolent just man sees" (177).

Thus, learning to look at the particular is a skill or discipline that can enhance one's moral sensitivity and thus change one spiritually for the better, accomplishing thereby the metanoia or conversion to a higher state of being that Murdoch envisages. Such attention to the particulars of one's environment is morally progressive because it breaks down egotism and fosters compassion. "Moral change comes from an *attention* to the world whose natural result is a decrease in egoism through an increased sense of the reality of . . . other people, but also other things" (52).

There are several practices that can facilitate the development of attentive awareness, which Murdoch sees as an ascetic discipline, a kind of "purification of consciousness" (193), a "cleansing the mind of selfish preoccupation" (245). One of these is through the meditative practices of Zen Buddhism (242–44). Another is through literature and art. As we have seen, Murdoch maintains that great art teaches one to *see* the world, the particulars of the world in all their diversity, and to respect those particulars as having a being apart from one's ego (374).

Such attentiveness, which Murdoch feels is exhibited by the great scholar as well as by the great artist, sees and therefore allows to come into being entities that would otherwise remain concealed (to reprise Bigwood's reworking of Heidegger), rescuing things from what Cixous called "the nothing-being to which our blindness relegates them" (*L'Heure* 24). Such a process requires great patience and the disciplined ability to resist imposing one's own signifying text upon them. But the patience and discipline pay off; the gods thereby arrive.

Murdoch believes it is urgent that such an epistemological and thereby spiritual reorientation be fostered in the young. Meditation practices could be taught in the schools. "Reverence for life and being, for otherness, is something which can be taught or suggested very early. 'Don't kill the poor spider, put him out in the garden'" (*Metaphysics* 337). The baneful effects of television on youth should be recognized. It, like other modern technologies, impairs "our power to perceive" (377), "reduc[ing] rather than enhanc[ing] our ability to see the detail of our surroundings" (330).

The task, therefore, as I see it, for ecofeminist critics, writers, scholars, and teachers is to encourage the development of forms of attention that enhance awareness of the living environment, that foster respect for its reality as a separate, different, but knowable entity. Such a commitment entails reconceiving literature and literary criticism in the ways suggested in this essay as epistemological and moral practices that can contribute to the designed spiritual transformation, to *metanoia*.

One might question whether the process described in this article is too apolitical—that is, it fails to consider that all epistemological acts exist in a political context, and therefore that some I's are more powerful than the thou's and vice versa, which means a neutral existential encounter of the kind envisaged by Buber is not possible.[8]

In this essay, I assume, however, a political context. The purpose of the epistemological awakening described here is to sensitize dominators to the realities of the dominated, that is, to make the dominator-subject see/hear what has been construed as an object. It is not a matter of making the dominated sensitive to the realities of the dominator, which she generally knows only too well. But, most humans, even those who are themselves dominated because of gender or race, are dominators/exploiters of animals and other natural entities and therefore can benefit from learning the discipline of meditative awareness and the modes of contextual discourse I propose.

Notes

Reprinted with the permission of the author. A slightly longer version of this article appeared in *Hypatia* 11.2 (Spring 1996).

1. To the extent, however, that postmodernist/ poststructuralist theory retains the idealist assumptions of structuralism (in particular, the notion of human knowledge as a series of culturally constructed autotelic texts that are nonreferential) it is not amenable to ecofeminism. As Carol Bigwood suggests in her ecofeminist critique of Judith Butler, this vein of poststructuralist theory continues to privilege culture over nature.

2. Terry Eagleton characterized structuralism as "one more form of philosophical idealism" (108). I borrow the term from him.

3. It is interesting that nonliterate people (according to a study of Russian peasants done by A. R. Luria in the thirties) seem to retain an alternative, narrative epistemological mode. Instead of using deductive, generalizing signifiers to identify the signified, they tend to locate the signified within a pragmatic narrative. Thus when given four terms such as hammer, saw, log, and hatchet, the nonliterate subject would not group three under the generic term tool, excluding the log, but rather would envisage an operational story that involves all four items (Ong 51).

4. Another dialogical model of literary criticism is presented in Patrocinio P. Schweickart's "Reading Ourselves," in which she criticizes reader-response theory from a feminist point of view. Schweickart urges that we "construe the text not as an object"; however, the "thou" she identifies in the text is "the manifestation of the subjectivity of the absent author—the 'voice' of another woman" (47). In this Schweickart seems to be reverting to the romantic hermeneutic method of Schleiermacher and Dilthey, which has been criticized for its concern with author intentionality (see Kepnes 7–9).

5. At the turn of the nineteenth century some theorists even held the idea that the artist was a kind of "vivisector." Willa Cather, for one, embraced it early in her career, holding that "the links between [the] sword, the dissector's knife, the surgeon's scalpel, and the writer's pen are literal as well as metaphoric" (O'Brien 148). Cather "considered technology's victory over nature analogous to the 'virile' writer's praiseworthy triumph over recalcitrant subject matter" (389). Cather eventually moved toward a less dominative conception of the artist. (For further discussion of Cather's evolving ideas on the subject see Donovan "Pattern" and "Everyday").

6. For more on the fluidity of boundaries that characterizes certain women's art see Lauter and Donovan "Everyday."

7. For a discussion of empathy or sympathy as a basis for ethical treatment of animals see Donovan "Attention."

8. Grimshaw (239–40) criticizes Murdoch along these lines.

Works Cited

Adams, Carol J., ed. *Ecofeminism and the Sacred.* New York: Continuum, 1993.

———. *The Sexual Politics of Meat: A Feminist-Vegetarian Critical Theory.* New York: Continuum, 1990.

Bakhtin, Mikhail. *Problems of Dostoievsky's Poetics.* 1929. Trans. R. W. Rotsel. Ann Arbor: Ardis, 1973.

Bigwood, Carol. *Earth Muse: Feminism, Nature, and Art.* Philadelphia: Temple University Press, 1993.

Buber, Martin. *Between Man and Man.* 1947. Trans. Ronald Gregor Smith. New York: Macmillan, 1965.

———. *I and Thou.* Trans. Walter Kaufman. New York: Scribner's, 1970.

Cameron, Kenneth Walter. *Young Emerson's Transcendental Vision.* Hartford: Transcendental Books, 1971.

Cheney, Jim. "Eco-feminism and Deep Ecology." *Environmental Ethics* 9.2 (1987): 115–45.

———. "Postmodern Environmental Ethics: Ethics as Bioregional Narrative." *Environmental Ethics* 11.2 (Summer 1989): 117–34.

Cixous, Hélène. *L'Heure de Clarice Lispector: Précédé de vivre l'orange.* Paris: Des Femmes, 1989. Bilingual text; English trans. Cixous, Ann Liddle, and Sarah Cornell.

———. *Reading with Clarice Lispector.* Trans. Verena Andermatt Conley. Minneapolis: University of Minnesota Press, 1990.

Donovan, Josephine. "Attention to Suffering: Sympathy as a Basis for Ethical Treatment of Animals." *Beyond Animal Rights: A Feminist Caring Ethic for the Treatment of Animals.* Ed. Josephine Donovan and Carol Adams. New York: Continuum, 1996. 147–69.

———. "Breaking the Sentence: Local-Color Literature and Subjugated Knowledges." *The (Other) American Traditions.* Ed. Joyce Warren. New Brunswick, N.J.: Rutgers University Press, 1993. 226–43.

———. "Everyday Use and Moments of Being: Toward a Nondominative Aesthetic." *Aesthetics in Feminist Perspective.* Ed. Carolyn Korsmeyer and Hilde Hein. Bloomington: Indiana University Press, 1993. 53–67.

———. *Feminist Theory: The Intellectual Traditions of American Feminism.* Rev. ed. New York: Continuum, 1992.

———. "Jewett and Swedenborg." *American Literature* 65.4 (1993): 731–50.

———. "The Pattern of Birds and Beasts: Willa Cather and Women's Art." *Writing the Woman Artist.* Ed. Suzanne Jones. Philadelphia: University of Pennsylvania Press, 1991. 81–95.

Eagleton, Terry. *Literary Theory: An Introduction.* Minneapolis: University of Minnesota Press, 1983.

Grimshaw, Jean. *Philosophy and Feminist Thinking.* Minneapolis: University of Minnesota Press, 1986.

Homans, Margaret. *Bearing the Word: Language and Female Experience in Nineteenth-Century Women's Writing.* Chicago: University of Chicago Press, 1986.

Hunter, Kathryn Montgomery. *Doctor's Stories: The Narrative Structure of Medical Knowledge.* Princeton: Princeton University Press, 1991.

Jewett, Sarah Orne. *Deephaven.* Boston: James R. Osgood, 1877.

———. *Letters of Sarah Orne Jewett.* Ed. Annie Fields. Boston: Houghton Mifflin, 1911.

———. Letter to Theophilus Parsons, 24 Aug. 1876. Special Collections, Colby College Library, Waterville, Maine. Quoted by permission of the Colby College Library.

———. *Sarah Orne Jewett Letters.* Ed. Richard Cary. Rev. ed. Waterville, Maine: Colby College Press, 1967.

———. "A White Heron." *The Country of the Pointed Firs and Other Stories.* 1886. Garden City, N.Y.: Anchor Doubleday, 1956.

———. "A Winter Drive." *Country By-Ways.* Boston: Houghton Mifflin, 1881.

Kepnes, Steven. *The Text as Thou: Martin Buber's Dialogical Hermeneutics and Narrative Theology.* Bloomington: Indiana University Press, 1992.

Kowalski, Gary A. *The Souls of Animals.* Walpole, N.H.: Stillpoint, 1991.

Lauter, Estella. *Women as Mythmakers: Poetry and Visual Art by Twentieth-Century Women.* Bloomington: Indiana University Press, 1984.

Lorde, Andre. "Uses of the Erotic: The Erotic as Power." *Sister Outsider: Essays and Speeches.* Trumansburg, N.Y.: Crossing Press, 1984. 53–59.

Morson, Gary Saul, and Caryl Emerson. *Mikhail Bakhtin: Creation of a Prosaics.* Stanford: Stanford University Press, 1990.

Murdoch, Iris. *Metaphysics as a Guide to Morals.* New York: Viking Penguin, 1993.

———. *The Sovereignty of Good.* New York: Schocken, 1971.

———. "The Sublime and the Beautiful Revisited." *Yale Review* 69 (Dec. 1959): 247–71.

———. "The Sublime and the Good." *Chicago Review* 13 (Autumn 1959): 42–55.

Murphy, Patrick D. "Ground, Pivot, Motion: Ecofeminist Theory, Dialogics, and Literary Practice." *Hypatia* 6.1 (1991): 146–61.

———. "Prolegomenon for an Ecofeminist Dialogics." *Feminism, Bakhtin, and the Dialogic.* Ed. Dale M. Bauer and Susan Jaret McKinstry. Albany: State University of New York Press, 1991. 39–56.

O'Brien, Sharon. *Willa Cather: The Emerging Voice.* New York: Oxford University Press, 1987.

Ong, Walter J. *Orality and Literacy: Technologizing the Word.* New York: Routledge, 1982.

Perlina, Nina. "Mikhail Bakhtin and Martin Buber: Problems of Dialogic Imagination." *Studies in Twentieth-Century Literature* 9.1 (1984): 13–28.

Rich, Adrienne. *Diving into the Wreck—Poems.* New York: Norton, 1973.

Ruddick, Sara. *Maternal Thinking: Toward a Politics of Peace.* Boston: Beacon Press, 1989.

Scholtmeijer, Marian. "The Power of Otherness: Animals in Women's Fiction." *Animals and Women: Feminist Theoretical Explorations.* Ed. Carol J. Adams and Josephine Donovan. Durham: Duke University Press, 1995. 231–62.

Schweickart, Patrocinio P. "Reading Ourselves: Toward a Feminist Theory of Reading."

Gender and Reading: Essays on Readers, Texts, and Contexts. Ed. Elizabeth A. Flynn and Patrocinio P. Schweickart. Baltimore: Johns Hopkins University Press, 1986. 31–62.

Sontag, Susan. *Against Interpretation and Other Essays.* New York: Farrar, Straus, and Giroux, 1966.

Thompson, John B. *Studies in the Theory of Ideology.* Berkeley: University of California Press, 1984.

Warren, Karen J. "Feminism and Ecology: Making Connections." *Environmental Ethics* 9.1 (1987): 3–20.

Weil, Simone. *The Simone Weil Reader.* Ed. George A. Paniches. New York: George McKay, 1977.

Woolf, Virginia. "Modern Fiction." *Collected Essays.* Vol. 2. London: Hogarth, 1966. 103–10.

———. *Moments of Being.* Ed. Jeanne Shulkind. 2d ed. San Diego: Harcourt, 1985.

———. *A Room of One's Own.* 1929. New York: Harcourt, Brace, 1957.

5

"Buffalo Gals, Won't You Come Out Tonight":
A Call for Boundary-Crossing in Ecofeminist Literary Criticism

Karla Armbruster

THE DEVELOPING FIELD of ecofeminism has recently produced an impressive array of anthologies, special issues of journals, and articles devoted to exploring and explaining the field's history and potential.[1] The differing and sometimes contradictory approaches represented within this growing body of ecofeminist literature make clear that ecofeminism is a constantly changing field that has evolved from a diverse background, including not only ecology and feminism but also socialism, philosophy, women's spirituality, and grassroots political activism.[2] While the heterogeneous and dynamic nature of ecofeminism makes it difficult to define, ecofeminist writers do share a general conviction that there are important connections between the oppression of women and the destruction and misuse of nonhuman nature within male-dominated cultures. And, whether their work takes the form of theory, cultural analysis, or creative prose or poetry, they all give a sense that it is politically essential to explore and emphasize these connections if the dominations of women and nature are to be substantively challenged. Unlike other forms of feminism, though, ecofeminism has yet to evolve a significant body of literary criticism that reflects and helps to advance its political goals. Ian Marshall, one of the first literary critics to explore the potential of an ecofeminist approach, explains this phenomenon by suggesting that the theoretical task of defining the premises of ecofeminism has had to precede any critical application of those premises (49).

However, I believe that creative, complex ecofeminist interpretations of literary texts should be able to enhance the growth of ecofeminist theory rather than wait for its development. For the project of ecofeminist literary criticism to flourish, though, it must become more responsive to its position at the intersection of two broad fields—ecofeminism and literary theory and criticism—and simultaneously draw from and contribute to both. Currently, ecofeminist literary criticism is dependent on ecofeminist theory, which limits its capacity to meaningfully contribute to literary theory and criticism; in particular, it is limited by certain trends of thought in ecofeminist theory that are difficult to apply to the interpretation of literature in ways that result in complex and ideologically subversive readings. The trends I refer to are allegorically described by Val Plumwood in *Feminism and the Mastery of Nature*. As she explains, it is all too easy for the ecofeminist theorist "pilgrim" to "fall into the Ocean of Continuity on the one side or stray into the waterless and alien Desert of Difference on the other, there to perish" (3). As she suggests, there is a tendency within ecofeminist theory to emphasize the connections or continuity between women and nature at the expense of recognizing important differences between the two groups. Other tendencies within current ecofeminist theory go to the opposite extreme and emphasize differences based on aspects of identity such as gender, race, or species in ways that can isolate people from each other and from nonhuman nature.

The path between continuity and difference that ecofeminist theorists must walk is so narrow and difficult not because of inadequacies in the theorists or the theories, but because of the complexity of their task. Ecofeminism explicitly works to challenge dominant ideologies of dualism and hierarchy within Western culture that construct nature as separate from and inferior to human culture (and women as inferior to men).[3] While many ecofeminists identify such ideologies primarily as masculine, such a characterization is overly simplistic; as Val Plumwood explains, "it is not a masculine identity pure and simple, but the multiple, complex cultural identity of the master formed in the context of class, race, species and gender domination, which is at issue" (5). The ideologies of dualism and hierarchy that ground all these dominations are such pervasive forces within our culture that even a movement with the most subversive motives and concepts cannot help but reflect their influence. Within ecofeminism, an unproblematized focus on women's connection with nature can actually reinforce the "master" ideologies of dualism and hierarchy by constructing yet another dualism: an uncomplicated opposition between women's perceived unity with nature and male-associated culture's alienation from it. On the other hand, an unbalanced emphasis on differences in gender, race, species, or other aspects of identity can deny the complexity of human and natural identities and lead to the hierarchical ranking of oppressions on the basis of importance or causality.

Although many ecofeminist theorists are keenly aware of the pervasiveness of dominant ideologies of dualism and hierarchy, they are far more likely to note the ways that other fields manifest the influence of such forces than to search for their traces in ecofeminist discourse itself.[4] Thus, they risk unconsciously reinforcing the very cultural beliefs and attitudes that they wish to transform. To help fulfill the political potential of ecofeminism, ecofeminist literary critics must become more conscious of the ways that ecofeminist theory can be subtly diverted into the traps of continuity or difference and thus recontained by the pervasive force of dominant ideologies of dualism and hierarchy. And to make a significant impact on literary criticism and theory, ecofeminist literary critics must offer a perspective that complicates cultural conceptions of human identity and of human relationships with nonhuman nature instead of relying on unproblematized visions of continuity or difference.

One way that ecofeminist literary critics can work toward these goals is to expand their theoretical base beyond self-proclaimed ecofeminist theorists to other theorists and critics who have grappled with similar issues. Specifically, feminist theorists interested in poststructuralist thought, such as Teresa de Lauretis and Donna Haraway, are deeply concerned with the same issues of domination, gender, and nature that characterize ecofeminist theory. In this essay, I will examine how their work can help to identify the ways that ecofeminist theory is recontained by dominant ideologies and how such insights might help to avoid such recontainment. After offering this perspective, I will explore how these theoretical observations might be put into practice by formulating a model of poststructuralist ecofeminist reading and applying it to Ursula Le Guin's "Buffalo Gals, Won't You Come Out Tonight," which also offers its own insights into some of the central problems of ecofeminist theory and criticism. Ultimately, I hope to demonstrate that by crossing the boundaries of ecofeminist theory and engaging with the ideas of other theorists, ecofeminist literary critics can further ecofeminism's agenda by proposing new solutions to the problems of how to negotiate connection and difference while simultaneously contributing to literary criticism and theory by showing how complex questions about the relationship between human subjects and nonhuman nature can result in new and exciting ways to read literary texts.

The Limits of Subversion in Ecofeminist Theory

It almost goes without saying that the ecofeminist theorists most vulnerable to perpetuating dualism and hierarchy are those growing out of the tradition of radical or cultural feminism; by insisting upon essentialist connections between women and nature, such ecofeminists oppose women and nature to male-dominated culture in the most rigidly dualistic fashion. As Vera Norwood explains in *Made from This Earth: American Women and Nature*, ecofeminists who share the radical or cultural feminist viewpoint "focus on women's 'physical' connection with the earth as a result of their menstrual cycle, pregnancy, and childbirth" (265) to assert that women are inherently closer to nature than men.[5] While essentialist ecofeminists such as Andrée Collard adamantly reject dominant ideologies that might use an inherent, biological connection between women and nature to dominate both, their representations of such a connection often simply reverse the traditional cultural hierarchies. In addition, as Ynestra King explains, by separating women and nature from men and culture, such a form of ecofeminism "does not necessarily question the nature-culture dualism or recognize that women's ecological sensitivity and life orientation is a socialized perspective that could be socialized right out of us depending on our day-to-day lives" ("Ecology" 23).

As Greta Gaard points out in "Misunderstanding Ecofeminism," most ecofeminist writers are aware of the dangers inherent in essentialism and distance themselves from it (21). For example, Ynestra King's social ecofeminism displays a careful attention to the culturally as well as naturally constructed nature of women's identities. Even more interestingly, Susan Griffin—whose *Woman and Nature: The Roaring inside Her* has often been interpreted as a text of cultural ecofeminism—consistently goes beyond narrow, biological connections between women and nature in her writing. For example, in *Woman and Nature* she juxtaposes scenarios of the oppression of women and of nonhuman nature throughout the history of western civilization.[6] Thus, she highlights the connections between the *cultural* positions of women and natural entities, suggesting that male-dominated culture has created the bond between women and nature that she seeks to reclaim and use in a liberatory fashion. For both King and Griffin, it is women and nature's shared oppression within male-dominated Western culture rather than biology or essential identity that constructs a special closeness between them.

By avoiding or complicating biological essentialism in their conceptions of women and nature, King and Griffin move away from a dualistic elevation of women/nature over men/culture: neither writer explicitly excludes men from a connection with nonhuman nature; instead, both stress that men and women are subject to cultural forces that can blind them to the participation in nature that all humans share.[7] In addition, both are committed to overcoming a variety of other culturally encoded dualisms, such as mind/soul or intellect/emotion.[8] Despite the strong antidualistic bent of King's and Griffin's work, though, both writers are—like all subjects within Western culture—vulnerable to the pervasive and often subtle influence of dominant ideologies of dualism and hierarchy. By showing some of the ways the work of two such different yet antiessentialist ecofeminists fall into the traps of continuity and difference, thus yielding to the hegemony of the ideologies they explicitly set out to challenge, I hope to suggest in this section that the pervasiveness of these ideologies limits the subversive potential of ecofeminist undertakings and thus is an issue that should concern all ecofeminists.

Central to the ecofeminist agenda is the goal of individual, social, and ideological change—specifically, change that will improve the cultural standing of women and nature. As I have suggested, one of the primary problems that essentialism can cause for ecofeminists is that, in many ways, it seems antithetical to change. An identity based on essential qualities is unchanging, and the ways essentialist connections between women and nature support dominant ideologies also limit ecofeminists' capacity to catalyze social and cultural change. One way that ecofeminists such as King and Griffin support the possibility of change is through their acknowledgment of the historically and socially constituted nature of the (female) subject. In taking this view of subjectivity, they share one of the widely accepted insights of poststructuralist thought. Growing out of the work of thinkers such as Derrida and Foucault, the poststructuralist view that ideological forces construct our subjectivities through discourse can be interpreted as allowing for the possibility that individuals, and thus culture, can change in a way that essentialist views of identity do not allow.[9]

However, the possibility of change depends on a sense that the forces that construct subjectivity can shift, alter, and even conflict. Ecofeminists such as King and Griffin often fail to support a sense that the forces constructing women's subjectivities are diverse and shifting because they rarely explore the effect of forces (whether cultural or natural) other than women's cultural/historic association with nonhuman nature. Their intense focus on the connections between women and nature can lead them to erase all differences between the two, and thus they fall inadvertently into Plumwood's "Ocean of Continuity." While emphasizing the connections and potential for communion between any group of humans and nonhuman nature is an important step toward overcoming the dualisms that structure our culture's thinking, relying *only* on connection can collapse the self/other dualism into an undifferentiated whole. Such holism risks simply incorporating the other into the self, a move that Jim Cheney warns leaves no room for "respecting the other *as* other" (124).

The erasure of differences between women and nonhuman nature is perhaps most obvious when ecofeminists speak for women and nature as a group in such a way that they appropriate for all women nature's status within contemporary Western society as exploited victim of human culture. They emphasize the bond between women and nature to the extent that it completely determines the relationship between the two: they are represented as virtually one and the same. For example, in *Woman and Nature,* Griffin stresses the constructed association between the two to the extent that she creates an image of women/nature as a monolithic group consistently opposed to men. In one illustrative scenario, Griffin portrays a caged lion being examined by Western male scientists. The situation of this lion, for whose roaring the book is named, illustrates the basic opposition Griffin maintains throughout this work: "They wonder why she roars, and conclude that the roaring must be inside her. They decide to see it. She swings at them when they try to put her asleep. She has no soul, they conclude, she does not know right from wrong. 'Be still,' they shout at her. 'Be humble, trust us,' they demand. 'We have souls,' they proclaim, 'we know what is right,' they approach her with their medicine, 'for you.' She does not understand this language. She devours them" (187). Despite aspects and sections of her work in which she rejects hierarchy and dualism altogether, Griffin's consistent practice of opposing women/nature to male-dominated culture undermines the antidualistic aspects of her work.

When ecofeminists neglect to respect nature's differences from women, they can misrepresent the needs of natural entities and allow women to avoid acknowledging whatever complicity they might have in environmental degradation. As Vera Norwood explains in *Made from This Earth,* "some [ecofeminist writers] have cast women, along with nature, as an oppressed class that did not participate in the masculine agenda of domination" (276–77). While the degree of participation certainly varies from woman to woman, only an overly simplistic view of subjectivity can claim that any human is completely innocent of complicity in dominant ideologies; as the poststructuralist feminist Donna Haraway insists, "'We' cannot claim innocence from practising such dominations. . . . Innocence, and the corollary insistence on victimhood as the only ground for insight, has done enough damage" (157). Thus, even "the positionings of the subjugated are not exempt from critical re-examination, decoding, deconstruction, and interpretation" (191). Even Griffin and King, who emphasize that women's connection with nature is culturally constructed, rarely engage in such reexaminations and thus fail to explore the extent to which many women benefit from and participate in the ideological, political, and economic forces that sanction the domination and abuse of nonhuman nature. In a discussion of the feminist health movement and body consciousness, King does acknowledge that women have traditionally been complicit in such ideologies: "To the extent that we make our own flesh an enemy, or docilely submit ourselves to medical experts, we are participating in the domination of nature" ("Healing the Wounds" 1990, 119).[10] However, she does not discuss the extent to which women have participated in the "medicalization of childbirth" (118) to a much greater extent than simply by acquiescing to the tyranny of medical experts. In fact, more and more women are *becoming* such experts, participating in the dominant forces of Western science and medicine, as doctors and researchers, marketers who promote the technologies, nurses who administer them, and so on. Although such participation need not always reinforce dominant ideologies, it is important to note that many women actively contribute not only to their own oppression but also to the domination of nonhuman nature in some aspects of their lives.

By representing women's bond with nature as something all women share equally and that significantly shapes every woman's identity, writers such as King and Griffin perpetuate a vision of identity that lacks an attention to difference: not only the differences between women and nonhuman nature but among women as well. Specifically, as Norwood points out, dominant Western society has traditionally linked wild nature with marginalized groups like African Americans and Native Americans to place those groups outside the bounds of culture. Consequently, she explains, a sense of connection with nonhuman nature may be more problematic for African American or Native American women than for other American women (177). This lack of attention to difference is significant, for the differences between women and the rest of nature mean that women can participate in cultural attitudes and practices that are environmentally destructive, and the differences between women mean that some participate more fully and consciously in these attitudes and practices than others.

The limited view of identity reinforced when women and nature are even subtly conflated by antidualistic ecofeminists can undermine ecofeminism's potential for subverting dominant ideologies because the erasure of difference within the category "women and nature" simply displaces difference elsewhere, where it often serves to reinforce dualism and hierarchy. In particular, the "Desert of Difference" is revealed in the way such views oppose women and nature to male-dominated culture instead of seriously destabilizing such oppositions and rankings. However, it also arises when ecofeminists fail to account fully for the complex nature of identity and for the multiple ways oppression occurs in our culture. In their quest to emphasize the significance of the culturally inferior position of women and nature, both King and Griffin claim that one form of oppression is prior to or the source of all others. For King, it is oppression of women by men; for Griffin, it is human domination of nature.[11] While these two views may seem to set women and nature at odds, in competition for the position of "most oppressed," the ecofeminist emphasis on the woman-nature connection allows the qualities and position assigned to one group to be transferred to the other.

Of course, it is necessary for ecofeminists to stress that both the oppression of women and the domination of nature possess deep roots in Western culture, but the categorical assertion that any form of oppression is the ground of all others does little to challenge the ideologies responsible for dominations of all sorts. Although it is necessary to separate forms of oppression to discuss them, such a hierarchical and static approach goes beyond a sensitivity to difference to become a rigid code specifying which forms of difference should take political priority over others.[12] By giving in to the desire to establish such a code, even consciously antidualistic writers such as King and Griffin effectively enthrone gender and association with nature as the aspects of identity most vulnerable to oppression, thus implying that identity can be dissected into self-contained units that can be evaluated for severity of oppression. This need to rank aspects of difference inevitably alienates those who are foregrounding aspects of identity—such as race or sexual orientation—different from those selected as most oppressed. Thus, difference is again displaced rather than destabilized, serving to separate people from each other and from nature instead of encouraging them to form alliances for change on the basis of shared aspects of identity and experiences of oppression.

The challenge that faces ecofeminists who would avoid reinforcing dominant ideologies of dualism and hierarchy is to work toward a theory of human and natural subjectivity significantly more complex than the static concepts of identity that are found in both the "Ocean of Continuity" and the "Desert of Difference." While poststructuralism's emphasis on the changing, constructed nature of the subject helps to avoid essentialist notions that can lead to rigid, unchanging identity categories that promote dualism and hierarchy, it is in feminist approaches to poststructuralism that I see the most promising efforts to work toward a theory of identity that recognizes the interweaving of oppressions both within the human subject and among the outside, discursive forces acting on that subject. As Teresa de Lauretis explains in "Eccentric Subjects: Feminist Theory and Historical Consciousness," feminist theory has reconceptualized the subject of poststructuralism as "shifting and multiply organized across variable axes of difference" (116), axes that include but are not confined to gender, race, class, ethnicity, and sexual orientation. Like many other feminist poststructuralists, de Lauretis accepts "the interrelatedness of discourse and social practices, and of the multiplicity of positionalities concurrently available in the social field seen as a field of forces; not a single system of power dominating the powerless but a tangle of distinct and variable relations of power and points of resistance" (131). If we employ such a theory of subjectivity that affirms "the interweaving of oppressions rather than their hierarchical privileging" (Donaldson 8), we can acknowledge the ways that each person's socially constructed subjectivity is different from that of others without inevitably isolating us from each other. By viewing subjectivity as organized across multiple axes of difference, we can acknowledge the way that we foreground different aspects of our identity at different times. When I foreground a certain aspect or axis of identity, I can temporarily forge a connection with others who are foregrounding a similar axis of identity based on similar shaping forces in their own histories. I can establish connection without committing myself to a monolithic, static conception of identity—my own or others'.

While ecofeminists have much to gain by more fully integrating such a complex, shifting sense of the female subject into their theories of women's relationship to nature, they, in turn, can contribute to and complicate feminist poststructuralist thought. In particular, ecofeminists such as King and Griffin insist that nonhuman nature exerts a significant shaping force on human identity, even to the extent of representing aspects of identity such as psyche and sexuality as a kind of inner nature (King, "Healing the Wounds" 1989, 132). As SueEllen Campbell suggests, the poststructuralist insight that we are constructed by "all kinds of influences outside ourselves, that we are part of vast networks, texts written by larger and stronger forces" can easily be expanded to see nonhuman nature as one of those forces (209).[13] However, few poststructuralists—feminist or otherwise—have seriously considered the implications of including nature as one of these forces.[14] King and Griffin's refusal to leave nonhuman nature out of the process of constructing subjectivity productively challenges the human/nature dualism and could potentially expand the range of poststructuralist thought.

The Potential of Poststructuralism: An Ecofeminist Reading of "Buffalo Gals, Won't You Come Out Tonight"

Having explored some of the mechanisms through which ecofeminist theory can inadvertently and subtly reinforce dominant ideologies of dualism and hierarchy, the ways that the concerns and insights of feminist poststructuralists can help illuminate these mechanisms, and the possibility that ecofeminist theory might, in turn, enrich feminist poststructuralist thought, I now turn to the implications for ecofeminist literary criticism. By expanding the range of theorists that they draw on, ecofeminist critics can develop interpretive and analytical tools that will allow them to go beyond simply looking for literature that emphasizes women's or other marginalized people's sense of connection with nature (connections that are inevitably opposed to dominant culture's alienation from nature). One way of doing this would be to evolve approaches that ask questions that account for the complexity that poststructuralist feminist theory has accorded to human identity and that further develop that complexity in exploring the relationship between humans and nonhuman nature. These questions might include:

—Does the text convey a sense of the human subject as socially and discursively constructed, multiply organized, and constantly shifting?

—Does the text also account for the influence of nonhuman nature on the subject (and of the subject on nonhuman nature) without resorting to essentialism?

—Does the text avoid reinscribing dualisms and hierarchical notions of difference?

I do not mean to suggest that ecofeminist literary critics should confine their endeavors to texts that allow them to answer such questions in the affirmative; on the contrary, exploring ways that different texts both fail and succeed to construct subversive visions of human identities and nonhuman nature can help us to understand better the dynamics of domination, particularly as they are represented in discourse, and to learn better how we might disrupt them.

To demonstrate the potential for an ecofeminist literary criticism growing out of a broadened theoretical foundation, I offer a poststructuralist ecofeminist reading of Ursula Le Guin's "Buffalo Gals, Won't You Come Out Tonight," the first work in Le Guin's volume of stories and poems entitled *Buffalo Gals and Other Animal Presences.* I have chosen this novella not only because it allows me to demonstrate the potential of a critical framework that draws on theoretical works outside the boundaries of self-defined ecofeminist theory but also because the creative work itself can contribute to ecofeminist and other theoretical debates about identity, connection, and difference. In her introduction to *Buffalo Gals and Other Animal Presences,* Le Guin makes clear that her primary purpose is to write about animals and other nonhuman living things in ways that belie the cultural myth that "animals are dumb: have no words of their own" (9). In doing so, she addresses the problems caused by "Civilized Man's" deafness to the nonhuman voices that would remind him of the connectedness of all life. Significantly, though, Le Guin does not recommend a point of view that allows connectedness to erase all difference, criticizing the "sloppy identifications" (12) of Walt Whitman, which annihilate the otherness of nature by engulfing it in his own ego. Instead, in "Buffalo Gals," Le Guin creates a conception of human subjectivity and reality that engages with both connection and difference.

Le Guin's novella begins when a little girl, injured in a plane crash somewhere in a desert landscape in the American West, is discovered by a coyote, who tells the girl, "You fell out of the sky" (17). The coyote's unexplained command of human language creates the sense that this story will blur the boundary between humans and other animal species, a sense that grows as the little girl, Myra, follows the coyote back to her home. In the process, Myra's perception of the coyote is suddenly, inexplicably transformed from an animal "gnawing at the half-dried carcass of a crow, black feathers sticking to the black lips and narrow jaw" to a "tawny-skinned woman with yellow and grey hair and bare, hard-soled feet" (21).

Once Myra arrives at Coyote's village, she meets more characters who, despite predominantly human appearances, also possess qualities that identify them with particular species of nonhuman animals: Doe, for instance, could be identified as a deer simply by her walk—"a severely elegant walk, small steps, like a woman in high heels, quick, precise, very light" (33)—and the chipmunks live as a huge family in a dark, burrowlike house. In addition, these people possess characteristics that are distinctly supernatural: Blue Jay replaces Myra's eye, damaged in the plane wreck, with a new eye made out of pine pitch, and after a few healing licks from Coyote's tongue, it works quite well.

In creating such characters, Le Guin is drawing on Native American legends of the First People, whom the anthropological linguist William Bright describes as "members of a race of mythic prototypes who lived before humans existed" (xi). Le Guin's representation of these people, and especially Coyote, as ambiguous and irreducible to animals, humans, gods, or legends corresponds to the way Barre Toelken describes the Navajo conception of Coyote: "There is no possible distinction between Ma'i, the *animal* we recognize as a coyote in the fields, and Ma'i, the *personification* of Coyote power in all coyotes, and Ma'i, the *character* (trickster, creator, and buffoon) in legends and tales, and Ma'i, the symbolic character of *disorder* in the myths. Ma'i is not a composite but a complex; a Navajo would see no reason to distinguish separate aspects" (204). Ultimately, Le Guin's complex First People represent a worldview that resists definite boundaries and dualisms, neither choosing one side over the other nor collapsing difference. Nevertheless, this world is separated from the world of Myra's origin, a world inhabited by what the First People call the New People. This separation represents not an inevitable opposition between the two peoples, but rather the dualism that human culture has constructed, not only between itself and nonhuman nature, but also between its dualistic way of perceiving reality and a perceptual mode that refuses such boundaries. While the First People thus cannot be labeled "nonhuman" in the sense that they have no human aspects, they do represent the nonhuman to Myra in the sense that they offer an alternative to the dominant, dualistic human culture that she comes from. On this level, the story is about the process of Myra adapting to, learning about, and coming to love the nonhuman and to love Coyote in particular as their representative.

Significantly, although Myra is female, Le Guin does not suggest that her gender gives her an inherent or essential bond with Coyote or any of the other First People.[15] In addition, while Le Guin has transformed the traditionally male Coyote of Native American legends into a female who "adopts" Myra in some human senses of the word, many of Coyote's behaviors fly in the face of human expectations about nurturing mothers (including Mother Nature). Coyote possesses an irreverent and often crude sense of humor, she entertains a constant stream of "boyfriends"—sometimes in the bed right next to Myra— she is boastful and lazy, and she talks to her own excrement. Of course, all of these characteristics correspond to the way Coyote is represented in Native American legend, but for Myra, "a lot of things were hard to take about Coyote as a mother" (37) and require a great deal of adjustment.

Le Guin's introduction to the volume containing "Buffalo Gals, Won't You Come Out Tonight" makes it clear that, for her, it is more important that Myra is a child than that she is female: "for the people Civilization calls 'primitive,' 'savage,' or 'undeveloped,' including young children, the continuity, interdependence, and community of all life, all forms of being on earth, is a lived fact, made conscious in narrative (myth, ritual, fiction)" (10). Instead of predicating an ability to connect with the nonhuman on an exclusionary, gender-based essentialism, Le Guin acknowledges the biological and physical interdependence all humans have with the rest of nature. Of course, her sense that "Civilization" masks or destroys an inborn sense of this interdependence does set up a potentially dangerous opposition between nature and culture, but her focus on childhood as the prototypical state of openness to the nonhuman is liberating in the sense that it becomes a possibility for every person.

Despite Le Guin's assertion that children possess an awareness of the interdependence and community of all life similar to the worldview of the First People, Myra's identity is also clearly a construction of her "civilized" culture. Before falling asleep on her first night with the First People, Myra's last thought is "'I didn't brush my teeth'" (27). This sense that Myra, as a subject, is culturally constructed is heightened by the way she changes throughout the story in response to forces outside of herself. But by including nonhuman nature as an aspect of those forces, Le Guin avoids a human solipsism that refuses to acknowledge the power or effect of any force outside of human discourse. Instead, Myra's interactions with Coyote and the rest of the First People illustrate what Patrick

D. Murphy identifies as the "ecological process of interanimation": "the ways in which humans and other entities develop, change, and learn through mutually influencing each other day to day, age to age" ("Ground" 149).

As Murphy explains, to recognize the way nonhuman entities can participate in the ideological, discursive forces shaping human subjectivities, we must escape dominant constructions of the human-nature relationship that represent humans as superior to and separate from a passive, silent, nature: "just as that self enters into language and the use of *parole,* so too does the 'other' enter into language and have the potential, as does any entity, to become a 'speaking subject'" (151). To recognize the potential of the nonhuman to speak and act, it is important for humans to "work to render the signification presented us by nature into a verbal depiction by means of speaking subjects, whether this is through characterization in the arts or through discursive prose" (152). Donna Haraway, too, emphasizes the importance of being able to perceive nonhuman "actors" as powerful, active speakers: "Actors come in many and wonderful forms. Accounts of a 'real' world do not, then, depend on a logic of 'discovery' but on a power-charged social relation of 'conversation.' The world neither speaks itself nor disappears in favor of a master decoder. The codes of the world are not still, waiting only to be read. . . . Ecofeminists have perhaps been most insistent on some version of the world as active subject, not as resource to be mapped and appropriated in bourgeois, Marxist, or masculinist projects" (198–99).

In representing the First People as she does, Le Guin makes the move Murphy and Haraway recommend: she renders the natural world in the form of speaking, active subjects, thus questioning the idea of impermeable boundaries between human and animal (especially the boundary that excludes the nonhuman from discourse). Importantly, Coyote is portrayed as especially active in seeking connections with Myra. In the legends of Native American cultures, particularly those native to the American Southwest, the figure of Coyote has links with human culture beyond the human aspect all First People share. William Bright characterizes the legendary Coyote as "a Levi-Straussian 'mediator' who links the world of humanity, with all of its curiosity, self-awareness, and resultant 'cultural' baggage, to the 'natural' world of animals" (22). The legendary Coyote's affinity for humanity is paralleled to some degree by the relationship of the biological coyote to dominant human culture: it has shown an impressive ability to adapt to the changes human cultures have imposed upon its environment, often expanding its range to include areas where wolves have been eliminated or adapting to life in close proximity to human beings.[16] Even more incredibly, the species thrives in North America today despite persistent and brutal campaigns intended to eliminate it.[17]

True to this biological and legendary relationship with human culture, Le Guin's Coyote represents such an openness to interconnection, even when connecting means crossing hostile boundaries erected by human culture. As Myra figures out, "That was Coyote's craziness, what they called her craziness. She wasn't afraid. She went between the two kinds of people, she crossed over" (39). Eventually, Myra realizes that although some of the other People accept her, it is only with "the generosity of big families" (39). Coyote alone consciously chose to take care of her, a choice growing out of Coyote's "crazy" ability and desire to cross over and make connections with human culture. In response to Coyote's attitude and actions, Myra chooses to connect across the boundaries as well. She decides to stay with Coyote rather than Chipmunk or Rabbit, even though Coyote's house is filthy and her bed is smelly and full of fleas. Ultimately, as Myra lies listening to Coyote singing "one of the endless tuneless songs that wove the roots of trees and bushes and ferns and grass in the web that held the stream in the streambed and the rock in the rock's place and the earth together," she tells Coyote, "I love you" (56).

Although Myra clearly changes in response to the worldview represented by Coyote and the rest of the First People, the question remains how significant any such change can be. After all, these People reach her precisely because of the human aspects of their appearance and language, so how successfully can their effect on her subvert dominant cultural ideologies that privilege the human? Similarly, an important question for many feminists is how to imagine a way in which discourse—which most poststructuralists view as the primary force determining the nature of social institutions as well as constructing meaning and human subjectivity—can be used to subvert the very ideologies it works to maintain. As Teresa de Lauretis explains in *Alice Doesn't*, "That patriarchy exists concretely, in social relations, and that it works precisely through the very discursive and representational structures that allow us to recognize it, is the problem and struggle of feminist theory" (165). This problem is further complicated by the sense that an extreme poststructuralist view of identity as purely socially constructed leaves little room for agency. In a version of social constructionism taken to its extreme, individuals have no real control over their actions or identities, but are instead "written" by history and culture and thus seem unable to intervene in these forces or in the construction of their own subjectivities in a subversive way. If Myra changes only in reaction to the extraordinary forces acting on her in the First World, without real choice or agency, how helpful can her example be for the rest of us?

For poststructuralist feminist theorists such as de Lauretis, the key to a theory of identity that allows for the ability of the subject to participate subversively in the construction of her own and others' subjectivities through discourse is the insight that the subject is constantly changing as it is exposed to shifting ideological forces and different discursive structures. As Joan Scott explains, "Subjects are constituted discursively, but there are conflicts among discursive systems, contradictions within any one of them, multiple meanings possible for the concepts they deploy" (34). It is the contradictions and conflicts among discursive systems and among axes of difference, and thus within the individual subject, that allows for the possibility of multiple meanings, or in other words, for interpretation. And it is through the act of interpreting the discursive and ideological forces acting on her that the individual subject can participate in the construction of those forces in return.

More specifically, in "Eccentric Subjects: Feminist Theory and Historical Consciousness," de Lauretis explores how individuals may achieve their potential to interpret and thus participate in the construction of ideological forces and their own subjectivities; they can do so by taking what de Lauretis calls an "excessive critical position," a position "attained through practices of political and personal displacement across boundaries between sociosexual identities and communities, between bodies and discourses, by what I like to call the eccentric subject" (145). In this view, displacement gives the subject a new perspective, highlighting the discrepancies and possibilities of meaning that allow for interpretation.

Significantly, "Buffalo Gals" begins with Myra's displacement across a boundary, into a realm where she is asked to take a drastically different view of identity and community than that held in dominant human culture. Le Guin represents this boundary quite vividly by the change in Coyote's appearance from unambiguously animal—Myra first notes that the coyote is "a big one, in good condition, its coat silvery and thick. The dark tear-line from its long yellow eye was as clearly marked as a tabby cat's" (17)—to ambiguously human, animal, and supernatural. Near the end of the story, when Myra decides to try to reapproach the world of the New People, her experience suggests that the boundary between the two worlds extends beyond physical appearance to the way the people on either side of it perceive and name reality. As Myra draws near,

> It did seem there was a line, a straight, jerky line drawn across the sagebrush plain, and on the far side of it—nothing? was it mist?
> "It's a ranch," the child said. "That's a fence. There's a lot of Herefords." The words tasted like iron, like salt in her mouth. The things she named wavered in her sight and faded, leaving nothing—a hole in the world, a burned place like a cigarette burn. (46)

Because she has crossed this boundary, at Coyote's invitation, Myra is confronted with confusions and inconsistencies, with multiple interpretations of reality and of her own identity. Throughout the course of the story, she learns to negotiate these multiple interpretations in a way that allows her consciously to step beyond her culturally constructed human perception and, at least temporarily, perceive as the nonhuman. For example, at one point Myra wonders why Coyote sleeps in the night and wakes in the day like humans rather than the other way around, but "when she framed the question in her mind she saw at once that night is when you sleep and day when you're awake" (34–35). While the readers of Le Guin's story may never be physically displaced across a boundary in the way Myra is, her experience can lead us to imagine situations that would encourage us to take the perspectives of identities and positions different than those to which we are accustomed.

Significantly, Myra's displacement does not lead her dualistically to choose one side of the boundary over the other or to try to eradicate the boundary through some form of homogeneous union of the two sides. Her response is instead dialogic, in the sense that Patrick D. Murphy explains in "Ground, Pivot, Motion": "A dialogic method can recognize that the most fundamental relationships are not resolvable through dialectical synthesis: humanity/nature, ignorance/knowledge, male/female, emotion/intellect, conscious/unconscious" (148). Instead, a dialogic approach puts such "opposites" in conversation with each other, acknowledging similarities without erasing difference. When Coyote first meets Myra, she names her "Gal," and Le Guin suggests that Myra deals with the potential contradiction between her two names by trying to look at the situation from Coyote's point of view: "She said it as a name; maybe it was the child's name, Myra, as spoken by Coyote" (23). Although Myra becomes better and better at understanding and adopting the worldview of the First People, she never entirely rejects her human perspective, either, somehow dialogically positioning herself on the boundary between the two: "The child thought of herself as Gal, but also sometimes as Myra" (39).

Of course, Myra's guide in learning to resist both dualism and dialectical synthesis is Coyote, a figure whose potential for connections that do not erase difference has been recognized by several feminist theorists. As Stacy Alaimo points out, Donna Haraway's use of the Coyote Trickster of Native American legend "not only resists glorified mystification, . . . [but] also destabilizes the dualism of active/passive, resource/user, knower/known on which an epistemology and a politics of domination is based" (145). Haraway sees in the liminal figure of Coyote a way to perceive

that historically specific human relations with "nature" must somehow—linguistically, ethically, scientifically, politically, technologically, and epistemologically—be imagined as genuinely social and actively relational; and yet the partners remain utterly unhomogeneous. . . . Curiously, as for people before us in western discourses, efforts to come to linguistic terms with the non-representability, historical contingency, artefactuality, and yet spontaneity, necessity, fragility, and stunning profusions of "nature" can help us refigure the kind of persons we might be. These persons can no longer be, if they ever were, master subjects, nor alienated subjects, but—just possibly—multiple heterogeneous, inhomogeneous, accountable, and connected human agents. (3)

What Myra learns from Coyote in Le Guin's story is precisely how to be such a human agent, and she achieves this state by learning to perceive reality in a new way. Myra's two eyes, one original and thus linked to the world of her origin and one given to her by the people of the First World, come to symbolize the ways of seeing represented by those two worlds. When she uses just her original eye in the world of the First People, "everything [is] clear and flat"; she learns she must use them both together if she is to gain depth perception. Chickadee hints at the potential power of such perception when she explains that "'Things are woven together. So we call the weaver the Grandmother.' She whistled four notes, looking up the smokehole. 'After all,' she added, 'maybe all this place, the other places too, maybe they're all only one side of the weaving. I don't know. I can only look with one eye at a time, how can I tell how deep it goes?'" (50)

Of course, learning to use both eyes together is difficult in either world. The new eye does not work well until Coyote licks it, and Myra starts to feel like it is not seeing at all as she approaches the world of her origin. Adapting to her new eye, though, does not mean adopting from the First People some monolithic way of seeing that is opposed to her original mode of perception, for there is no one way of seeing among the First People. Just as Myra sees them as human in form, they all see everyone as resembling their own species: As Coyote explains, "Resemblance is in the eye. . . . So, to me you're basically greyish yellow and run on four legs. . . . To Hawk, you're an egg, or maybe getting pinfeathers" (35). It is clear Myra cannot abandon her old eye, her human perception. Instead, she learns to see with both eyes at once, adopting the realization that there are many ways of seeing and learning to figure that realization into her own perception. This alteration of perspective is not a simple integration of opposites, however, for the two eyes and the two worlds they represent cannot be reduced to a dualistic opposition. One eye roots her in her human origins, while the other gives her depth perception: the knowledge of her interconnections with other species and other spiritual planes, an understanding of the multiple ways of seeing related to those other species and places, and the ability to respect the differences among those ways of seeing. In his article "Voicing Another Nature," Patrick D. Murphy gives us the term "another-otherness" for this perception of otherness that respects difference without using it to justify domination or prohibit connection: "'Anotherness' proceeds from a heterarchical—that is, a nonhierarchical—sense of difference" (63).

Le Guin's story deals with the possibility of integrating the two worlds represented by the two eyes more overtly as well. Chickadee tells Myra that once the boundary between the two did not exist: "'When we lived together it was all one place,' Chickadee said in her slow, soft home-voice. 'But not the others, the new people, they live apart. And their places are so heavy. They weigh down on our place, they press on it, draw it, suck it, eat it, eat holes in it, crowd it out" (49). But the idea of resolving the dualism between culture and its oppressed and repressed "others" by returning to some Edenic state when there are no discernible differences between humans, animals, and spirits is not a feasible one. As Donna Haraway explains, the answer to dualism is not to give into the seduction of such "origin myths," which promise the return to some original "organic wholeness through a final appropriation of all the powers of the parts into a higher unity" (150). While such a promise of the possibility of holism might seem the antidote to the hierarchical domination that proceeds from our culture's dualistic ideology, that sort of unity often requires that some entities be appropriated by or incorporated into others. Such an erasure of difference is just another kind of domination.

Le Guin, too, rejects the possibility that dualism may be resolved by returning to an original state of unity. Chickadee predicts that "Maybe after a while longer there'll only be one place again, their place. And none of us here. I knew Bison, out over the mountains. I knew Antelope right here. I knew Grizzly and Greywolf, up west there. Gone. All gone" (49–50). Thus, the possibility of achieving one place again is presented only as negative, as predicated on the eradication of the First People. The story also refuses the possibility of ending human culture's alienation from its "other" by rejecting the world of the New People. Myra has learned to adapt to and value the world of the First People, primarily through her emotional attachment to Coyote. Soon after Myra confesses to Coyote that she loves her, Coyote eats a poisoned salmon set out by one of the New People and suffers through an agonizing death. In her grief, Myra wants to reject all her connections with the world that killed Coyote; looking out at the town of New People, she pronounces, "I hope you all die in pain" (58).

However, Myra learns she cannot abandon her identity as a New Person; Chickadee and the spider-like Grandmother tell her that Coyote was in the process of taking her back to her own people before she was killed. Going back to the New People, though, does not mean leaving behind all her new connections with the First People or her newly learned way of seeing. They tell her she can keep her new eye, and Chickadee promises she will come if Myra makes gardens for her. Grandmother promises, "I'll be there too, you know. In your dreams, in your ideas, in dark corners in the basement" (60). Myra learns she may even reencounter her beloved Coyote, who, true to her legendary prototype, "gets killed all the time" (59). Corresponding to the persistence of the coyote species, this lack of finality to Coyote's death may seem to undercut the importance of human culture's need to transform its destructive behavior toward nonhuman nature. Yet, as Chickadee has revealed, species like Bison and Greywolf have been unable to survive the pressures of human culture. And as Myra's experience attests, any diminishment of the diversity of the world of the First People represents a loss to all people.

In the end, Myra becomes one of the hybrid "buffalo gals" of the novella's title, with allegiances to the worldviews of both First and New People. Her experience demonstrates a way that human beings can forge a relationship with nonhuman nature for political ends without positing essential or static connections that erase difference and reinscribe dualism or hierarchy. In *Simians, Cyborgs, and Women*, Donna Haraway turns to a model of political identity formulated by Chela Sandoval called oppositional consciousness: a kind of postmodern identity constructed out of "otherness, difference, and specificity" (155). Importantly, "this identity marks out a self-consciously constructed space that cannot affirm the capacity to act on the basis of natural identification, but only on the basis of conscious coalition, of affinity, of political kinship" (157). Ultimately, Le Guin's story provides us with a sense in which we can each act as conscious agents of political change. Through an openness to viewpoints and communities outside dominant human cultural experience, Myra becomes, and accepts the necessity of remaining, what Haraway would call a "split and contradictory self." Such a self holds the potential for subverting dominant ideologies because her divisions and contradictions allow her to connect without oversimplifying her identity in ways that reinscribe those ideologies in new forms; such a self is the one Haraway describes as able to "interrogate positionings and be accountable, the one who can construct and join rational conversations and fantastic imaginings that change history" (193).

In this way, the work of poststructuralist feminists can complement and complicate the ideas most commonly associated with ecofeminism by providing an approach to identity that encourages neither the erasure of difference by representing women and nature as a homogeneous, continuous whole nor its overemphasis, which can lead to alienation and the dominations of humans and nature. Such a sense of identity destabilizes views of both human subjectivity and nature, refusing static, definite boundaries between nature and culture, myth and reality, or any other traditionally constructed dualisms. Given this transformed vision of identity, differences between humans and the rest of nature as well as the differences among humans, including gender, race, ethnicity, and sexual orientation, need not be the roots of conflict; instead, they can be the potential source of new and more sustainable relationships both within human culture and between culture and nonhuman nature. Thus, by going beyond the boundaries of self-defined ecofeminist theory, ecofeminist literary criticism can strengthen its potential to offer us models of human identity and human relationships with nonhuman nature that can disrupt and challenge dominant ideologies, both through literary interpretations and through the politicized perceptions and actions that texts and interpretations can inspire.

Currently, ecofeminist literary criticism exists primarily in potential form, and the potential it holds for contributing to ecofeminism's agenda of political change as well as for expanding and complicating literary criticism's scope and methodology is significant. However, critics must work not only to apply the principles of ecofeminist theorists but also to cross boundaries to put those principles into dialogue with other theories and critical approaches as well as with the literary texts themselves. In this way, ecofeminist literary critics can become, like Myra, buffalo gals who choose to form alliances across boundaries of difference. Such alliances will inevitably involve opening ourselves up to a variety of approaches and viewpoints, and negotiating the ways these approaches and viewpoints interact with our own will allow ecofeminist literary critics to engage in a process of constant self-interrogation and transformation. In this way, by exploiting our position at the intersection of ecofeminism and literary theory and criticism, we can encourage theorists, critics, and readers alike to cross boundaries, building on our connections with each other while using our differences to expand the range of what we can imagine for our future.

Notes

1. In "Living Interconnections with Animals and Nature," Greta Gaard lists many of these publications. Notable among them for representing the diversity within ecofeminism are Caldecott and Leland, Diamond and Orenstein, and Plant. The 1993 collection edited by Gaard, *Ecofeminism: Women, Animals, Nature,* expands ecofeminism's focus to include animals in particular (as opposed to a previous tendency to discuss "nature" in general).

2. For a graphic representation of some of the differences of opinion within ecofeminism, see Salleh "Second Thoughts" and Biehl.

3. I use dualism in the sense of radical dichotomy; as Plumwood explains, "Dualism is the process by which contrasting concepts (for example, masculine and feminine gender identities) are formed by domination and subordination and constructed as oppositional and exclusive" (31). Plumwood goes on to explain why dualism is inevitably linked with hierarchy: "In dualism, the more highly valued side (males, humans) is construed as alien to and of a different nature or order of being from the 'lower', inferiorized side (women, nature) and each is treated as lacking in qualities which make possible overlap, kinship, or continuity. The nature of each is constructed in polarised ways by the exclusion of qualities shared with the other; the dominant side is taken as primary, the subordinated side is defined in relation to it. . . . The effect of dualism is, in Rosemary Radford Ruether's words, to 'naturalize domination'" (32).

4. For example, a number of ecofeminist writers have noted a masculine bias in the field of deep ecology, a branch of environmental philosophy that shares with ecofeminism the goal of ending humans' alienation from nonhuman nature. As the ecofeminist theorist Jim Cheney points out, though, deep ecologists' failure to question the role that patriarchal thought has played in human alienation from nature presents "inherent dangers, not the least of which is the possibility (or inevitability) that the methods employed for overcoming alienation . . . will be precisely those methods which originally produced or now sustain that alienation" (118). For introductions to the principles of deep ecology, see Naess, Fox, and Devall and Sessions. The ecofeminism–deep ecology debate has taken place largely within the pages of *Environmental Ethics*. In particular, see the work of Cheney, Salleh, and Zimmerman. For examples of ecofeminist critiques of deep ecology that occur elsewhere, see the work of Birkeland and Kheel.

5. Among ecofeminist theorists, there exists a spectrum of feminist positions on the issue of women's relationship to nature. The essentialism of radical or cultural feminists lies at one end; as Greta Gaard explains in "Misunderstanding Ecofeminism," embracing the woman/nature connection "has been the path of cultural feminists, who seek to wash themselves clean of the masculine public realm entirely, and exalt, instead, all those attributes of feminine culture—darkness, the wild, nature, animals, spirituality, the body, emotion" (21). At the opposite end is the position that "you can reject it, which has been the strategy of liberal feminists, who seek to abandon anything attributed to the feminine realm and leap headlong into the public male realm of reason, to go 'where the rights are'" (21). However, ecofeminists do sometimes disagree on the labels they give to these positions. In "Healing the Wounds: Feminism, Ecology, and the Nature/Culture Dualism" (both 1989 and 1990 versions), Ynestra King suggests feminists who embrace the woman-nature connection should be called *radical cultural feminists* or simply *cultural feminists* to distinguish them from *radical feminists* who repudiate the woman-nature connection to claim women's place in the realm of culture. Plumwood uses the terms *radical* and *cultural* for those who embrace the woman-nature connection and claims that those who repudiate that connection follow "the feminism of uncritical equality" (30). Carolyn Merchant calls this second group *liberal feminists:* "Historically, liberal feminists have argued that women do not

differ from men as rational agents and that exclusion from educational and economic opportunities have prevented them from realizing their own potential for creativity in all spheres of human life" (100).

6. As several critics have pointed out, the construction of women, nature, and Western culture found in *Woman and Nature* is far more complex than an unproblematized assertion of an essential, biological connection between women and nature. Ynestra King notes in "Healing the Wounds" (1989) that *Woman and Nature*, which is "located ambiguously between theory and poetry, has been read much too literally and at times invoked wrongly to collapse the domination of women and the domination of nature into a single, timeless phenomenon. Griffin collapses the rigid boundaries of the subject and the object, suggesting a recovery of mysticism as a way of knowing nature immanently" (125). King also notes, in "The Ecology of Feminism and the Feminism of Ecology," that *Woman and Nature* is "antidualistic, struggling to bridge the false oppositions of nature and culture, passion and reason" (28n12). In "Voicing Another Nature," Patrick D. Murphy argues that, in *Woman and Nature*, Griffin "employs a postmodernist metanarrative structure, polemically critiques what she observes, posits a utopian conclusion, and includes humans as part of the nature they study" (68); according to Murphy, Griffin's text is self-consciously about "the relationship of ideology to the constraints on dialogue about nature" (69).

7. In her theoretical essay "Split Culture," Griffin makes clear that, despite the historical association between women and nature in Western culture, neither men nor women are "safe" from the "divided habit of mind" that sees humans as separate from the earth (12). In "The Ecology of Feminism," King is careful to point out that if men feel more alienated from nonhuman nature than women do, it is a result of culture and history rather than an inherent aspect of men's identities. And thus ecofeminism should work toward "a dynamic, developmental theory of the person—male *and* female—who emerges out of nonhuman nature, where difference is neither reified or ignored and the dialectical relationship between human and nonhuman nature is understood" ("Healing the Wounds" 1989, 131). In addition to avoiding the dualism between men/culture and women/nature we see in more essentialist versions of ecofeminism, King is concerned with bridging the gap between rationality and spirituality she sees represented by socialist and cultural feminists. According to King, socialist feminists tend to share the rationalist bias of Marxist theorists and thus "have not seriously attended to the domination of nonhuman nature, nor to the domination of inner nature" ("Healing the Wounds" 1989, 128). Cultural feminists, with their focus on personal transformation and empowerment, account for the "inner nature" of human beings but fail to see women as social historical agents. For King, it is crucial for ecofeminism to go beyond the dualistic opposition implied by the extremes of these two positions: "we are not talking heads, nor are we unself-conscious nature" (128).

8. King's work demonstrates a consistent, explicit commitment to "the organic forging of a genuinely antidualistic . . . theory and practice" ("Healing the Wounds" 1989, 130). Griffin, in the preface to *Woman and Nature*, explains that one of her goals

is to deconstruct the "separations that are part of the civilized male's thinking and living" (xvi).

9. As Stacy Alaimo explains, "the poststructuralist idea that there is no 'outside' of the text, nothing that is not discursive," can actually be interpreted as broadening the possibilities for political effects and analyses because "breaking down the thought/reality opposition casts discourse as material" (151n3).

10. Note that this essay, as published in Diamond and Orenstein's 1990 collection *Reweaving the World: The Emergence of Ecofeminism,* is a later version of the essay that appears in Jaggar and Bordo's 1989 *Gender/Body/Knowledge: Feminist Reconstructions of Being and Knowing.* Although I cite the earlier version elsewhere in this essay, here I am citing the 1990 version because the earlier version does not include the discussion of body consciousness.

11. While King acknowledges that "the domination of sex, race, and class, and the domination of nature are mutually reinforcing" in "The Ecology of Feminism" (20), elsewhere she backs away from her commitment to the equal importance of all sources of difference and declares that "the mind-set of hierarchy" that allows domination to occur has "its material roots in the domination of human by human, particularly women by men" ("Healing the Wounds" 1989, 115–16). Similarly asserting that a certain form of oppression is prior to or the source of all others, Susan Griffin turns to the domination of nature as the original form of dualism and oppression in "Split Culture." She roots Western society's enslavement of African people in the cultural association of Africans with nonhuman nature (14).

12. Donna Haraway sees a similar tendency on the part of socialist feminists to search "for a single ground of domination to secure our revolutionary voice" (160–61) and identifies it as a form of essentialism.

13. In "Ground, Pivot, Motion: Ecofeminist Theory, Dialogics, and Literary Practice," Patrick D. Murphy even suggests a way to conceive of natural forces as acting on the subject through a form of discourse; using Bakhtin's theory of the utterance, he proposes, "If emotion and instinct arise from historical natural influences on the evolution of the species, then their exertions on our behavior, their entering into consciousness, are a form of the natural world 'speaking' to us through signs that our conscious renders verbally" (152).

14. Donna Haraway is a prominent exception to this trend.

15. Other stories in *Buffalo Gals and Other Animal Presences* may be more likely to create the impression of an essentialist connection between women and nature. In particular, "She Unnames Them" opposes women and nature to patriarchal culture and language. However, I believe the ingenious way in which Le Guin rewrites one of the dominant myths grounding Western culture's anthropocentrism (Adam's naming of, and consequent authority over, the animals in the Garden of Eden) can also be read as an exploration of the potential of language to subvert dominant cultural ideologies.

16. See Bright for more extensive discussions of the similarities between the biological coyote and the coyote of Native American legend.

17. In *Of Wolves and Men,* Barry Lopez describes how "the unrestrained savagery that was once a part of wolf killing in the United States continues with efforts in America to control 'brush wolves' or coyotes. These animals are hunted down by ranchers from helicopters with shotguns. Their dens are dynamited. Their mouths are wired shut and they are left to starve. They are strung up in trees and picked apart with pistol fire. They are doused with gasoline and ignited" (196).

Works Cited

Alaimo, Stacy. "Cyborg and Ecofeminist Interventions: Challenges for an Environmental Feminism." *Feminist Studies* 20 (Spring 1994): 133–52.

Biehl, Janet. *Rethinking Ecofeminist Politics.* Boston: South End Press, 1991.

Birkeland, Janis. "Ecofeminism: Linking Theory and Practice." *Ecofeminism: Women, Animals, Nature.* Ed. Greta Gaard. Philadelphia: Temple University Press, 1993. 13–59.

Bright, William. *A Coyote Reader.* Berkeley: University of California Press, 1993.

Caldecott, Léonie, and Stephanie Leland, eds. *Reclaim the Earth: Women Speak Out for Life on Earth.* London: Women's Press, 1983.

Campbell, SueEllen. "The Land and Language of Desire: Where Deep Ecology and Poststructuralism Meet." *Western American Literature* 24 (Nov. 1989): 199–211.

Cheney, Jim. "Eco-feminism and Deep Ecology." *Environmental Ethics* 9.2 (1987): 115–45.

Collard, Andrée, with Joyce Contrucci. *Rape of the Wild: Man's Violence against Animals and the Earth.* Bloomington: Indiana University Press, 1989.

Daly, Mary. *Gyn/Ecology: The Metaethics of Radical Feminism.* Boston: Beacon Press, 1978.

de Lauretis, Teresa. *Alice Doesn't: Feminism, Semiotics, Cinema.* Bloomington: Indiana University Press, 1984.

———. "Eccentric Subjects: Feminist Theory and Historical Consciousness." *Feminist Studies* 16 (Spring 1990): 115–50.

Devall, Bill, and George Sessions. *Deep Ecology: Living as if Nature Mattered.* Salt Lake City: Peregrine Smith Books, 1984.

Diamond, Irene, and Gloria Feman Orenstein, eds. *Reweaving the World: The Emergence of Ecofeminism.* San Francisco: Sierra Club Books, 1990.

Donaldson, Laura E. *Decolonizing Feminisms: Race, Gender, and Empire-Building.* Chapel Hill: University of North Carolina Press, 1992.

Fox, Warwick. *Towards a Transpersonal Ecology: Developing New Foundations for Environmentalism.* Boston: Shambhala, 1990.

Gaard, Greta, ed. *Ecofeminism: Women, Animals, Nature.* Philadelphia: Temple University Press, 1993.

———. "Living Interconnections with Animals and Nature." *Ecofeminism: Women, Animals, Nature.* Ed. Greta Gaard. Philadelphia: Temple University Press, 1993. 1–12.

———. "Misunderstanding Ecofeminism." *Z Papers* 3.1 (1994): 20–24.

Griffin, Susan. "Split Culture." *Healing the Wounds: The Promise of Ecofeminism.* Ed. Judith Plant. Philadelphia: New Society Publishers, 1989. 7–17.

———. *Woman and Nature: The Roaring inside Her.* New York: Harper and Row, 1978.

Haraway, Donna J. *Simians, Cyborgs, and Women: The Reinvention of Nature.* New York: Routledge, 1991.

Kheel, Marti. "Ecofeminism and Deep Ecology: Reflections on Identity and Difference." *Reweaving the World: The Emergence of Ecofeminism.* Ed. Irene Diamond and Gloria Feman Orenstein. San Francisco: Sierra Club Books, 1990. 128–37.

King, Ynestra. "The Ecology of Feminism and the Feminism of Ecology." *Healing the Wounds: The Promise of Ecofeminism.* Ed. Judith Plant. Philadelphia: New Society Publishers, 1989. 18–28.

———. "Healing the Wounds: Feminism, Ecology, and the Nature/Culture Dualism." *Gender/Body/Knowledge: Feminist Reconstructions of Being and Knowing.* Ed. Alison M. Jaggar and Susan P. Bordo. New Brunswick: Rutgers University Press, 1989. 115–41.

———. "Healing the Wounds: Feminism, Ecology, and the Nature/Culture Dualism." *Reweaving the World: The Emergence of Ecofeminism.* Ed. Irene Diamond and Gloria Feman Orenstein. San Francisco: Sierra Club Books, 1990. 106–21.

Le Guin, Ursula. "Buffalo Gals, Won't You Come Out Tonight." *Buffalo Gals and Other Animal Presences.* New York: Penguin Books, 1987. 17–60.

Lopez, Barry. *Of Wolves and Men.* New York: Charles Scribner's Sons, 1978.

Marshall, Ian. "Literal and Metaphoric Harmony with Nature: Ecofeminism and Harriet Prescott Spofford's 'Circumstance.'" *Modern Language Studies* 23 (Spring 1993): 48–58.

Merchant, Carolyn. "Ecofeminism and Feminist Theory." *Reweaving the World: The Emergence of Ecofeminism.* Ed. Irene Diamond and Gloria Feman Orenstein. San Francisco: Sierra Club Books, 1990. 100–105.

Murphy, Patrick D. "Ground, Pivot, Motion: Ecofeminist Theory, Dialogics, and Literary Practice." *Hypatia* 6.1 (1991): 146–61.

———. "Voicing Another Nature." *A Dialogue of Voices: Feminist Theory and Bakhtin.* Ed. Karen Hohne and Helen Wussow. Minneapolis: University of Minnesota Press, 1994. 59–82.

Naess, Arne. "The Shallow and the Deep, Long-Range Ecology Movement: A Summary." *Inquiry* 16.1 (1973): 95–100.

Norwood, Vera. *Made from This Earth: American Women and Nature.* Chapel Hill: University of North Carolina Press, 1993.

Plant, Judith, ed. *Healing the Wounds: The Promise of Ecofeminism.* Philadelphia: New Society Publishers, 1989.

Plumwood, Val. *Feminism and the Mastery of Nature.* London: Routledge, 1993.

Salleh, Ariel. "Class, Race, and Gender Discourse in the Ecofeminism/Deep Ecology Debate." *Environmental Ethics* 15.3 (1993): 225–44.

————. "Deeper than Deep Ecology: The Eco-Feminist Connection." *Environmental Ethics* 6.4 (Winter 1984): 339–45.

————. "Second Thoughts on *Rethinking Ecofeminist Politics:* A Dialectical Critique." *ISLE: Interdisciplinary Studies in Literature and Environment* 1.2 (1993): 93–106.

Scott, Joan W. "'Experience.'" *Feminists Theorize the Political.* Ed. Judith Butler and Joan W. Scott. New York: Routledge, 1992. 22–40.

Toelken, Barre. "Ma'i Joldloshi: Legendary Styles and Navajo Myth." *American Folk Legend.* Ed. Wayland Hand. Berkeley: University of California Press, 1971. 203–11.

Zimmerman, Michael. "Feminism, Deep Ecology, and Environmental Ethics." *Environmental Ethics* 9.1 (Spring 1987): 21–44.

6

"Skin Dreaming":
The Bodily Transgressions of Fielding Burke,
Octavia Butler, and Linda Hogan

Stacy Alaimo

A DISTURBING SCENE in Fielding Burke's 1932 *Call Home the Heart* raises potent questions about how environmental feminism can negotiate the racially inflected ideologies of nature and the body. Because the discursive links between "nature," the "body," and racist hierarchies have, historically, been so firmly forged, it is crucial not only to understand how these discourses have functioned but also to determine the possibilities for transforming this volatile space. Burke's novel demonstrates how two predominant ideologies of nature, the social Darwinist and the romantic, employ a racially marked body to bolster white supremacy. Her novel exemplifies the discursive territory that Octavia Butler and Linda Hogan disrupt through their bodily transgressions. While Burke narrates a tale of white flight from the debased "natural" body, Butler and Hogan occupy corporeality to recreate it as a space of liminality and resistance.

Burke's *Call Home the Heart,* a socialist-feminist novel, narrates the struggles of Ishma, a young woman who leaves her husband and her beloved mountains because she "'couldn't go on living like an old cow. Fodder in winter and grass in summer and a calf every year'" (393). She flees from the "animality" of her existence, especially the endless reproduction. Fortunately, while participating in the Gastonia mining strikes, Ishma befriends a communist doctor who provides her with the information she needs to control her own reproduction. Yet, ideologically, it is not until the strangely pivotal scene with Gaffie Wells that Ishma gains freedom from her body. After having courageously saved Gaffie's husband from lynching by a KKK group, Ishma ungraciously receives her outpouring of gratitude:

Gaffie Wells was very fat and very black. Her lips were heavy, and her teeth so large that one needed the sure avouch of eyes to believe in them. It was impossible to associate her with woe, though tears were racing down her cheeks. As her fat body moved she shook off an odor that an unwashed collie would have disowned.

"Bressed angel, bressed angel ob de Lawd," she kept repeating, and with a great sweep enveloped Ishma, her fat arms encircling the white neck, her thick lips mumbling at the quivering white throat. "We'll all be in heaben togeddah! Sistah! sistah! Yo' sho' got Jedus in you!"

The fleshy embrace, the murky little room, the smoking ashes, the warm stench, the too eager faces shining greasily at the top of big, black bodies, filled Ishma with uncontrollable revulsion. She thought of a high, clean rock on Cloudy Knob, half covered with sweet moss and red-tipped galax. She shut her eyes and saw a cardinal flying over the snow. (383)

Ishma recoils from Gaffie, who becomes in her eyes a horrific, racist signifier of the body. Gaffie's earthly, massive, black flesh threateningly encircles the white "angel's" fragile neck. Ishma escapes the claustrophobic entrapment of the flesh by imagining a "high, clean rock" and an ethereal cardinal soaring over (white) snow. Ishma's white, romanticized view of an aesthetic, spiritual, liberating nature thus displaces the "low" aspects of the natural, the inescapable corporeality of human beings, onto the "lower" race.[1]

This scene demonstrates how even though "the body" has been persistently coded as female in Western culture, white women have fled from corporeal connections with a debased nature by displacing that nature onto the bodies of African Americans and others. While illustrating the interlocking ideologies of race and gender, this scene also manifests the counterposed ideologies of a "romantic" versus a social Darwinist nature that have persisted in the United States. Social Darwinism—as a popularized ideology, not as a strictly scientific theory—places humans, like other life forms, in a struggle for the survival of the "fittest," which serves to justify capitalism by naturalizing it. Indeed, the "survival of the fittest" metaphor naturalizes racist social inequities by categorizing types of bodies. Once race is accepted as a natural classification, social Darwinism can employ racial hierarchies to mitigate anxieties about human corporeality—anxieties fostered by the theory of evolution. Darwin toppled "man" from his Adamic role as master of the animals by stressing the kinship between humans and other primates. To ease their anxieties about being related to a nature they assumed they had risen above, whites interposed the "lower races" to serve as a border zone. Social Darwinism, then, takes the Cartesian hierarchy between mind and body and stretches it into a racist and anthropocentric scale, in part by imagining that evolution is teleological.

Romantic conceptions of nature,[2] on the other hand, invoke nature as a disembodied space, a place in which the individual can mentally or spiritually find respite, a place to feel that "unity with nature." If social Darwinism negotiates humans' troublesome corporeality by placing human bodies on a hierarchical scale in which some bodies are closer to "nature" than others, the romantic view of nature flees the physical realm altogether by seeking a mental or spiritual communion with nature. Yet this "unity" with nature denies nature its own specificity: nature serves as a mirror for the human subject who does not seek connection across difference but merely wishes to confirm a preconceived image. Or, as Chaia Heller puts it, our "idea of nature has become the small, blue pool into which Narcissus gazed, enamored of his own reflection" (231). When Ishma fantasizes about a cardinal flying against snow, for example, that serves to mirror (and produce) her own "clean" whiteness. Moreover, such romantic musings usually emanate from a disembodied Cartesian self, who is, by definition, radically severed from all that is "natural."

The pivotal scene in *Call Home the Heart* illustrates how the dual images of nature, the idealized and the debased, work as two sides of the same system, a system that maps a Cartesian dichotomy onto nature: the idealized version of nature is associated with the human mind or spirit, while the debased version of nature is associated with the human body.[3] Dividing nature into the ethereal and the abject allows the "higher" races and classes to use nature as a dumping ground,[4] even while reserving another nature as an idealized place to which only they have privileged access. During the back-to-nature movements in the early twentieth century, for example, many middle- to upper-class white males in the United States, such as the conservationist William T. Hornaday in *Our Vanishing Wildlife: Its Extermination and Preservation*, reiterated that the wilderness properly belonged to white men, even as they depicted blacks, Italians, and other "lower races" as savages "closer" to nature.

Thus, historically, nature has been mapped by dichotomies coded by gender and race, associating women and people of color with abject bodily resources. Negotiating such an ideologically mined terrain is extremely difficult, especially when the idealized version of nature seems to be complicitous in maintaining its mirror image. If every action has an equal and opposite reaction, perhaps leaping into an ethereal realm as Ishma does can be accomplished only by propelling "nature" onto the bodies of others. Taking disembodied, romantic flight strengthens the dichotomies between the corporeal and the ethereal, the body and the mind, nature and culture.

Occupying the space of the abject body, however, offers the potential for disrupting this constellation of ideologies. Precisely because the body has been so intimately associated with racially, sexually, and environmentally destructive ideologies of nature, it offers a potent site for contestation and transformation. In *Volatile Bodies* Elizabeth Grosz argues that reconceptions of the body, which regard it as "the threshold or borderline concept that hovers perilously and undecidably at the pivotal point of binary pairs," can disrupt our most basic and enduring oppositions: "The body is neither—while also being both—the private or the public, self or other, natural or cultural, psychical or social. . . . This indeterminable position enables it to be used as a particularly powerful strategic term to upset the frameworks by which these binary pairs are considered" (23–24). Linda Hogan and Octavia Butler evoke the body precisely in this way: they rewrite the body as a liminal, indeterminate space that disrupts the opposition between nature and culture, object and subject. At the same time, they conjure nature-body connections in which neither nature nor the body is fallen, denigrated, or exiled. Although stressing the connections between the body and nature could reinforce the same system of oppositions coded by gender and race, Hogan and Butler rewrite the body in ways that disrupt historically ingrained patterns. They invoke the body not as a mute, passive space that signifies the inferior part of our natures but as a place of vibrant connection, historical memory, and knowledge. By rewriting the body they also displace social Darwinist vertical hierarchies with horizontal relationships. The verticality of the racially coded Cartesian split shown in *Call Home the Heart* is toppled and a variety of horizontal parallels, transformations, and "crossings" take its place: Hogan charts the parallel and intersecting paths of humans, mountain lions, and whales, while Butler transforms her female protagonist into dolphins and leopards. Instead of peering down at other creatures, they look across, from within, and—importantly—away from. As the paths of humans and animals intersect, the body becomes a threshold, a site of elemental connections, and a space for "skin dreaming."

Bodily (In)Vestments versus Bodily Knowledges in Octavia Butler's *Wild Seed*

In a passage that could serve as an epigraph for Octavia Butler's work, Trinh T. Minh-ha writes: "Ego is an identification with the mind. When ego develops, the head takes over and exerts tyrannical control over the rest of the body. . . . But thought is as much a product of the eye, the finger, or the foot as it is of the brain" (39). Butler's *Wild Seed* dramatizes a battle between two modes of knowing and being: the tyrannical force of an egotistical, disembodied mind and the transformative powers of an utterly embodied woman. Doro, an immortal creature whose vocation is to breed human beings for extraordinary physical or mental strengths, keeps his people like slaves; he owns them, he controls their reproduction, and he even consumes some of them. In a later book in the same series, *Mind of My Mind,* Doro confesses to one of "his" people that he began breeding humans because people with a "certain mental sensibility" simply tasted the best (90). The "wild seed" of the title is Doro's name for the people he collects for their genetic potential, people who are "too valuable to be casually killed" (13). Doro represents a slavemaster ideology that treats humans as seeds to be sown and harvested, as farm animals to be used and bred by their owners. Although Doro breeds people of all races, his practices suggest the treatment of African slaves in the United States and the racist and capitalist ideologies that naturalized the institution of slavery. "Wild seed" encapsulates the capitalist response to nature that slave owners extended onto African bodies: wild seed, like other "natural resources," supposedly has no value until the entrepreneur discovers it, appropriates it, and transforms it into something "valuable."

Representing a horrific Cartesian subjectivity, Doro must kill to obtain new bodies; he needs a fresh supply of bodies to "wear" until they are worn out. Radically severed from his own corporeality, he exists as an amalgam of mind and will that prospers by subjugating other human bodies. Doro would agree with his fellow breeder John Hammond, the "creator" of the dinosaurs in the film *Jurassic Park,* who contends, "creation is an act of sheer will." The desire simply to will beings into being is no doubt motivated by the wish to obliterate or deny women's power to give birth. Although Doro often mates with women himself, using his body-of-the-week to impregnate them, it is his will that drives his plan to create a master race. As the metaphor "wild seed" suggests, he treats humans the way humans have treated nature, as a space evacuated of mind: "Cartesian thought declares non-human nature *terra nullius,* uninhabited by mind, totally available for annexation, a sphere easily molded to the ends of a reason conceived as without limits" (Plumwood 192). In other words, Cartesian thought defines nonhuman nature as that which is devoid of mind or intention, so that humans can fashion themselves as the only creatures endowed with "reason" and, moreover, to justify reason's unchecked use, alteration, and even destruction of nonhuman nature. Doro extends the Cartesian territory of *terra nullius* onto human bodies, bodies that he can colonize, breed, and control with his disembodied mind. For Doro, both a Cartesian and a capitalist, bodies are nothing but vestments and investments.

Butler counterposes Anyanwu to Doro: she is the only one sufficiently strong and immortal to be a match for him. Unlike Doro, she does not require a perpetually new wardrobe of bodies for her journey through the millennia. Anyanwu's body is no mere vestment—it is her greatest strength. When first threatened by Doro's power she realizes that neither God nor prayer would save her, "she had only herself and the magic she could perform with her own body" (36). That magic includes healing herself, healing others, manufacturing medicines within her body, and transforming herself into many different bodies, old and young, male and female, black and white, human and animal. As in her Xenogenesis Trilogy, Butler radically challenges the oppositions between body and mind, nature and culture by creating bodies that know. Anyanwu's body "reads" the information embodied in other creatures (80), suggesting that corporeality, like culture, is coded and bodies, not just minds, have the power to interpret these codes. By describing the body as a place that is not only written upon but an entity that also reads, Butler stresses the body's agency and "mind." For example, by eating dolphin flesh for the first time, Anyanwu's body learns dolphinness: "for her, the flesh of the fish told her all she needed to know about the creature's physical structure—all she needed to know to take its shape and live as it did. Just a small amount of raw flesh told her more than she had words to say. Within each bite, the creature told her its story clearly thousands of times" (79). Although rather gruesome, this scene collapses the dichotomies between nature and culture, body and mind, subject and object, as each bite gives an enlightening gustatory-narrative jouissance. Carol J. Adams has argued that the "traffic in animals" functions, in part, by ontologizing animals into "meat" as a "mass term" that naturalizes the eating of animals by denying them their uniqueness and individuality (201–2). While Anyanwu does consume the dolphin, the passage as a whole works against the ontology of animals as a mass term because the dolphin is hardly a slab of mute flesh—significantly, it has its own story to tell. This story is told in a mode of signification that not only transgresses the nature-culture divide but also surpasses the usual forms of communication: Anyanwu "thought her flesh-messages even more specific than . . . books" (80).

She ingests so much information that her body is able to transform itself into a dolphin, which thereby allows her to experience a different way of seeing and breathing and to enjoy the "tricks" that her dolphin body "knew" (82). She realizes that dolphins have a complex system of communication, do not enslave their own people as humans do, and enjoy rather seductive mating rituals, as she is swept into a mating dance with a charming male dolphin. Unfortunately, a human male takes her back to the ship before she can consummate this relationship. When Isaac, the man whom Anyanwu will later marry, jumps into the water to bring her back, Anyanwu (as a dolphin) finds him a "clumsy thing, stiff and strange"—hardly as tempting as the male dolphin she was just courting (85). Instead of extolling bestiality, this scene demonstrates to what extent embodied perspectives shape our desires and judgments, as does a later scene in which a now white Anyanwu is horrified to realize that she walked by a slave market without noticing the slaves (211).

Embodied knowledges effect ethical commitments as well as blind spots; Anyanwu's experience as a dolphin compels her to vow never to eat dolphin again. By emphasizing to what extent bodily perspectives shape our perceptions, Anyanwu's experiences critique the epistemological ideal of objectivity, which asserts that the "truest," most reliable knowledge results from processes that are "beyond" a particular perspective. Similarly, Donna Haraway condemns the ideals of objectivity that relativism and totalization promote as irresponsible "god-tricks" that promise "vision from everywhere and nowhere equally and fully" (191). She argues that "only partial perspective promises objective vision": "Feminist objectivity is about limited location and situated knowledge, not about transcendence and splitting of subject and object. In this way we might become answerable for what we learn how to see" (190). Instead of assuming that the most "true" knowledge emanates from a disembodied knower who is somehow both "nowhere" and "everywhere," Haraway argues for knowledges that take into account their own limited perspectives and are responsible for their own positions. Rather than value a transcendent distance between the subject (the knower) and the object (the known), "situated knowledges" account for their limited positions in part by considering the interrelations between subject and object. Similarly, Anyanwu's transformations refuse rigidly to divide subject from object, knower from known. Since Anyanwu understands "dolphinness" only after she has transformed herself into a dolphin, her way of knowing collapses the very division between subject and object, as one transforms into the other. Anyanwu's transformations dramatize an embodied epistemology that acts as an antidote to willful separations and masterful machinations.

Wild Seed paints a monstrous portrait of Cartesian subjectivity while creating an alternative in Anyanwu, whose name invitingly sounds like "anyone-you." By shapeshifting into eagles, dolphins, and leopards, Anyanwu transgresses the human-animal divide, traveling horizontally across into different, but not inferior, forms that offer alternative ways of seeing the world. Anyanwu enacts María Lugones's argument for "traveling to someone's 'world'" as a way to understand *what it is to be them and what it is to be ourselves in their eyes.* She contends that only "when we have traveled to each other's 'worlds' are we fully subjects to each other" (401; Lugones's emphasis). In Butler's work, animals are not objects for appropriation but subjects living in "worlds" of their own. Furthermore, Anyanwu, like several feminist epistemologists, dramatizes the extent to which knowledges are embodied and suggests a model of knowing that sees animal and human bodies as active, signifying forces, not abject, mute, passive resources. Butler casts off the body as a mere vestment or investment and transforms it into a liminal space that blurs the divisions between humans and animals, subjects and objects, nature and culture.

Linda Hogan's "Terrain of Crossed Beginnings"

In an interview with Patricia Clark Smith, Linda Hogan stated that after participating in a research project on wolves in northern Minnesota she realized that "wolves really are the projection of people's inner fears or desires." She also discovered how "difficult it is for people to see difference—between one human being and another, between species. What people look for is similarities—or shadow—the shadow-self, as Jung says, so you can look for evil on the outside and not have to acknowledge your inner evil" (151). These projections, of course, are no mere psychological matter—they have contributed to the extermination of many thousands of wolves in the United States alone. It is therefore important for environmental philosophy to create conceptions of nature that neither radically sever it from humanity nor pose it as a tabula rasa for human inscriptions.[5] While Hogan's poetry evokes profound connections with nature, it strives to affirm nature's differences, in part by refusing to engulf it within human projections. As it represents human-nature relations with a difference, Hogan's poetry rejects both the romantic and the debased versions of nature, offering us *The Book of Medicines* for Cartesian dis-ease.

"Mountain Lion," for example, eschews a mystified moment of unity as it describes the speaker's fearful encounter with the mountain lion. Hogan grants the mountain lion her own perspective that reverses the usual categories of the civilized and the wild, a perspective in which the human "was the wild thing / she had learned to fear" (19–20). The speaker of the poem acknowledges that the mountain lion does not desire her presence, in fact, "Her power lived / in a dream of my leaving" (21–22). The recognition that her presence is unwelcome to the mountain lion gives the speaker a self-consciousness about the consequences of her gaze, as the look she first aims at the mountain lion and then turns away serves as a metonym for their vexed relation.

> It was the same way
> I have looked so many times at others
> in clear light
> before lowering my eyes
> and turning away

from what lives inside those
who have found
two worlds cannot live
inside a single vision.
   (23–31)

The "clear light" signals Enlightenment models of knowing in which the distance between the subject and the object looks like mere empty space. This emptiness then presumes to offer perfect access to transparent knowledge, as nothing impedes the viewer's penetrating gaze. The speaker rejects this paradigm, however, by turning away and lowering her eyes. By looking away, she does not entrap the lion within the parameters of her gaze, but instead acknowledges the mountain lion's integrity and the substantial differences between the worlds they inhabit.

As John Berger explains, the human gaze has objectified animals: "animals are always the observed. The fact that they can observe us has lost all significance. They are the objects of our ever-extending knowledge. What we know about them is an index of our power, and thus an index of what separates us from them. The more we know, the further away they are" (16). Paradoxically, by diverting her gaze and choosing to know less, not more, she does not push the lion further away by reducing her to an object of knowledge. Instead, she acknowledges that they exist in separate, but parallel worlds. She deflects the romantic desire to feel a sense of unity with the lion or to use the lion as a mirror to reflect back her own consciousness. She also refuses to colonize the lion's territory or self by subsuming it into her view. The colonizing response to nature operates, in part, through "denying and canceling [nature's] independence of self" (Plumwood 191). These responses to the lion would destroy her: "two worlds cannot live / inside a single vision" (30–31).

In "Naming the Animals," it is language, not vision, that entraps the animals. Leaving Eve out, Hogan rewrites the story of Adam naming the animals by suggesting that naming is a proprietary act that both distances and circumscribes that which is named. After Adam calls "legs, hands, / the body / of man out of clay and sleep" (1–3), he continues to name other creatures:

these he named; wolf, bear, other
as if they had not been there
before his words, had not
had other tongues and powers
or sung themselves into life
before him.

These he sent crawling into wilderness
he could not enter.
    (7–14)

Naming captures the animals in language, seemingly to fence them within the
sphere of human territory, yet the final act sends them "crawling into wilderness / he could not enter." Whereas acknowledging the integrity of the mountain lion's vision allows the poet and the lion to retain a parallel relationship,
naming the animals within human language paradoxically inscribes them as
the not-human. Moreover, although the animals had "been there / before his
words," the act of naming constitutes an ersatz "creation" that negates the
animals by conjuring them into language only to expel them. Descartes appears to incite this process, since naming "the body / of man" (2–3) allows man
to forget the "clay of his beginnings" (5). Thus, man forgets his own earthy
origins, divorcing himself from the corporeal and the animal, while constructing a wilderness to contain the exiled.

The animals' abject status would then be transferred to certain groups of
humans: the children of Adam "would call us pigs" (22). While one would expect the speaker to deny this appellation, she abruptly affirms the misnomer:

I am a pig,
the child of pigs,
wild in this land
of their leavings,
drinking from water that burns
at the edge of a savage country
of law and order.
    (23–29)

By affirming a connection to one of the most abject animals, Hogan underscores a historical truth, that Christians treated Native Americans with disdain
and brutality, as "pigs"; but she also takes refuge in a space that is not the territory of a "savage country / of law and order." In her interview with Smith,
Hogan discusses how "women and Indians are often equated with animals, in
ways that have negative connotations for all three." When Smith suggests this
underlines "the horror people have of the physical" Hogan responds, "and of
the body, of all matter. Matter is not our primary concern in this country, or
in Western thinking" (148–49). Instead of distancing herself from the abject,
Hogan animates matter itself. Like the animals "at the fierce edge of forest"
who "know the names for themselves" (18–19), the speaker, at the end of the
poem, finds her power through physicality:

From somewhere I can't speak or tell,
my stolen powers
hold out their hands
and sing me through.
   (35–38)

Just as the animals had already "sung themselves into life" (11) before their naming by man, the speaker is recreated. Although she cannot articulate where the source of her powers lies, perhaps because (the English) language itself enforces the mind/matter split, the metaphor of her powers holding "out their hands" suggests an embodied passage "through," to a time "before" Cartesian, Adamic separations, to a time when "there [were] no edges to the names" (33).

Because she is living in an age when matter does not matter, it seems crucial for Hogan to accentuate human embodiment. In an interview with Joseph Bruchac, Hogan explained the fundamental importance of physicality: "We're here on earth with our bodies. We're not meant for outer space physically or spiritually. People who go into the mental can go off too far into the mental. I don't know many people who can go off too far into the physical (I don't mean athletically or sexually, I mean awareness of the body)" (130). Awareness of the body not only offers a sense of grounding for humans but also holds out the possibility for connections with nature that neither obliterate its differences nor reinforce hierarchies of beings.

Along with "Naming the Animals," several other poems capture a yearning to experience bodily ties with nature and to cross over to a time when those corporeal connections were most evident. "Crossings" reverses the teleological and anthropocentric misconception that "ontogeny recapitulates phylogeny,"[6] in which the (human) fetus replays the entire evolutionary procession by developing from fish to human. Instead of a human fetus with fishlike characteristics, Hogan describes a fetal whale with human features.

Not yet whale, it still wore the shadow
of a human face, and fingers
that had grown before the taking
back and turning into fin.
   (11–14)

Wearing a "shadow / of a human face," the fetal whale is hauntingly human-like; caught in a frozen, illuminating moment, on a "block of shining ice" (10), the creature embodies a corporeal "crossing" between whale and human. Significantly, the human form is not the ultimate destination: the fingers are taken back and transformed into fin, a more fitting form for whale life.

Seeing the fetal whale evokes a longing for the "terrain of crossed beginnings":

Sometimes the longing in me
comes from when I remember
the terrain of crossed beginnings
when whales lived on land
and we stepped out of water
to enter our lives in air.
    (18–23)

The corporeal crossings embodied by the human features of the fetal whale parallel the geographic, evolutionary paths of humans and whales that crossed in the past. Although the poet longs for the time when the paths crossed and humans and whales met at the intersection, the narrator does not envelop the whale in her longing, but instead charts the separate, but intersecting paths that the two species have taken. Hogan thus displaces a ladder of beings with a horizontal nonhierarchical model of difference.

"Skin Dreaming" and "Great Measures" also evoke a mythical past of corporeal crossings. In "Skin Dreaming," skin, which is "the oldest thing" (12), is also the

    closest thing to God
touching oil, clay,
intimate with the foreign land of air
and other bodies.
    (1–4)

Skin is "godly" not because it is transcendent or ethereal, but because of its liminality, its intimacy with the "outside" world of oil, clay, "other bodies," and the "foreign land of air." The juxtaposition of intimacy with the "foreignness" of something as common as air depicts the skin as a brave corporeal ambassador, crossing borders. Skin, somehow, has a memory: "It remembers when it was the cold / builder of fire" (13–14). The skin blends into the cold air that chills it. As a liminal zone, the skin both "*was* the cold" itself and was also the "cold / builder of fire" as the line break suggests. Since fire is a common icon for human achievement, these lines make skin an agent of culture. No gift from the gods on high, fire is created by the skin that it will warm.

Skin is not only spatially liminal but temporally liminal; it emerges from the past, from ancestors and forests, paradoxically embodying a history of what no longer is.

It has fallen through ancestral hands.
It is the bearer of vanished forest
fallen through teeth and jaws
of earth
where we were once other
visions and creations.
    (22–27)

Skin falls from the "ancestral hands" as if it were an unplanned gift from the ancestors, a gift that has escaped the predatory "teeth and jaws / of earth." As a liminal zone the skin is part of the clay it touches, yet it has escaped being absorbed back into the earth itself. Skin "bears" vanished forest in that it somehow brings forth the forests of the past that it has been intimate with, but it also must "bear" that the forest has vanished. Born from its ancestors, skin brings forth both the presence and the absence of the forests "where we were once other / visions and creations." The final lines suggest skin dreams recall a time and place where humans were not human; the skin as a liminal boundary dissolves, dissolving a distinctly human identity.

Although it has genealogical "roots" in the past, Hogan's image of the skin is similar to Gilles Deleuze and Felix Guattari's notion of a rhizome, which "connects any point to any other point, and its traits are not necessarily linked to traits of the same nature; it brings into play very different regimes of signs, and even nonsign states" (21). The skin connects with oil, clay, air, cold, ancestors, and forests—both signifying and nonsignifying states. More importantly, like the rhizome, it is "always in the middle, between things, interbeing, *intermezzo*" (25). By being precisely in the middle, skin disrupts the old dichotomies that sever nature from culture, subject from object, body from mind. Grosz explains that in Deleuze and Guattari's writing, "subject and object can no longer be understood as discrete entities or binary opposites. Things, material or psychical, can no longer be seen in terms of rigid boundaries, clear demarcations; nor, on an opposite track, can they be seen as inherently united, singular or holistic" (167). Similarly, Hogan transforms the skin from a boundary that contains the human form into a liminal zone that connects across and dissolves boundaries.

"Great Measures" dissolves the boundaries of the human into corporeal connections with substances and elements of the earth. The voice of the poem describes the "first time a lover held me" (1) as an elemental transformation into body and liquid.

I was hand, body, liquid
ruled by dark seas

that swallow the edges of land
and give them up to another place.

I am still this measure of brine,
ancient carbon, the pull of iron
across linked and desperate distances,
beginning and end together
the way sunlight on skin
is still connected
to the fiery storms of its origins.
      (5–15)

The speaker defines herself as a "measure" of the basic fluids and elements of life. The word *measure* suggests the materiality of the definition, in that places, substances, and ingredients are measured, yet it also suggests a section of music, a section made up of the same basic elements as the other measures and related to them through patterns of melody and harmony. This is a profoundly antiromantic definition in that the images of brine, carbon, and iron are not prettified, lofty, or ethereal: no rainbows or flowers here. Again the skin suggests to the poet the origins of life itself; the fiery storms recall cauldrons of lava deep in the earth. The connection is an embodied, sensual one: sunlight on skin does not look like fire, it *feels* like fire. But most significantly, the speaker defines herself as "the pull of iron / across linked and desperate distances"; her body becomes not a self-enclosed place but a magnetic force that pulls together "desperate distances." "Desperate" suggests the strong desire for these severed distances to reconnect, yet the images of brine, carbon, and iron disrupt any lingering desire for a holistic unity that would contain and govern these dispersed elements. Like Deleuze and Guattari's "body without organs" that is not a "fragmented, splintered body," but instead "nonstratified, unformed, intense matter" (164, 153), the body in "Great Measures" transgresses ordinary physical boundaries by becoming a multiplicity of nonstratified, elemental matter. Such matter—which profoundly "matters"—traverses the categories of animal, vegetable, and mineral, and thus calls such divisions into question.

The body is a crucial site for contestation and transformation, precisely because ideologies of the body have been complicit in the degradation of people of color, women, and nature. Octavia Butler's *Wild Seed* and Linda Hogan's poetry in *The Book of Medicines* challenge the dominant dichotomies by envisioning bodily transgressions and corporeal crossings. They transform the body from a site of abjection into a means of connection. Instead of displacing corporeality onto the bodies of racially marked others, as Ishma does in

Call Home the Heart, they displace the Cartesian and social Darwinist ideologies that cast the body as abject by rewriting the body as a place of power, knowledge, and liminality. Rosi Braidotti describes a "new form of corporeal materialism" in which "the body is seen as an inter-face, a threshold, a field of intersection of material and symbolic forces" (219). For this corporeal materialism to effectively challenge the system of dichotomies that sever nature from culture, it is important that the body be not just a place that has been inscribed by cultural forces but a threshold where nature and culture dissolve, a rhizomatic place that connects "desperate distances" through elemental relations to such things as brine, carbon, and the pull of iron. Not exactly abject and certainly not sublime, images of brine and carbon suggest another way of envisioning nature that neither engulfs it within a romantic vision nor severs it from humanity altogether. By refusing to divide nature from culture, body from mind, subject from object, Linda Hogan and Octavia Butler encourage us to find new ways of understanding the places we inhabit, the places we are.

Notes

I would like to thank Greta Gaard and Patrick Murphy for their constructive and thought-provoking comments.

1. In my book manuscript in progress, "Undomesticated Ground: Nature and Feminism in Fiction, Theory, and Culture," in which I argue that "nature" has served as a crucial zone for the cultural work of feminism, I extensively discuss *Call Home the Heart* and analyze Octavia Butler's Xenogenesis Trilogy, along with several other literary, theoretical, and popular culture texts.

2. I am using the term *romantic* in a rather broad sense to describe an idealized and elevated version of nature that exists outside the human self. For an interesting feminist critique of how nature has been portrayed within ideologies of romantic love, see Heller.

3. It is ironic that the Cartesian dichotomy would be replicated on nature, since the Cartesian mind, as Plumwood explains, defines itself against nature. "Descartes enforces . . . a strict and total division not only between mental and bodily activity, but between mind and nature and between human and animal. As mind becomes pure thought—pure *res cogitans* or thinking substance, mental, incorporeal, without location, bodiless—body as its dualised other becomes pure matter, pure *res extensa*, materiality as lack" (115).

4. Several aspects of Julia Kristeva's conception of the abject resonate with this essay: the abject is that which is banished from, opposed to, and thus helps define the human self; the abject often signals "those fragile states where man strays on the territories of *animal*"; and the abject functions as a border that obscures the self's relation to and unsettling dependence on the "other" (1, 12, 9–10).

5. See Murphy for an important model of the "other" that is based on "ecological processes of interanimation" rather than on psychoanalytic constructs.

6. Thanks to Rajani Sudan for helping me remember this phrase.

Works Cited

Adams, Carol J. "The Feminist Traffic in Animals." *Ecofeminism: Women, Animals, Nature.* Ed. Greta Gaard. Philadelphia: Temple University Press, 1993. 195–218.

Berger, John. *About Looking.* New York: Vintage International, 1980.

Braidotti, Rosi. *Patterns of Dissonance: A Study of Women in Contemporary Philosophy.* Trans. Elizabeth Guild. New York: Routledge, 1991.

Burke, Fielding. *Call Home the Heart.* 1932. New York: Feminist Press, 1983.

Butler, Octavia. *Mind of My Mind.* New York: Warner Books, 1977.

———. *Wild Seed.* New York: Warner Books, 1980.

Deleuze, Gilles, and Felix Guattari. *A Thousand Plateaus: Capitalism and Schizophrenia.* Trans. Brian Massumi. Minneapolis: University of Minnesota Press, 1987.

Gaard, Greta, ed. *Ecofeminism: Women, Animals, Nature.* Philadelphia: Temple University Press, 1993.

Grosz, Elizabeth. *Volatile Bodies: Toward a Corporeal Feminism.* Bloomington: Indiana University Press, 1994.

Haraway, Donna. *Simians, Cyborgs, and Women: The Reinvention of Nature.* New York: Routledge, 1991.

Heller, Chaia. "For the Love of Nature: Ecology and the Cult of the Romantic." *Ecofeminism: Women, Animals, Nature.* Ed. Greta Gaard. Philadelphia: Temple University Press, 1993. 219–42.

Hogan, Linda. *The Book of Medicines.* Minneapolis: Coffee House Press, 1993.

———. Interview with Patricia Clark Smith. *This Is about Vision: Interviews with Southwestern Writers.* Ed. William Balassi, John F. Crawford, and Annie O. Eysturoy. Albuquerque: University of New Mexico Press, 1990. 141–55.

———. "To Take Care of Life." Interview with Joseph Bruchac. *Survival This Way: Interviews with American Indian Poets.* Ed. Joseph Bruchac. Tucson: Sun Tracks and University of Arizona Press, 1987. 119–33.

Hornaday, William T. *Our Vanishing Wildlife: Its Extermination and Preservation.* New York: Charles Scribner's Sons, 1913.

Kristeva, Julia. *Powers of Horror: An Essay on Abjection.* Trans. Leon S. Roudiez. New York: Columbia University Press, 1982.

Lugones, María. "Playfullness, 'World'-Traveling, and Loving Perception." *Making Face, Making Soul/Haciendo Caras: Creative and Critical Perspectives by Women of Color.* Ed. Gloria Anzaldúa. San Francisco: Aunt Lute Books, 1990. 390–402.

Murphy, Patrick D. "Ground, Pivot, Motion: Ecofeminist Theory, Dialogics, and Literary Practice." *Hypatia* 6.1 (1991): 146–61.

Plumwood, Val. *Feminism and the Mastery of Nature.* New York: Routledge, 1993.

Trinh T. Minh-ha. *Woman, Native, Other.* Bloomington: Indiana University Press, 1989.

7

Ecocritical Chicana Literature:
Ana Castillo's "Virtual Realism"

Kamala Platt

Our mission is to redefine environmental issues as social and economic justice issues, and collectively set our own agenda to address these concerns as basic human rights.

PODER Mission Statement

You can't really separate issues of ecology from feminism or from human rights or from development, or from issues of ethnic and cultural diversity.

Vandana Shiva, *India Progressive Action Group Newsletter*

SINCE THE EARLY 1980S, a growing movement led by people of color—often working-class women—has been critiquing "traditional" environmental organizing and advocating for environmental justice. International and national calls summon us to reevaluate race, class, and gender issues as we assess the degradation of the habitats of human and nonhuman environmental communities. In the last few years other discourses—including literary texts—have joined forces with this activist analysis in linking environmental injustice with structural racism and patriarchy and historically identifying environmental racism as the outcome of colonialism and imperialist capitalism.

Images of environmental injustice and resistance are prominent in the contemporary Chicana novel *So Far from God* by Ana Castillo.[1] Castillo situates environmental justice issues within the larger field of race, class, and gender justice, thereby embracing the "virtual realities" encountered by a Nuevo Mexicano community. In examining her portrayal of environmental justice issues, I hope to present histories, pedagogies, and strategies that inform and critique ecofeminism and ecocriticism from a cultural perspective that has historically been silenced.

Before discussing the fiction it will be helpful to discuss two terms that I will use frequently—*environmental justice* and *environmental racism*—within the context of current environmental and ecofeminist agendas. Linguistically and historically the words *environmental* and *justice* mark two separate areas of social discourse. When environmental concerns and a concern for justice are combined, new issues are raised. The coined term *environmental justice* poses questions for environmentalism. Whose environment is protected? Whose environment is neglected? For those involved primarily with social justice the term signals the necessity for more extensive inclusion of environmental issues in their agendas. For those who have never separated the two concepts in the first place, *environmental justice* names and thus underscores the importance of their work. Similarly, *environmental racism* draws attention to neglected agendas.

As the following definitions demonstrate, the term *environmental racism* is more than just the antithesis of *environmental justice*. The term *environmental racism* was coined in 1982 during demonstrations against a PCB landfill slotted for Warren County, North Carolina, a predominantly African American area. Benjamin F. Chavis Jr. explains the context in which the term developed: "For the more than 500 protesters who were arrested, the behavior of county officials was seen as an extension of the institutional racism many of them had encountered in the past" (3). Chavis's subsequent definition of *environmental racism* is similar to others:

> Environmental racism is a racial discrimination in environmental policy making. It is racial discrimination in the enforcement of regulations and laws. It is racial discrimination in the deliberate targeting of communities of color for toxic waste disposal and the siting of polluting industries. It is racial discrimination in the official sanctioning of the life-threatening presence of poisons and pollutants in communities of color. And it is racial discrimination in the history of excluding people of color from the mainstream environmental groups, decision making boards, commissions, and regulatory bodies. (3)

Chavis's definition demonstrates that environmental racism pervades environmental concern as well as environmental culpability. Environmental racism has only recently been named, but this does not suggest that the phenomenon is recent. Rather, Mary Lee Kerr and Charles Lee map the beginnings of environmental racism in the southern United States onto European colonization: "the first Southerners to experience environmental racism were Native Americans—Cherokees, Choctaws, Chickasaws, Creeks, Tuscaroras, Catawbas, Seminoles, Natchez, and other Southern Indians who inhabited the region long before Columbus lived in complex, self-sustaining communities" (10). But while the institutions and attitudes that create environmental injustice have been around for centuries, the material effects due to unregulated industrial and technological production have become more lethal in recent years.

Like others aligned with environmental justice organizing, Ana Castillo maps the effects of environmental racism onto gendered human bodies by describing how environmental injustice and degradation are not gender neutral. Examples of this gender asymmetry include the extensive damage that many toxins cause to women's reproductive systems. In the Third World, occupational divisions of labor created by invasive "development" programs have different effects on women than on men. Women are less likely than men to profit from the introduction of a cash economy and more likely to experience increased manual labor. And in the move from a rural to an urban environment necessitated by environmentally destructive development, women are more likely than men to have to turn to prostitution as the only form of employment open to them. This presents another set of economic, legal, and health issues with which women must contend. Analysis from a social environmentalist perspective has demonstrated that many environmental issues are intrinsically linked to other issues of structural violence (Shiva, *Staying Alive;* Omvedt).

In short, one might borrow a slogan from AIDS activism that links AIDS with other social justice issues: "Diseases don't discriminate; people do." Transposed to environmental racism, it would proclaim: "Toxins don't discriminate; people do." In other words, women do not give birth to unwhole or unhealthy children because toxins are drawn to their more complex reproductive systems. Women give birth to children who have been poisoned because few of the chemicals used by industry have been tested—not to mention banned—for toxic effects to workers of either gender and especially because the Western medical profession has rarely made research on women's health issues a priority. Knowledge is missing; furthermore, accumulated knowledge is not being dispersed to many who could directly benefit from it. These are both environmental and feminist issues; they are the grounds for the structural interrogation of societies' discrimination against women. In response, women have rallied politically to fight environmental racism, often leading their communities in resistance. As I shall demonstrate shortly, Ana Castillo engages just such a complex web of issues in her fiction.

Ecofeminists and social environmentalists share a related thesis: the best analysis must articulate lived experience. Ariel Salleh observes that "some ecofeminism . . . is contiguous with radical or socialist paradigms, but by going back to women's lived experiences in a time of global crisis, it brings fresh understandings to these movement ideologies" (202). The environmental justice movement extends the argument that ecofeminists posit, adding the recognition that the experience in question is racially and economically defined, as well as gendered. Lourdes Torres's explains the importance of this crucial addition:

> It is not enough to speak of double or triple oppression; rather, women of color are themselves theorizing their experience in radical and innovative terms. Their condition as women, as people of color, as working-class members, and in some cases as lesbians, has led them to reject ... theories ... which have failed to develop an integrated analysis sensitive to the simultaneous oppression that women of color experience. Rather, third world women are making connections between the forces of domination which affect their lives daily and are actively participating in the creation of a movement committed to radical social and political transformation at all levels. (275)

Many women share Torres's perspective and have addressed the issue of mainstream feminism's exclusion of women of color (see Saldívar-Hull; Russo; Torres; and Anzaldúa).

Additionally, as noted by Laura Pulido, an environmental geographer and urban planning and Chicano studies scholar, the environmental justice movement has the prerogative to develop further through redressing the weaknesses to which other organizations, in related areas, have succumbed: "Unlike traditional trade unionism, [the environmental justice movement] should both combat racism and discrimination and attend to the environmental impact of development. Unlike the mainstream environmental movement, it should both emphasize economic equity and community empowerment" (125).

In India, Vandana Shiva—the foremost scholar on environmental justice, a dynamic participant in environmental activism, and an ecofeminist—has consistently focused on the ways in which environmental devastation has affected women's lifestyles and the subsequent roles women have played in fighting for environmental justice. The roles of ethnicity and class are integral to her gendered critique of environmental issues. Shiva, although recognized as an ecofeminist worldwide, defines environmental justice from the context of her work in support of environmental justice in rural India.

Shiva has constructed a polemical relationship between "environmental justice" and what she entitles "green imperialism" (*India* 2). The choice between the two is a choice "between a common future for all or continued economic and environmental apartheid" (*India* 3). Shiva clarifies her use of the term *apartheid* with a rhetorical question: "Are we going to move into a[n] era of environmental apartheid, where the North becomes clean and stays rich while the South stays poor and becomes the toxic dump of the world?" (*India*

3). Like her activist peers in the United States, Shiva uses terms that are familiar in current liberal and left political circles to redefine environmental issues. Her language reiterates that, in the Third World, environmentalism, when transported from the First World, often merely reinscribes structural violence such as imperialism and apartheid. Joni Seager makes an observation and a suggestion that reiterate the presence of structural violence within the First World as well: "In action-oriented environmental groups, it is difficult to ask questions about relationships between men and women, whites and African Americans, and our environmental crisis. It is not easy to ask about masculinity and militarism, privilege and power, and it is not considered polite to point out that white men . . . have been far more implicated in the history of environmental destruction than women. But there is too much at stake to stick to the easy questions and polite conversation" (65). Environmental justice groups in the United States have initiated this agenda by identifying race and class as determining factors in a community's likelihood of experiencing the effects of environmental racism.[2] This assertion parallels ecofeminism's acknowledgment of gender as a determining factor in environmental health.

Gender considerations have also been addressed by these and other environmental justice activists, but often to a lesser extent than has occurred within ecofeminism's gendered focus. Shiva, who pays allegiance to both groups, has made an assessment of the causes of environmental degradation that remains the most comprehensive examination (of which I am aware) in terms of identifying multiple sites of vulnerability. However, she does not extensively address the situation of the "Third World within the First World" in the United States. Perhaps neither those within ecofeminism nor the environmental justice movement has taken full advantage of the possibilities that an alliance of agendas addressing the junction of gender and race would allow. Such an alliance would expand both groups' understandings of the causes and effects of global and local environmental degradation and would empower their struggles against environmental racism.

Internationally and nationally, race and ethnicity are pivotal points in constructions of environmental justice politics, demonstrating that gender issues cannot be extracted from other social issues that affect one's environmental vulnerability. In the United States, and perhaps worldwide, a similar spectrum of environmental oppression affects the lifestyles, livelihoods, and life spans of various social groups of people differently. The formula in each context is nearly identical: being poor, a person of color, an indigenous person, and a woman are factors which work against one's chances of having an economically and ecologically sustainable lifestyle in a relatively unpolluted, noncarcinogenic environment. This means that intrinsic to the struggle to attain

environmental justice is the discernment of the complex involvement of gender, class, coloniality, and race issues. In the exchange that takes place in examining environmental justice issues raised by literature, activism, art, and
theory further concerns become evident: rurality/urbanity, caste, sexuality,
religion, nation, immigration status, and sedentarism are agendas that have a
bearing on the portrayals of social environmentalism found in literature by
women of color.

As the theorist Christine J. Cuomo has pointed out in "Unravelling the Problems in Ecofeminism,"

> A plurality of resistance targets abuses of power on a multiplicity of levels and in a
> multiplicity of places. This kind of resistance also originates from diverse perspec-
> tives, includes a variety of goals, and takes many shapes. While continually challeng-
> ing each other and working to create an ecologically astute and feminist ethic,
> ecofeminists should respect, encourage, and learn from a multitude of effective
> methods and theories. In that way, ecofeminism could then become an alliance of
> varied theories and methodologies that share common goals and values, rather than
> a unified movement. (363)

An investigation of literature, conjoined with the study of less "traditional"
genres of cultural texts, contributes to the theoretical, artistic, and practical
bases of oppositional consciousness; thus these texts act in alliance to resist
environmental racism. The analytical focus on a shared project, in these different types of texts, breaks down the critical division between "literary" and
popular/grass-roots cultural texts and thus suggests the possibility of reciprocal relationships. Fiction that illuminates social justice issues, such as environmental justice, may serve as a medium for raising awareness in a variety
of different, but overlapping, audiences and "classrooms."

Tracking the course of environmental racism often exposes scars of past co-
lonial encounters and thus underscores the interconnections of environmental
racism and colonialism. In current literary studies, Chicana/o literature is often
studied within the larger field of ethnic literature from the United States; however, "Greater Mexico" is also a postcolonial site.[3] Although in the past postcolonial literary and critical theory focused primarily on areas that experienced
British colonialism, recently such theory has been occasionally extended to
Chicano/a literature. As colonialism has been replaced by imperialism, the disenfranchisement, instead of being expunged, has shifted somewhat.

Currently, agricultural workers displaced by environmental degradation
migrate to urban areas. These disenfranchised urban communities—already
under the siege of poverty and often also in industrial toxic dumping zones—
are common to Greater Mexico. A complex set of social disenfranchisement

and displacement issues has sometimes pitted the rural, often immigrant poor against indigenous peoples. In Greater Mexico, local alliances between indigenous, mestizo, and other societally marginalized groups—sometimes specifically in environmental justice struggles—have proved to be a means of developing resistance to outside domination.

Within socially engaged cultural traditions, I find that environmental justice is being established as a recurring and foundational necessity for working toward the creation of local, and ultimately global, equity and enfranchisement. Women have been key players in conceptualizing and disseminating cultural work that promotes environmental justice. Specifically, Chicanas, such as Ana Castillo, are currently generating a rich body of socially engaged cultural poetics extending a tradition that speaks out against colonialism, imperialist capitalism, and environmental and other racisms.

So Close to the United States: Fe's Death by Environmental Injustice in the "Land of Enchantment"

In all of her novels, Ana Castillo uses fiction to document social issues and to narrate how various types of injustices play themselves out in Latina/o as well as other ethnic communities. In *So Far from God,* Castillo examines the environmental health of high tech industry workers in a "Silicon Valley age" Nuevo Mexicano community.

So Far from God takes place in and around Tome, New Mexico.[4] The story focuses on Sofia and her family: four daughters, each of whom die young, and her gambling, rambling husband, Domingo. Sofia, in her youth, married Domingo against the wishes of her family and friends; she spends most of her married life holding her family together alone. La Loca, the youngest daughter, dies and is resurrected at age three. After her resurrection, she stays at home and will let no one except her mother touch her; she does, however, have a healthy social life with animals, spirits, and her sisters, both before and after their deaths. The three elder daughters, Esperanza, Caridad, and Fe, have relationships with men who jilt them; the termination of a relationship is repeatedly a turning point for characters in the novel. Esperanza gets a college degree in Chicano studies and an M.A. in communications; after being a local TV anchor, she goes to Washington, D.C., to continue her career as a news reporter. She is sent to cover the Gulf War and disappears on the job in Saudi Arabia. While her physical body is never found, her spiritual/ghostly body returns to visit family and friends. Caridad attracts, but cannot keep men; she is married, is cheated on, has three abortions, and is brutally attacked in the first chapter. She barely survives molestation by her attacker but months later she regains her former beauty miraculously and goes on to become a clairvoyant and to fall in love with a woman. Fe is the compulsively conventional daughter for whom things never work out conventionally. Her first fiancé abruptly terminates their relationship, causing Fe to scream for years and thus earn the title La Gritona;[5] Fe dies from cancer that she contracts after exposure to chemicals at her workplace. In the midst of supporting her daughters and her husband (when he is home), Sofia decides to run for mayor of Tome; she wins and slowly begins to turn around the struggling town with a series of cooperatives and an organization of mothers called M.O.M.A.S.

I offer this summary as a basic grounding in the novel, especially for those unacquainted with the work, but such a linear synopsis is hardly appropriate for the text of a writer whose work is "never linear" because life is not "that way." Rather, Castillo sees life and text as a freeway: "You have a million variations and exits, like on the freeway, where you can keep making choices or redoing them" (*Mester* 154). Further, the language of the novel is missing from my account. With the usual mix of Spanish phrases, and an unusual borrowing from the religious language of Castillo's rendition of New Mexican Catholicism, Castillo portrays a cultural regionalism largely through almost formulaic caricatures.

In the tradition of Castillo's earlier epistolary novel, *The Mixquiahuala Letters,* which provides charts for three different readings of the text, I would like to suggest three possible and predominant readings for *So Far from God:* a religious reading that sees the novel as a New Mexican Catholic text; an aesthetic reading that sees the text as an example of magical realism; and the third—the kind I will attempt—a "political" reading of social justice issues. The allegorical depiction of the Stations of the Cross, the religious influence in the language, and the examination of spirituality and miracles are brought into conjunction with social justice and material everyday existence; except at these junctures, the religious aspects are largely beyond the scope of my reading. The implications of describing the text as "magical realism" are also important, but Castillo suggests her texts are about Mexican Catholic reality, not magical reality.[6] The descriptive category *magical realism* may stereotype the text by situating it in the historical tradition of Latin American literature; this may assimilate the historically specific experience of Chicana/os into the larger Latin American tradition of *realismo marveloso* that has too often been depoliticized in the United States. Castillo's texts are, therefore, more adequately described as "virtual realism": a realism that virtually encompasses lived experience and propels it into postmodern fiction.

Two extended narratives of environmental justice run through *So Far from God,* one that foregrounds environmental racism, and one that foregrounds resistance and the development of oppositional consciousness. Environmental injustice plays its most elaborate role in chapter 11, "The Marriage of Sophia's Daughter to Her Cousin, Casimiro, Descendant of Sheepherders and Promising Accountant, Who, by All Accounts, Was Her True Fated Love; and of Her Death which Lingers among Us All Heavier than Air." As the lengthy title indicates, the chapter begins with what its protagonist, Fe, believes is a dream come true at last. She begins married life happily, and for her, this means not just an introduction to post-matrimonial bliss but full membership in consumer culture: "Fe got the long-dreamed-of automatic dishwasher, microwave, Cuisinart, and the VCR" (171) as well as a new corporation job to pay for it all. However, this new job, after a mere year of married life, causes her death. The reference to her death lingering "heavier than air" identifies the characteristics of a chemical that she has been using in her job at ACME International.[7]

The essence of the air is important. The chapter begins with a stereotypical description of the air in New Mexico during "that month in the 'Land of Enchantment' when it smelled of roasted chiles everywhere" (170). Two paragraphs later the smell of chiles in the air each year is the recurring emotional connection for her friends to both Fe's death and her wedding: "that month would always be remembered by everyone who had known her as the one in which la Fe died right after her first anniversary" (171). The connection between the hot and healthful spice and the chemically hot "cleanser" that Fe used to degrease weapons parts is a symbolic dichotomy that has been created materially.

Suzanne Ruta reports in *The Nation* that "traces of plutonium have been detected in chilies" downstream from New Mexico's Los Alamos National Laboratory, where 2,400 sites are "suspected of contamination with plutonium, uranium, strontium 90, tritium, lead, mercury, nitrates, cyanides, pesticides and other leftovers from a half century of weapons research and production" (9). Castillo's narrator twists the travel poster "Land of Enchantment" to portray the actual state of New Mexico that Ruta has described: Most people "didn't understand what was slowly killing them, too, or didn't want to think about it . . . despite dead cows in the pasture, or sick sheep, and that one week . . . when people woke up each morning to find it raining starlings. . . . Unlike their abuelos and vis-abuelos who thought that although life was hard in the 'Land of Enchantment' it had its rewards, the reality was that everyone was now caught in what it had become: The Land of Entrapment" (172).

Since Tome is only seventy-five miles downriver from Los Alamos, the sense of impending doom seems apt. At such points in Castillo's fiction, there is no need to "suspend disbelief"; "real life" does the job for the writer. In an interview, Castillo reports how "real life" portrayals in her fictions were rejected because of their anticipated "real life" effects:

I am dealing with environmental issues in New Mexico which are very serious for all of us. But they were afraid of the possibility of someone recognizing himself in there and going after the big New York publisher and the rich novelist. I said, "Wait a minute! What rich novelist?" So, I had a telephone conference with my editor and their lawyer and they recommended that one particular chapter had to be redone, to protect them. . . . They were concerned that one of the characters—and I don't know these people personally—was based on somebody that might say, "This is me." (*Mills College* 4)

It seems likely that chapter 11 was rewritten, which is significant if indeed the published version is a "watered down" narration of environmental racism. The environmental saga begins as Fe's dream job becomes a nightmare: she discovers that she has developed terminal cancer from exposure to toxins on the job. Meanwhile, Fe is being investigated by the FBI and is "almost" subpoenaed by the government for having used the deadly chemical, even though she was using it upon the orders of her corporate superior, who is not being investigated. She has not been told the potential danger of the lethal chemical, which her ACME superiors had indicated was only "ether." Readers are left to wonder which agent on Suzanne Ruta's list caused Fe's problems. Or did unlisted toxins destroy the environment and Fe's life?

By not knowing the specifics, readers are forced to fathom a broad expanse of possible problems: production of industrial toxic wastes seems likely to stop only with the demise of the humans who "produce and multiply" them and in many cases their toxicity far outlasts their production. Having been told "Yeah, it'll make you sleepy, but that's all" (182), Fe learns of the full toxicity of the chemical only when she is finally allowed to look at its data sheet in the corporate manual. Her fight for the information reveals much about corporate culpability in environmental racism; in this case, sexism is particularly involved. We are told that obtaining access to the manual "took a lot of determination on Fe's end, calling and coming by and each rotating foreman hiding and telling the girls to tell Fe that he was out to lunch, until she finally left a message . . . not to give her no more crap about that chemical having been ether or *she* with her lawyer would sue each little rotating ass there" (188).

Given Fe's history with gender abuse, readers know she will not take ill treatment quietly, however much she may strive to be a conventional woman. Fe's gender critique in this section is subtle, but important: the fore*men* give orders to those considered the "girls," their "inferiors" (in gender status as well as job status). But Fe is just another girl who, besides suffering from cancer, has become ACME's scapegoat for the FBI. Despite her dire situation, she turns the tables on the men in charge by threatening to "sue each little rotating ass." In making diminutive and slang reference to the men's body parts, she transfers—to their bodies—the description of their "rotating" the responsibility to answer her request. As both Fe and the reader know, they "rotate" responsibility to "keep their asses covered." In this passage, Fe transforms containment into empowerment; she "uncovers their asses," defies her status as victim, and, most importantly, gains access to the truth about the chemical with which she's been working—that it was, among other deadly things, *"heavier than air"* (188). Castillo uses italic type not only to emphasize an idea but also to set it off as incongruous. The weight of the chemical seems to be a figurative as well as an empirical property. The chemical's toxicity *weighs* upon Fe as the empirical truth about it is finally released to her: the chemical is life-threatening; air as symbolic of life is no match for this heavyweight toxin.

Living conditions, specifically working conditions, are absurd in the novel, but the absurdity is a political indictment. Fe dies spectacularly, but her textual death serves to document "real" world conditions that cause "real" deaths. In *So Far from God*, death comes to each sister on unusual terms. Each death is an allegorical lesson dealt with sinister grace.[8] On one level, Fe's death is the most "realistic" and probable. The description of her working conditions is not very different from those protested by people involved in the environmental justice struggle in Greater Mexico. Absurd events, such as Caridad's flight off the mesa to her death/transcendence into another state of being and Esperanza's after-death appearances happen often in *So Far from God;* such events have been identified by critics as magical realism. As Castillo herself has put it, "magical realism becomes realism."[9] It is materialized in the progressive media's reports on high tech industries' abominable conditions for its lowest paid workers. For instance, in an article entitled "High-Tech's Dirty Little Secret," which was published shortly after *So Far from God*, Elizabeth Kadetsky reports that "electronics assemblers work with a collection of toxic substances that can contain anything from arsenic to cadmium oxide. Medical complications from exposure to these substances range from loss of smell to scarring of the lungs to cancer" (517).

Similarly, Castillo depicts a Halloweenesque scene in which workers used chemicals "that actually glowed in the dark" (181). Protective gear does not prevent a "red ring around her nose and breath that smelled suspiciously of glue" (181). While these may be plausible chronic symptoms of chemical poisoning, they are also figuratively significant: the red ring around her nose could be read as a nose ring by which an independent-minded animal is controlled—the means by which a bull is led around by its master or a pig is kept from "rooting around." Likewise the smell of glue signifies the threat of adhesion—being stuck in a job/lifestyle from which there is escape only through death. It is also significant that the limited protection measures recommended by the corporation were aimed at protecting the weapons, rather than the workers; herein Castillo's political irony is functioning.

The narrator tells us that when Fe is given her particularly tough job (which later leads to her trouble with the FBI), she is sent from the upstairs work-rooms—with everyone else—down to the basement. In the room where she is to clean some large and very dirty high tech weapons parts, she finds that there is only "an excuse for a vent at the far end of the wall." Fe attempts makeshift protection with a hanky, a mask, and gloves from her previous workroom but the chemical ate through the gloves and "dissolved her mani-cure, not only the lacquer but the nails themselves!" (183–84). Such descrip-tions reveal the nature of the dangerous working conditions to the reader, who already knows that Fe is going to die from the toxic exposure. For Fe, who naively goes about her job without much questioning, the risky conditions merely mean inconvenience. But her symptoms are heightened by her fastid-ious conventionalism; such details mark the illusions created by the lifestyle she has adopted. Although the dangerous conditions seem preposterous, they are matched in Kadetsky's report: "at a small contract assembly house, U.S.M. Technology, . . . workers handled potentially hazardous solders and solvents with no masks, gloves or safety sheets in violation of state safety and health laws" (517). And like ACME International, the main offender in *The Nation*'s report is a subcontracting company (Kadetsky 517).

With each daughter, a different point, both empirical and philosophical, is tied in with fate.[10] If we focus on Esperanza, we might read *So Far from God* as an antiwar novel. Caridad's experiences with abusive men, both supernatural and (we cannot say) natural, force readers to ponder what is "natural" in het-erosexual relationships; if we use a feminist analysis we might read her subse-quent existence as a clairvoyant, as La Armitaña, and as a lesbian as a more constructive, if not exactly "stable," phase in Caridad's life. After Fe's death, La Loca, who after an inexplicable childhood death and resurrection will al-low no one except her mother to touch her, contracts AIDS.

Castillo interconnects a sisterhood of social ills (environmental racism, war, AIDS, and patriarchal domestic violence) through the four sisters, whose ex-periences with these social ills contribute to their deaths. In her acknowledg-ments, Castillo expresses her indebtedness to those involved in the "SouthWest Organizing Project who assisted in [her] research; above all, for the inspira-tion [she] received from their consciousness, ongoing commitment, and hope." The SouthWest Organizing Project coordinates support for the eco-nomic and environmental justice movement. Castillo's relationship with them suggests her commitment, as a writer, to these struggles.

The wisdom Sofia has attained through her life experience is part of what makes successful the chain of cooperatives she institutes as mayor. Laura Pulido in "Sustainable Development at Ganados del Valle" describes the similar insights of a community in northern New Mexico. Both communities strive to attain self-determination and sustainability and retain a symbiotic relationship between the needs of the people and the needs of nature. In fact, Castillo's narrator tells us that the fictional town's community development is modeled on the Ganados del Valle community: "Sofi's vecinos finally embarked on an ambitious project, which was to start a sheep-grazing wool-weaving enterprise, 'Los Ganados y Lana Cooperative,' modeled after the one started by the group up north that had also saved its community from destruction" (146).

Pulido reports that the significance of the "group up north"—the Ganados del Valle community—"besides its economic success, is that it has allowed people to develop to their fullest potential" (131). In particular, she notes that "women who previously saw themselves solely as housewives have acquired numerous other talents and skills and greatly expanded their horizons. Moreover, they now have a sense of ownership in Ganados, which, more than anything, means they have hope for the future" (131). Castillo's use of this cooperative as a model for the fictional one extends to the changes that the community development brings, which parallel the changes that Pulido attributes to Ganados; and gender roles are critiqued in both.[11] We see in each community that women benefit most from sustainable development, so environmental justice not only curtails increased oppression of women but also provides empowerment for social, political, personal, economic, and gender equality. This is accomplished through revamping and revaluing—not dismissing or discrediting—women's traditional roles, at least to the extent that these roles can be used constructively.

Fe's story, in its allegorical sense—and we catch this from her name—is the story of the demise, the resurrection, the death, and the final burial of "faith." Initially Fe's faith in her fiancé's dedication to their relationship is devastated. However, when she recovers from this—remembering it only as a long illness— she has lost a consistent voice. Because her vocal chords have been damaged by months of screaming, not all her words are audible. Due to this impairment, she is not given a raise at the bank where she works. Here Castillo's subtle critique attends to structurally endemic discrimination. Seen as not fit to deal with customers, she moves instead to ACME International, where she is seen as quite fit to deal with chemicals, in fact, the most deadly of chemicals.

Although Fe knows that ACME International is doing the dirty work for other companies who are contracted to build weapons by the Pentagon, she sees it initially as "very important work, when you thought about it" (181). In contrast, her sister Esperanza, the activist/reporter seen by most in her community as a *mitotera,* might have had a more substantial analysis of the role such work played in one's world, both personally and politically.[12] Esperanza, as Hope, having disappeared in the Gulf War, comes back as a spirit to visit the more spiritual of her sisters, however she does not appear to warn Fe about her job. And Fe ignores all the signs of looming trouble, she even ignores the "nausea and headaches that increased in severity by the day" (178), which she and many of her fellow workers experienced. Fe finds out that she had been pregnant only when she miscarries, and when she gets back to work, she discovers that many of her fellow workers can no longer have children. At this point, she recognizes that "there did seem to be something eerie and full of coincidence about it all" (180). However, it is not until her husband smells glue on her breath that she is really bothered, not until her role as perfect wife is jeopardized that she begins to question whether the job is worth the suffering. By then it is too late; not only has she lost her chance to have the "big familia" they wanted but the toxins have taken their toll and cancer has started to grow in her body. She slowly loses her faith in the benign nature of the system that she had earlier embraced for allowing her to buy into a related system—mass consumer culture. Thus, Castillo underscores the importance of personal responsibility for lifestyle in reducing the global vulnerability of environmental destruction.

Therefore, Fe too is being held accountable to her lifestyle and her "faith" in a system of structural oppression. After all, Fe's labor does not produce seemingly benign products like grapes or even computer chips, which to varying degrees meet basic needs despite the harm to workers, sometimes consumers, and the environment when the industries are unregulated and those in charge are unconscionable. Rather, Fe is involved in the production of the deadliest of weapons—one of which may even have killed her sister Esperanza during the Gulf War.

Although Fe's lifestyle is critiqued, Castillo at the same time implicitly endorses transformation of Fe's unintentional involvement in structural violence through progressive education and knowledge about appropriate technology that would meet the community's needs. The critique underscores the necessity of community openness to analysis of the power structure that dominates it. As in the critique of Fe's consumerist tendencies, Castillo demands accountability from the community. This saves her fiction from shallow celebration of the grass-roots communities she describes. Despite her caricatures of the ideal activist (in Sofia) and the epitome of victimization (in each of the sisters), the consequences of their actions are not based on charades but on real life.

Castillo provides political critiques in another way. By the end of the novel we realize that we as readers must question where we are: while we hear the land called New Mexico, we know from the title that we are "so far from God" and we know from the epigraph—if not from our history lessons—that means we are also "so near the United States"; if that is the case, then we cannot also be *in* the United States. Castillo has implicitly denied the legitimacy of the U.S.-Mexican border. The book's title marks a second ironic space: if anything, their strong adherence to Mexican Catholicism suggests that the characters in *So Far from God* are, in fact, "much closer to God" than most of us.

Near the end of the novel, the town turns out for a "Way of the Cross Procession" that is as much a political statement as a spiritual one. The symbiotic relationship of spiritual with material justice is stressed through transformation of tradition to express the community's reality. In place of the traditional photos of Mary, "some, like Sofi, who held a picture of la Fe as a bride, carried photographs of their loved ones who died due to toxic exposure hung around the necks like scapulars; . . . people spoke on the so many things that were killing their land and turning the people of those lands into endangered species" (241–42). The passage reads like a litany that parallels environmental devastation in (mostly) communities of color with the events of the Stations of the Cross. Jesus' condemnation to death is accompanied by an address from a spokesperson from the committee "working to protest dumping radioactive waste" (242). Jesus' first fall is paralleled by "people all over the land . . . dying from toxic exposure in factories" (242). Instead of meeting his mother, Jesus meets "three Navajo women [who] talked about uranium contamination on the reservation, and the babies they gave birth to with brain damage and cancer" (242). They affirm their "responsibility to 'Our Mother,' and to seven generations" (242), but ask whether those who care about saving rain forests and whales do not also care about the genocide of Navajo people.

"Livestock drank and swam in contaminated canals" (242) and, again, Jesus falls. As the women console Jesus, "children also played in those open disease-ridden canals" (243), dying as a result. And Jesus' third fall brings air "contaminated by the pollutants coming from the factories" (243). Environmental holocaust seems eminent as Jesus is nailed to the cross and finally dies: "Nuclear power plants sat like gargantuan landmines among the people" (243). Finally, in allusion to the farm workers' situation, "deadly pesticides were sprayed . . . on the vegetables and fruits and on the people who picked them" (243).

The assertive roles that women play in assuring community survival throughout the novel are intensified here. The women around Jesus console him but, unlike Mary, the New Mexican women—whose children are also dying—speak out. When one of the three Navajo women speaks of the eco-cide of Navajo communities through uranium contamination, she broadens and builds upon the connection between the spiritual and environmental justice drawn in the passage. The concern over the poisoning of the earth and her people aligns communities in protest; religious, geographic, and ethnic differences broaden the horizon of the struggle.

Castillo's portrayal of environmental justice succeeds at several levels: it portrays environmental justice issues in detail and it portrays resistance in lifestyle choices that are modeled on real life community cooperatives, in demonstrations of protest, and in the development of oppositional consciousness. Hence, Castillo's text is instructive and foreboding in its depiction of the reality of the "Land of Entanglement," but ultimately celebratory: it celebrates resistance built through alliance. And in doing so, it maps out local environmental justice battles well fought, won, and yet to be won.

Finally, then, I want to return to "virtual realism" by offering an extended definition of the concept as I see it actualized in *So Far from God*. In using this approach, I am situating environmental justice in a current cultural context—albeit one that is (to my knowledge) situated primarily in the First World—by suggesting that fiction that presents environmental justice foregrounds local historiographies in a kind of "virtual reality" frame. I apply this techno-art term while recognizing that "virtual reality" of the nonfictional variety has a very different—if not contradictory—result: the technology of "virtual reality" is about escaping reality through a simulation of reality. "Virtual realism" in fiction borrows from reality to create a fiction that commands its readers to confront the political reality of "real life." Thereby Castillo, among other authors, maps environmental justice issues, not just in real space, by pinpointing "toxic hot spots" on a world atlas, but also in real time, by pinpointing local struggles against degradation of human/natural habitats. She portrays environmental degradation to habitats and communities, and she portrays the acts of people who are rising up to counter environmental destruction. She shows how the effects of crimes against the environment are explicitly tied to sexist, racist, capitalist, and colonialist ideologies and acts. The ramifications of this cartography are important for anyone with an interest in literature, the environment, feminism, and justice.

Notes

1. Other fiction that addresses environmental justice issues includes Nina Sibal's *Yatra* and Leslie Marmon Silko's *Almanac of the Dead;* many of the short stories of Mahasweta Devi address land and resource rights issues that are at the heart of envi-

ronmental justice. In her translation of three of Mahasweta's stories in *Imaginary Maps*, Gayatri Chakravorty Spivak observes that the stories are "linked by the common thread of profound ecological loss" (198).

2. Such environmental justice groups include the Mothers of East L.A./Madres Del Este De Los Angeles Santa Isabel, People Organized in Defense of the Earth and her Resources (PODER), SouthWest Organizing Project (SWOP), Concerned Citizens of South Central Los Angeles (CCSCLA), and the umbrella group Southwest Network for Environmental and Economic Justice (SNEEJ), all in the Southwest; People for Community Recovery in South Chicago; the Gulf Coast Tenants Organization in Louisiana; and the White Earth Land Recovery Project (WELRP) in Minnesota. Many of these organizations are discussed in Bullard and Hofrichter.

3. Américo Paredes has coined the geopolitical delineation "Greater Mexico," which identifies historically marked boundaries that primarily coincide with territory that once belonged to Mexico but is currently under the rule of the United States; however the term has been extended to all communities of people of Mexican descent within the United States. César Augusto Martínez explains that Paredes's concept acknowledges that "there are indeed two Mexicos: one a recognized republic, and the 'other' a 'lived reality' in the United States (also referred to as the 'Greater Mexico North') 'constructed' by people of Mexican descent . . . negotiating geopolitical borders, or *fronteras*" (28).

4. Tome is a real city off Highway 25 south of Albuquerque.

5. *Gritona* is literally translated as "crying woman" or "woman who cries"; however La Gritona is also used as a synonym for La Llorona, the mythic woman who cries for her dead children. The stories about La Llorona/La Gritona vary, but a lover or husband is often involved. Fe acquires the name after her soured romance, but the name also predicts her later misfortunes, in particular her miscarriage and lost opportunity to have the family she anticipated.

6. For instance, in an interview published in *io,* Castillo responds to the suggestion that her work is magical realism: "The women in *So Far from God* are modeled on the martyrs in the history of the Catholic Church. We are made to believe in these miracles. I wasn't making anything up—it's not magical fiction; it is faith" (Miller and Walsh 27).

7. ACME International evokes the language of U.S. popular culture—ACME provided Wile E. Coyote with equipment to catch the Roadrunner in cartoons beginning in the 1960s. Kurt Vonnegut uses the same acronym for his portrayal of a corporate bureaucracy. Castillo's use of the acronym acts as a smoke screen to veil the "real life" corporation that figures in an incident of environmental injustice upon which Castillo bases this chapter. At the same time it calls attention to the fact that the story could have taken place anywhere within an organization that had adopted certain values and developed anonymity toward its workers.

8. Grace functions here both as a description of the prose and a description of the Mexican Catholicism that imbues the novel.

9. My appreciation to Elsa Saeta for providing this information.

10. Castillo has explained that figuratively Sofia's daughters represent martyred saints, but I am not interested here in matching daughters with saints, but in how contemporary renditions of the martyrs are involved in issues of social justice.

11. María Varela, who in 1990 won a MacArthur Foundation fellowship for her work as cofounder of Tierra Wool, one of the cooperative branches of Ganados del Valle, could be seen as a "real life" model for Sophia's activism. According to *Vista* she "has devoted the last 20 years to helping some 100 families in her community achieve economic equality" ("Weaving").

12. Castillo uses the Spanish word *mitotera* to describe how Esperanza was viewed by the Tome community. *Mitotera,* here, can be translated as a female political agitator or rebel rouser, but is considered pejorative. The term derives from *mitote,* a word Aztecs used to describe a *fiesta baile,* or dance party. A *mitotera* was a woman who drummed up enthusiasm for the party. Although the male counterpart *mitotero* is also used pejoratively in contemporary Spanish, it is much less common; this invites a gender critique that is beyond the scope of this essay. My appreciation to Hector Pérez for providing the information that enabled this extended definition.

Works Cited

Anzaldúa, Gloria, ed. *Making Face, Making Soul/Hacienda Caras: Creative and Critical Perspectives by Women of Color.* San Francisco: Aunt Lute Books, 1990.

Bullard, Robert D., ed. *Confronting Environmental Racism: Voices from the Grassroots.* Boston: South End Press, 1993.

Castillo, Ana. "Entrevista a Ana Castillo." Interview with Jacqueline Mitchell, et al. *Mester* 20.2 (1991): 145–56.

———. Interview. *Mills College Review: A Publication of the Walrus Literary Magazine* 2.2 (1992): 1–4.

———. *So Far from God.* New York: W. W. Norton, 1993.

Chavis, Benjamin F., Jr. Foreword. *Confronting Environmental Racism: Voices from the Grassroots.* Ed. Robert D. Bullard. Boston: South End Press, 1993. 3–5.

Cuomo, Christine J. "Unravelling the Problems in Ecofeminism." *Environmental Ethics* 14.4 (1992): 351–63.

Devi, Mahasweta. *Imaginary Maps: Three Stories by Mahasweta Devi.* Trans. Gayatri Chakravorty Spivak. New York: Routledge, 1995.

Hofrichter, Richard, ed. *Toxic Struggles: The Theory and Practice of Environmental Justice.* Philadelphia: New Society Publishers, 1993.

India Progressive Action Group Newsletter (Austin, Tx.) 3.2 (1992): 2–3.

Kadetsky, Elizabeth. "High-Tech's Dirty Little Secret." *The Nation* May 19, 1994: 517–20.

Kerr, Mary Lee, and Charles Lee. "From Conquistadors to Coalitions: After Centuries of Environmental Racism, People of Color Are Forging a New Movement for Environmental Justice." *Southern Exposure* 21.4 (1993): 8–19.

Martínez, César Augusto. "*Citings from a Brave New World:* The Art of the Other Mexico." *New Art Examiner* 21 (May 1994): 28–32, 56–57.

Miller, Kate, and Sean Patrick Walsh. "So Far, So Good: Ana Castillo, Novelist, Essayist, Poet, Painter." *io* 1.2 (1994): 24–27.

Omvedt, Gail. "'Green Earth, Women's Power, Human Liberation': Women in Peasant Movements in India." *Close to Home: Women Reconnect Ecology, Health, and Development Worldwide.* Ed. Vandana Shiva. Philadelphia: New Society Publishers, 1994. 99–112.

Pulido, Laura. "Sustainable Development at Ganados de Valle." *Confronting Environmental Racism: Voices from the Grassroots.* Ed. Robert D. Bullard. Boston: South End Press, 1993. 123–40.

Russo, Ann. "'We Cannot Live without Our Lives': White Women, Antiracism, and Feminism." *Third World Women and the Politics of Feminism.* Ed. Chandra Talpade Mohanty, Ann Russo, and Lourdes Torres. Bloomington: Indiana University Press, 1991. 297–313.

Ruta, Suzanne. "Fear and Silence in Los Alamos." *The Nation* Jan. 4–11, 1993: 9–13.

Saldívar-Hull, Sonia. "Feminism in the Borderlands: From Gender Politics to Geopolitics." *Criticism in the Borderlands: Studies in Chicano Literature, Culture, and Ideology.* Ed. Héctor Calderón and José David Saldívar. Durham: Duke University Press, 1991. 203–20.

Salleh, Ariel. "The Ecofeminism/Deep Ecology Debate: A Reply to Patriarchal Reason." *Environmental Ethics* 14.3 (1992): 195–216.

Seager, Joni. "Creating a Culture of Destruction: Gender, Militarism, and the Environment." *Toxic Struggles: The Theory and Practice of Environmental Justice.* Ed. Richard Hofrichter. Philadelphia: New Society Publishers, 1993. 58–66.

Shiva, Vandana. *Staying Alive: Women, Ecology, and Development* London: Zed Books, 1988.

Silko, Leslie Marmon. *Almanac of the Dead.* New York: Simon and Schuster, 1991.

Torres, Lourdes. "The Construction of the Self in U.S. Latina Autobiographies." *Third World Women and the Politics of Feminism.* Ed. Chandra Talpade Mohanty, Ann Russo, and Lourdes Torres. Bloomington: Indiana University Press, 1991. 271–87.

"Weaving a Better Future." *Vista* 22 (Sept. 22, 1990).

8

Rethinking Dichotomies in
Terry Tempest Williams's *Refuge*

Cassandra Kircher

IN HER WORK of creative nonfiction, *Refuge,* Terry Tempest Williams seems to embrace many of the dichotomies that have long been standard in Western thought: throughout the book she often connects women with nature and men with culture, each in opposition to the other. Williams sees women's connection to nature as virtuous, empowering, comforting, and good while portraying the institutions she identifies with the patriarchy as harmful or, at least, problematic. For example, she depicts the Utah landscape—the Great Salt Lake, the mountains, the desert, the earth itself, and the sky above it—as female while she often depicts the manipulation of the landscape for political, religious, or military ends as male. Besides these implicit dichotomies, Williams also explicitly announces an alliance between the female and nature against the male during a discussion that she has with one of her friends:

> We spoke of rage. Of women and landscape. How our bodies and the body of the earth have been mined.
>
> "It has everything to do with intimacy," I said. "Men define intimacy through their bodies. It is physical. They define intimacy with the land in the same way."
>
> "Many men have forgotten what they are connected to," my friend added. "Subjugation of women and nature may be a loss of intimacy within themselves." (10)

Two hundred fifty pages later, as if to remind the reader of her political stance, one ultimately grounded in deep ecology, Williams once again explicitly aligns women with nature: "The Earth is not well and neither are we," she says to her grandmother. "I saw the health of the planet as our own" (263), a message she repeats in the book's final chapter when describing her dream about women understanding "the fate of the earth as their own" (288) and "that to deny one's genealogy with the earth was to commit treason against one's soul" (288).

In spite of my love and admiration for this book, a response that might even stem, in small part, from Williams's romanticized valorization of women and nature (especially from my vantage point as a woman reader), I also question her apparent investment in male/female, culture/nature oppositions, as I imagine many other readers do. For one, Williams's decision to plot women and nature against men and culture in a work of nonfiction, and the way that she orchestrates this plotting, can be seen as simplistic. As the ecofeminist Maureen Devine suggests, when explaining the need to move beyond "such obviously defined dualisms":

> we have detailed accounts of parallel use and abuse of women and nature through the centuries. The images are easily available to us: nature as nurturing mother, the mother earth, virgin woods, images associated with the premodern organic world. It would be simple enough to cast these in the role of the protagonists, with the antagonist (villain?) being modern patriarchal mechanistic society; the market economy, industrialization, technology, progress. In short everything we identify with our present culture. (29)

Williams, it could be argued, relies, in part, on prefabricated dualisms to structure her book, a decision that reveals an either/or sensibility on her part and a penchant for cliché

Her depiction of women and their connection to nature, for example, results from a fairly basic equation: through figurative language Williams consistently associates the natural world with the female and through her presentation of herself, her mother, her grandmother, and other women, she associates the female characters in the book with the natural world. By describing women characters who easily commune with nature, Williams taps into what Sherry Ortner identifies as cultural constructs that envision women as closer to nature because of their body and natural procreative functions (73). And by describing the Utah landscape as female, Williams uses metaphoric descriptions that fall in line with age-old accounts that objectify the land as woman, either virgin or mother. Just as some writers and explorers (primarily male) have described voluptuous female landscapes, Williams, too, sees sand dunes as female, sporting "sensuous curves—the small of a woman's back. Breasts. Buttocks. Hips and pelvis. They are the natural shapes of Earth" (109). And just as these same writers, philosophers, and explorers also depict the maternal aspect of the land, Williams often describes the Great Salt Lake as mother (122, 151) and refers to the earth being ripped open by a backhoe as

"Mother Earth" (204). By perpetuating these woman/land connections that Annette Kolodny and others have labeled as regressive, and by relying on cultural assumptions that Sherry Ortner feels must be transcended, Williams, in a sense, strengthens harmful stereotypes when she could, in fact, be reinscribing the landscape with her own metaphors.

Williams also sets up a second easy equation in *Refuge:* any oppressive forces in the book are male or, more often, are related to patriarchal urban culture. She illustrates this equation in a number of ways. The "beergut-over-beltbuckled men" (12) associated with the Gun Club in the book's first chapter demonstrate their opposition to nature in their needless destruction of the burrowing owl's nest and in their flippant discussion with Williams: "you gotta admit those ground owls are messy little bastards. They'll shit all over hell if ya let 'em. And try and sleep with 'em hollering at ya all night long. They had to go. Anyway, we got bets with the county they'll pop up someplace around here next year" (12). Because they are the first men depicted in the book, their behavior resonates and they set the tone for what follows. Later, as Williams introduces powerful religious, political, and scientific components of culture, she depicts them, more often than not, as out of sync with nature in the same way that the men from the Gun Club are.

Williams represents the simplicity of male/female, culture/nature dichotomies in her description of two antithetical sculptures. The first represents the male. Described in phallic terms, the "newly erected" (127) piece of art by Karl Momen resembles an eighty-three-foot-high lightning "rod" (127) complete with colored spheres Williams dubs tennis "balls" (127). From a distance, the sculpture rises "like a small phallus dwarfed by the open space that surrounded it" (127). In contrast, a second sculpture embodies the femaleness, the roundness and circularity Williams sees as intrinsic in the land and in herself. Created by Nancy Holt, "Sun Tunnels," comprised of four tunnels laid upon the ground, can be entered by the viewer. Holes cut through the walls in the upper half of each tunnel frame the Great Basin landscape "within circles" (269), allowing light from the sun and moon to enter. While the narrator sees the first art piece as oppressive, ugly, and destructive—something that has no relationship to the land, something that casts shadows "across the salt flats like a mushroom cloud" (127)—she experiences the second piece in a blissful trance. Clearly, the first sculpture is meant to represent the enemy while the second depicts communion between women and the landscape. And clearly, these art pieces are meant to reinforce and exaggerate the dichotomies that Williams consistently portrays in *Refuge*, dichotomies that can be seen to falsify the relationships between men, women, nature, and culture.

Finally, in light of ecofeminism, Williams's dichotomies become even more problematic. Though ecofeminists tend to agree "that the same patriarchal attitudes which degrade nature are responsible for the exploitation and abuse of women" (Salleh 98), they disagree about the usefulness and wisdom of equating women and nature. Whereas radical feminists, such as Mary Daly in *Gyn/Ecology*, reinforce the dichotomies by emphasizing the morally superior character of woman and nature in relation to the patriarchal culture that dominates them, most critics believe that this sort of valorization leads to problems. Equating nature with women, they say, objectifies women and "relegates them [nature and women] to a position of 'otherness,' inferiority, and powerlessness relative to culture and male" (Devine 1). Furthermore, "most ecofeminists believe a real political shift means letting go of the culture vs. nature polarity altogether," in part because it "preserves the artificial separation of masculine and feminine genders" (Salleh 98). These critics, including Ynestra King, Carolyn Merchant, and Chaia Heller, who rely on historical analysis to support their arguments, hope to reconceptualize these male/female, culture/nature dualisms and would most likely look upon *Refuge* and its embracing of dualisms with more than skeptical eyes.

Fortunately, my criticisms of Williams's dichotomies do not adequately capture the intrinsic complexity of *Refuge*. The ways that Williams problematizes both the female/nature and male/culture alliances and, more importantly, the way she moves beyond dichotomies to depict a circular notion of family keeps the book from being essentialist. Although Williams, unfortunately, never questions the cultural representation of nature as feminine, and although she much more closely connects all women (herself, her mother, womenkind in general) to nature than she connects the men in the book, she also moves women out of an exclusive collaboration with nature by linking them to nondestructive institutions, such as the Utah Museum of Natural History and the Mormon church, which offers women a valuable community within a patriarchal framework. As Sherry Ortner realizes, it would be impossible for women not to participate in culture somehow (73); Williams's allegiance to certain cultural institutions, in fact, may even demonstrate her attempt to forge a synthesis between nature and culture.

Furthermore, Williams seems to understand that linking women to nonpowerful cultural institutions or giving them subordinate roles within powerful institutions is not enough. She further problematizes the alliance between women and nature by depicting women, including herself, who challenge the destructive patriarchal powers—religious and political—that they despise or, at least, question. She knows that by confronting her religious and political enemies and, thus, connecting herself to culture through activities such as organized protests, change can best occur, even if it means being arrested or paying another kind of price. Obviously, the actual writing of *Refuge* places Williams within the cultural realm, especially because the book does more than document her experiences with cancer and floods; it also works as a critique of twentieth-century culture.

In the case of Mormonism, Williams and other women, who uphold many beliefs of the Mormon church, often defy the traditional, patriarchal doctrines that keep their gender from full participation in religious rituals. Although Williams rarely depicts women overtly challenging church protocol, she, along with her mother and grandmother, secretly give each other the Mormon blessings (158), which are taboo for women to give in public. Williams herself challenges deep-seated Mormon beliefs, not just church practices, by reenvisioning the Holy Ghost as female, as a mother in heaven who can balance the sacred triangle. Although Williams does make these moves to criticize the Mormonism that is so much a part of her life, she stops short of doing an all-out critique of patriarchal religion the way feminists Judith Plaskow and Carol P. Christ do in their work. Completely dismissing Mormonism for Williams would mean becoming what she calls "a member of a border tribe among [her] own people" (268) or breaking family connections altogether—a price she does not want to pay, even if it means deceiving herself about her own religion. So, Williams keeps one foot in Mormonism while looking often to the natural world for religious consolation. Besides seeing the Holy Ghost as female, for example, Williams sees birds as her guides, comforters, and intercessors, what she calls "mediat[ors] between heaven and earth" (18), what can be thought of as the spirit of God manifested in this world. Williams also considers the landscape religiously charged. In one scene she drives past the Mormon church's temple and practices her own brand of religion—one that is animistic—on the shores of the Great Salt Lake, that "spiritual magnet that will not let [her] go" (240).

When Williams challenges the political powers in *Refuge*, she is, generally, more confrontational. Several times in the book she criticizes the Utah legislature's decisions on flood control and questions the legislature's understanding (or lack of understanding) of the natural world. In the book's last chapter, she and nine other women loudly and angrily condemn the government's testing of atomic bombs after learning about the ravaging of the Utah desert; this is when Williams finally reveals that this testing may have caused Utah's unnatural cancer epidemic along with her mother's death.[1] In *Refuge*, Williams never portrays herself as a victim of the patriarchy or as an agentless female object, but as a fighter who knows that "tolerating blind obedience in the name of patriotism or religion ultimately takes . . . lives" (286) and that the lessons taught her as a child—"not to make waves or rock the boat" (285)—need to be rejected. As a fighter, she is connected both to nature and to culture.

Williams also problematizes the female/nature and male/culture alliances by challenging the metaphoric equation of woman and nature. Though she never presents the landscape in as radical a way as, for instance, Gretchen Legler argues Gretel Ehrlich does by portraying the Wyoming wilds as an erotic, primarily male, lover with its own desire and autonomy (45–55), Williams often does complicate the equation of women and the land handed down from early American explorers and writers by specifically placing either herself or her mother into the generalized woman's slot in the dichotomy and thereby personalizing the metaphor and connecting it to actual women. In the passage below Williams undercuts her clichéd, virginal description of the land once she attempts to become one with the sand dunes in paragraph two. At this point, the landscape's status changes from an objective female "other" to much more of a subjective agent as Williams works to experience existence from the land's point of view:

> There are dunes beyond Fish Springs. Secrets hidden from interstate travelers. They are the armatures of animals. Wind swirls around the sand and ribs appear. There is musculature in dunes.
>
> And they are female. Sensuous curves—the small of a woman's back. Breasts. Buttocks. Hips and pelvis. They are the natural shapes of Earth. Let me lie naked and disappear. Crypsis.
>
> The wind rolls over me. Particles of sand skitter across my skin, fill my ears and nose. I am aware only of breathing. The workings of my lungs are amplified. The wind picks up. I hold my breath. It massages me. A raven lands inches away. I exhale. The raven flies. (109)

This kind of complication, where Williams binds or attempts to bind nature with herself rather than with women in general, abounds: "I am desert," she writes, "I am mountains. I am Great Salt Lake" (29). And later, "I want to see the Great Salt Lake as woman, as myself, in her refusal to be tamed" (92). She links herself to birds when describing herself as a "woman with wings" (273), admitting that she would rather be a bird than a human (266), and she also links herself to the celestial world when moving from a general image to one that is more specific: "As women, we hold the moon in our bellies. It is too much to ask to operate on full-moon energy three hundred and sixty-five days a year. I am in a crescent phase" (136).

Just as Williams's representation of land can be inextricably bound up with herself, in the passage below, her representation of land is inextricably connected, not stereotypically with Mother Earth, but with her own mother as earth:

> The pulse of Great Salt Lake, surging along Antelope Island's shores, becomes the force wearing against my mother's body. And when I watch flocks of phalaropes wing

their way toward quiet bays on the island, I recall watching Mother sleep, imagining the dreams that were encircling her, wondering what she knows that I must learn for myself. The light changes, Antelope Island is blue. Mother awakened and I looked away.

   Antelope Island is no longer accessible to me. It is my mother's body floating in uncertainty. (64)

Here Williams writes about the land as if it were her mother's body in the same way that she uses her own body in the sand dunes passage to connect with the natural world. Whereas in the sand dune landscape a connection exists because of the similar shape of dunes and women, in this passage the island landscape and her mother's body merge because both face a similar fate of disappearance. The island, pristine and populated by wild animals, may flood. Her mother's body, invaded by "wild" cancer and weakened by chemotherapy treatments, may die. Williams does not even need to inscribe the land as a body to see her mother in the landscape. After her mother dies, she sees her dead mother's spirit radiating from natural matter: "I am reminded that what I adore, admire, and draw from Mother is inherent in the Earth. My mother's spirit can be recalled simply by placing my hand on the black humus of mountains or the lean sands of desert. Her love, her warmth, and her breath, even her arms around me—are the waves, the wind, sunlight, and water" (214). By depicting the natural world as her own mother, Williams breaks new ground. Not only does it allow her to challenge Peter Fritzell's assertion that "nature writers have generally dissociated their central narrating figures from familial . . . relations and concerns" (306) but it also allows her to challenge "pornographic" representations of nature as violated woman by reinscribing them as familial.[2]

   Throughout *Refuge* Williams also problematizes many pairings of individual men with culture and, by doing so, validates the men in her life, particularly those she loves. Outside of a few men in the book whom she presents as villainous, most men, such as her husband, father, brothers, friends, and colleagues, are described as admirable, likable, and feminist in many of their viewpoints. Though most play minor roles in this book about three generations of women, these men are individuals separate from the political, religious, and scientific institutions that Williams depicts as nature's antagonists. These men are not solely aligned with culture; rather, in a similar way that Williams's women characters thrive in their relationships with nature, most of the individual men she depicts also have connections to and a love for the natural world. Although the Tempest family's pipe-laying business could be seen as a violation of the landscape, Williams does not see it that way. What she sees are men whose work outdoors brings them closer to nature. Many men, in fact, serve as her guides and companions into the natural world: for example, her father as well as her mother introduced her to camping and hiking, and her husband often joins her in exploring the wilderness.

Whereas many feminist texts depict individual men as sympathetic human beings and the institutions they are associated with as destructive, Williams challenges such simplistic descriptions. Outside of Mormonism, which her male family members enthusiastically participate in and which Williams describes, at least partially, as sexist, she positively portrays many of the cultural institutions associated with the individual men she knows. For example, the medical field, often represented in feminist texts as harmful or threatening to women (see Daly; Piercy; and Gilman, among others), is affirmed. Although Williams expresses frustration and anger about her mother's disease, she does not blame the medical establishment treating her. Rather she respects the physicians in the book, considering them friends and acknowledging Dr. Gary Smith as "family" (295). Archeology also receives favorable ratings. Williams portrays the men involved in this field as knowledgeable about and respectful of the artifacts they find as well as curious about past cultures' relationships to the land and to modern peoples. One of the male archeologists, because of his scientific knowledge and curiosity, is able to help Williams imagine herself more clearly in relation to an Anasazi woman who has been exhumed; without his expertise, she would not have gained the self-knowledge she does (though she gains knowledge by appropriating it from a "defenseless" ruin just as she also appropriates feathers from a dead curlew). In the case of archeology as well as medicine, scientific technology is used benevolently by men for something other than building atomic bombs or other such horrors found in the book's more destructive patriarchal institutions.

These shifts in the female/nature, male/culture paradigm, however, are not nearly as crucial to understanding *Refuge* as is Williams's primary trope of the circle, which binds the book together. This trope, which has been drawn so often and by so many writers and thinkers, is obviously nothing new. Although much celebrated and used in the twentieth century, the circle—what Emerson calls "this first of forms" (179)—stems from a tradition that seems to cut across time and space and is reflected in such diverse sources as Ecclesiastes in the Bible and Native American beliefs as spoken by Black Elk.

Just as many nature writers use this circle trope to explain the way the world works, Williams, too, depicts the circularity of the natural world in *Refuge:* the life and death of the women she loves and the rebirth of their souls, the migration of the birds, the pattern of her grief. Perhaps most ubiquitous is her circular presentation of the Great Salt Lake: "Great Salt Lake is cyclic. At winter's end, the lake level rises with mountain runoff. By late spring, it begins to

decline when the weather becomes hot enough that loss of water by evaporation from the surface is greater than the combined inflow from streams, ground
water, and precipitation. The lake begins to rise again in the autumn, when
the temperature decreases, and the loss of water by evaporation is exceeded
by the inflow" (6–7). As depicted in this passage, the lake's annual rhythm is
naturally circular, but even when its waters flood, as they do throughout *Refuge,* the Great Salt Lake rises and falls in a cyclic pattern. Williams, like so many
other nature writers,[3] also chooses a circular structure for her book when she
organizes her chapters according to the ebb and flow of the flooding Great Salt
Lake, a point she emphasizes by including lake level depths on the contents
pages and as chapter subtitles. When *Refuge* begins, the lake measures 4204.70
feet, the exact depth that it measures at the book's end.

In many ways, Williams's appreciation of the circle differs little from how
other nature writers have used it. In another way, however, Williams reenvi-
sions the circle through her metaphor of the extended family, a metaphor that
expands upon and uses as a starting point the strong notion of family that she
grew up with and which she has transferred to her thinking and writing about
nature: "When I talk about writing natural history," Williams admits during
an interview, "I must begin where I have always begun, and that is with my
family" (Lueders 41). It is with this background that Williams extends her
notion of family from relatives and people of other cultures whose history, like
her own, is "tied to the land" (14) to include the landscape of Utah's Great Basin
as well as the birds who stop there, birds whom she calls "relatives" (19) and
with whom she shares what she calls the "same natural history" (21). By focusing on this notion of the extended family, Williams positions herself within a site of patriarchy that she is determined to revise. Instead of depicting a
family in which the father is an authoritarian figure, the top point of a triangle, as her father seems to be, she depicts an ever-expanding family in which
all members are equal, merely small parts of an intricately interconnected system of life that promotes diversity, precludes hierarchy, and includes even the
ravaged: "The headless snake without its rattles, the slaughtered birds, even
the pumped lake and the flooded desert, become extensions of my family"
(252). In Williams's extended family, life is not more valuable for humans than
animals or, for that matter, for animate than inanimate objects: "There are
other lives to consider; avocets, stilts, and stones. Peace is the perspective found
in patterns. When I see ring-billed gulls picking on the flesh of decaying carp,
I am less afraid of death. We are no more and no less than the life that surrounds us" (29). As opposed to the linear configuration of dichotomies, the
sort of configuration that, for example, places nature on one end of a spectrum and culture on another, the metaphor of the extended family is circular,

encompassing inside its boundaries the values of nature and even of culture that Williams believes in.

Throughout *Refuge*, Williams often explicitly depicts the circle metaphor as she does in the image of her family spreading out its "sleeping bags in a circle, heads pointing to the center like a covey of quail" (15); at other times she depicts larger, more abstract circles expanding outward:

> In the blue light of the Basin, I saw a petroglyph on a large boulder. It was a spiral. I placed the tip of my finger on the center and began tracing the coil around and around. It spun off the rock. My finger kept circling the land, the lake, the sky. The spiral became larger and larger until it became a halo of stars in the night sky above Stansbury Island. A meteor flashed and as quickly disappeared. The waves continued to hiss and retreat, hiss and retreat.
>
> In the West Desert of the Great Basin, I was not alone. (190)

Here the narrator's circling includes everything within her vantage point—the rock, the land, the lake, the sky, and the ancient Fremont peoples represented by the petroglyph. Although many people may see the boundaries between the natural, animal, and human worlds as uncrossable, Williams crosses them within the bounds of the circular family. Outside its boundaries lies all that she does not believe in—the "disconnectors" of the universe, religious and political—which she associates with her vision of patriarchy.

Instead of creating a literary metaphor in *Refuge* in the way Thoreau and others do, Williams ultimately posits the circle as a working metaphor that she hopes will have specific, direct cultural and political consequences instead of apolitical, private, and muted ones. This is to a great extent Williams's project in *Refuge*—to reconceptualize her relationship with the world in language to change the world or, at least, to try to change the way that her readers perceive the relationship between humans and nature. It seems to be a valuable project.

Yet, because Williams often fails to examine the circular connections she makes, her method of merging her human family with the family of nature, represented by the lake and the birds, is not without its limitations. Although her notion that all life forms are equal, that "we are no more and no less than the life that surrounds us" (29), can be seen as noble, it can also be seen as romantic and risky. When, for example, Williams equates her mother's death and the death of three birds, she seems to be asking for criticism and weakening the metaphor of the extended family. Before her mother dies, she finds, in three separate instances, a barn swallow, a swan, and a curlew who are dying or have just died. The birds serve to prepare her for her mother's death and the connection between birds and mother seems deliberate. At one point, Williams even explicitly connects her dying mother to one of the birds: "Her head was turned now, and with each breath her head drew back, reminding me of the swallow I beheld at Bear River, moments before it died" (230). In another example, Williams spreads out a dead whistling swan on the beach with the same pains she used to prepare her mother's body after her death. In the following scene, however, she sits down to an elaborate turkey dinner without any hint of regret or sorrow. By suggesting that these two dead birds—the swan and the turkey—are somehow of a different class, Williams romanticizes one bird while consuming another and fails to see the relationship between them. Failing to make this sort of connection lies at the heart of the environmental crisis Williams seems to want to address. In a last example, when Williams and her husband happen upon a dead curlew, they perform an impromptu ceremony later mirrored in the ceremony performed for her mother:

> We kneel down and run our fingers down its long, curved bill. Brooke ponders over the genetic information a species is born with, the sophistication of cells and the memory held inside a gene pool. It is the embryology of a curlew that informs the stubby, straight beak of a chick to take a graceful curve down.
>
> I say a silent prayer for the curlew, remembering the bond of two days before when I sat in their valley nurtured by solitude. I ask the curlew for cinnamon-barred feathers and take them. (151–52)

In this passage, as well as the one that follows, kneeling, touch, and prayer honor the dead as both bird and human are similarly mourned. "We knelt around her body. Dan held Mother's head in his lap. Our father offered a prayer for the release of her spirit and gave thanks for her life of courage, of beauty, and for her generosity, which enabled us to be part of her journey. He asked that her love might always be with us, as our love will forever be with her. And with great humility, he acknowledged the power of family" (231). Although Williams assumes, in the pages of *Refuge,* that this sort of metaphoric connection is credible, that the death and suffering of a human equals that of a bird in type as well as importance, it is the circular metaphor—not any sort of thoughtful revelation—that forces her to make a connection that she might not otherwise have been prepared to make. If not for the power of metaphor, and its ability to overcome both the text and its intentions, Williams might have been hesitant to make such a romantic comparison between her mother's death and that of a curlew.

Williams also fails to examine the consumerism she depicts in *Refuge* or to acknowledge that, because of this preoccupation with material goods, the human members of her extended family are intrinsically different from the nonhuman ones. Thoreau, who led a life of simplicity antithetical to the materialism already evident in nineteenth-century America, set an antimaterialist precedent in nature writing. *Walden,* especially its first chapter, "Economy," in which he meditates upon the necessities of life, can be read as a critique of America's materialistic values. In the book's later chapters, Thoreau moved more to a presentation of the philosophical, to an awareness of transcendent moral and spiritual values antithetical to materialism. Since Thoreau, most nature writers, almost as if an unspoken rule exists, have followed his footsteps, perhaps not critiquing materialism or even necessarily living lives of simplicity, but by avoiding materialism in their work and concentrating on the natural world. Williams, however, if not explicitly promoting materialistic values, at least makes frequent allusions to material possessions such as fine clothes, cars, and cosmetics, often calling attention to their quality and cost through her use of specific details: her gloves, for example are "deer-skinned" (121), her pistol, "pearl-handled" (148). While many nature writers write about their rustic Walden-like cabins or the flimsy tents they carry, with a few other essentials, into the backcountry, Williams writes about the new home she and her husband have bought up the canyon, about shopping in elite department stores, about eating in expensive restaurants. With these allusions Williams seems to suggest that spirituality, which is so prevalent in *Refuge,* can still exist in twentieth-century materialistic America. On the one hand she should be commended for being honest, for not trying to hide details that might be antithetical to the genre she is writing in. On the other hand, it seems possible either that Williams's class privilege, which is evident and perhaps offensive to many readers of *Refuge,* might not be evident to her. Or, it seems possible that she deliberately fails to acknowledge her class privilege because acknowledging it means that she must accept that her own conspicuous consumption may be destroying the earth she loves.

Throughout *Refuge* Williams moves randomly back and forth between these two configurations that I have been discussing: the confrontational, linear dichotomies (which she often problematizes) and the circularity of the extended family, not being quite able to let go of the former while she experiments with the latter. Because she is doing two things at once *Refuge* is slippery, so slippery that many readers, especially ecofeminists committed to exposing the negative implication of linking women with nature, may be tempted to dismiss the book. Whereas Maureen Devine argues in *Women and Nature* that the seven novels she studied all begin with a premise of dualistic opposition before their authors question and reject this same premise, Williams's strategy does not involve setting up dichotomies just so that she can attack them. Rather, by failing to abandon either dichotomies or the circle, Williams presents a confused picture of humans and their relationship with nature at the same time that she presents a confused picture of herself and her politics.

Paradoxically, perhaps, I believe that this confusion not only is interesting and challenging but also opens up *Refuge* as a site for critical debate. By including both dichotomies and the circle metaphor, Williams creates a nonauthoritative space for readers to consider the issues in the book more critically, since her own word cannot be entirely accepted.

Notes

1. Cancer, which has probably always been a part of the human experience, does not seem natural in the kinds and quantities we see it today. In 1900 cancer of all kinds counted for 4 percent of all deaths in the United States. Now, after heart disease, it is the second biggest killer. Fifty years ago a woman's chance of getting breast cancer was one in twenty, but today it is one in eight (Clorfene-Casten 52–56; Brady).

2. For a discussion of the way traditional American nature writing portrays the landscape in a "pornographic" manner, see Legler 45–46.

3. Thoreau, for example, lived at Walden Pond for two years, but condensed the experience into one year to obtain a form that related to nature's cycles. Other writers, such as Sue Hubbell, follow this seasonal structure. Besides relying on the cyclical pattern of time, nature writers also structure their work circularly in other ways to convey Emerson's axiom "that there is not an end in nature, but every end is a beginning" (179). Ann Zwinger, for example, who seems to be linearly organizing *Run, River, Run* from the birth of the Green River in the Wyoming backcountry to its "death" when it merges with the Colorado River, ultimately depicts what Aldo Leopold calls "the never-ending circuit of life" (175): "And, as it rose in rock, so it ends in rock, not in the hard, shattered gray granites, but the sediments from more ancient mountains, layered, worked, reworked" (279). In the last chapter of *Beyond the Aspen Grove*, Zwinger's organization takes on another permutation of the circular as she describes the layers of ecosystems and history encircling the rock she is sitting on.

Works Cited

Black Elk Speaks. Trans. John G. Neihardt. Lincoln: University of Nebraska Press, 1932.

Brady, Judith, ed. *One in Three: Women with Cancer Confront an Epidemic*. San Francisco: Cleis Press, 1991.

Christ, Carol P., and Judith Plaskow, eds. *Womanspirit Rising: A Feminist Reader in Religion*. San Francisco: Harper and Row, 1979.

Clorfene-Casten, Liane. "The Environmental Link to Breast Cancer." *Ms.* May–June 1993: 52–56.

Daly, Mary. *Gyn/Ecology: The Metaethics of Radical Feminism*. Boston: Beacon Press, 1978.

Devine, Maureen. *Women and Nature*. Metuchen: Scarecrow Press, 1992.

Ehrlich, Gretel. *Islands, the Universe, Home*. New York: Viking, 1991.

Emerson, Ralph Waldo. *Essays: First Series*. Ed. Joseph Slater, Alfred R. Ferguson, and Jean Ferguson Carr. Vol. 2 of *The Collected Works of Ralph Waldo Emerson*. Cambridge, Mass.: Belknap Press of Harvard University Press, 1979.

Fritzell, Peter. *Nature Writing and America*. Ames: Iowa State University Press, 1990.

Gilman, Charlotte Perkins. *"The Yellow Wallpaper" and Selected Stories of Charlotte Perkins Gilman*. Ed. Denise D. Knight. Newark: University of Delaware Press, 1994.

Heller, Chaia. "For the Love of Nature: Ecology and the Cult of the Romantic." *Ecofeminism: Women, Animals, Nature*. Ed. Greta Gaard. Philadelphia: Temple University Press, 1993. 219–42.

Hubbell, Sue. *A Country Year: Living the Questions*. New York: Random House, 1986.

King, Ynestra, and Adrienne Harris, eds. *Rocking the Ship of State: Toward a Feminist Peace Politics*. Boulder: Westview, 1989.

Kolodny, Annette. *The Lay of the Land: Metaphor as Experience and History in American Life and Letters*. Chapel Hill: University of North Carolina Press, 1985.

Legler, Gretchen. "Toward a Postmodern Pastoral: The Erotic Landscape in the Work of Gretel Ehrlich." *ISLE: Interdisciplinary Studies in Literature and Environment* 1.2 (1993): 45–55.

Leopold, Aldo. *A Sand County Almanac*. New York: Oxford University Press, 1966.

Lueders, Edward, ed. *Writing Natural History: Dialogues with Authors*. Salt Lake City: University of Utah Press, 1989.

Merchant, Carolyn. "Earthcare." *Environment* 23.5 (1981): 6–12, 38–40.

Ortner, Sherry. "Is Female to Male as Nature Is to Culture?" *Woman, Culture, and Society*. Ed. Michelle Rosaldo and Louise Lamphere. Stanford: Stanford University Press, 1974. 67–87.

Piercy, Marge. *Woman on the Edge of Time*. New York: Fawcett Crest, 1976.

Plaskow, Judith, and Carol P. Christ, eds. *Weaving the Visions: New Patterns in Feminist Spirituality*. San Francisco: Harper and Row, 1989.

Salleh, Ariel. "Second Thoughts on *Rethinking Ecofeminist Politics*: A Dialectical Critique." *ISLE: Interdisciplinary Studies in Literature and Environment* 1.2 (1993): 93–106.

Thoreau, Henry David. *Walden and Resistance to Civil Government*. Ed. William Rossi. 2d ed. New York: Norton, 1992.

Williams, Terry Tempest. *Refuge*. New York: Pantheon, 1991.

Zwinger, Ann. *Beyond the Aspen Grove*. New York: Harper and Row, 1981.

———. *Run, River, Run*. Tucson: University of Arizona Press, 1975.

9

In Search of Common Ground:
An Ecofeminist Inquiry into Christa Wolf's Work

Deborah Janson

In this essay I will address the continuing relevance of the East German writer Christa Wolf by drawing parallels between her work and that of well-known ecofeminists from the West, including Susan Griffin, Starhawk, and Riane Eisler. Wolf, who was born in 1929, was raised in Nazi Germany, and joined the Communist party in 1949, became the German Democratic Republic's (GDR) most widely read and highly respected author. Having established her literary reputation in 1961 with her first novel, *The Divided Heaven,* Wolf gradually became more and more critical both of the East German state and of patriarchy generally, while at the same time remaining a committed socialist. In the GDR she was extremely popular among the reading public, but was at times tolerated only grudgingly by government officials. In the West Wolf has for several decades been a favorite among feminist scholars of German literature, and prior to unification she also received high praise from the West German literary establishment. In 1990, however, prominent West German critics engaged in a vicious media attack against her that sparked a long and heated debate.[1] Their sudden reversal indicates that following unification Wolf was no longer considered a welcome critic of the East German state but an influential representative of a pan-German (or international) Left whose political views posed a threat to the status quo. In other words, Wolf was targeted by a once doting media because her feminist brand of socialism offers a critique of androcratic social structures that is just as valid for unified Germany as it had been for the GDR.

This change in the West's perception of Wolf underscores certain features common to capitalism and communism. Many countries in eastern and western Europe, as well as in North America and other parts of the world, are industrialized, patriarchal, and white supremacist. Furthermore, their dominant social institutions are largely characterized by competition, a lack of respect for difference, and a lack of concern for the planet and most of its inhabitants. As a result, women *and* men of either political system are threatened by poverty, warfare, environmental illness, and impoverishment of the spirit. This situation has in turn produced the common desire for a different kind of society—one based on cooperation, community, and recognition of the intrinsic value of each individual. Longings such as these—clearly expressed in Wolf's texts—correspond closely to the ecofeminist concept of a partnership-based society that advances communication and mutual respect; pursues the development of life-sustaining rather than life-destroying technologies; and emphasizes relationships rather than hierarchies, linking rather than ranking. While most scholars are currently emphasizing cultural differences, I find these two feminist visions for social change close enough to warrant a cross-cultural, interdisciplinary, and comparative examination.

Yet in view of the broad range of perspectives subsumed under the term *ecofeminism*, I would like first to clarify which aspects are relevant to this discussion. Since I will focus only on those matters also important to Wolf, I will not address issues such as population, bioregionalism, animal liberation, or women's ecological movements in the Third World. Instead I will compare ideas in Wolf's texts with some ecofeminist views on the conceptual basis of mainstream science, the detrimental effects of certain types of technology, the desirability of a partnership-based society, and the preference for an immanent rather than a transcendent spirituality.

Common to all varieties of ecofeminism is a critical awareness of the connections between the domination of women and the domination of nature that characterize rationalism. This worldview regards the exploitation of nature as a means to achieve human liberation and relies on a nature-culture dualism that ranks differences instead of valuing them. Adherents of rationalism generally consider themselves superior to nonhuman life and often by extension to women or other groups they deem closer to nature. Employing the "logic of domination," this perspective maintains that superiority justifies subordination. It prevents its supporters from appreciating the uniqueness of all life forms and sanctions the abuse and neglect of those they regard as inferior.

In a 1991 interview with David Macauley, the ecofeminist author Susan Griffin objects to the continuing dominance of rationalist thought among many of today's scientists, for this perspective blinds some researchers to the interconnectedness and intrinsic value of all living things. Trained to esteem only the mind, these people purposely distance themselves from their emotions and in so doing adopt a cold and uncaring attitude toward others. Griffin maintains that this detachment from others turns scientists into beings incapable of experiencing love and, therefore, incapable of knowing others ("On Women" 119).

Griffin's objections find resonance in several of Wolf's works. In a 1973 short story entitled "Self-Experiment," the protagonist, a successful female scientist who is transformed into a man after voluntarily taking a new drug called Bepeter Masculinum 199, decides to abandon the experiment after she discovers that her superior always manages to maintain a cool and calm composure by detaching himself completely from his emotions, as if life were a film. Upon returning to her original female state, the protagonist, who had had to sacrifice a partner and family to succeed in her male-dominated profession, determines in the last few lines of the story to undertake a new experiment—to see what will happen if she learns to love.

The desire to be known and loved is also a central theme in Wolf's examination of the German Romantics, a study prompted by the sense of disillusionment she felt when her government became increasingly repressive in the late 1970s. Searching for the source of conflict between the artist and the state, Wolf uncovers various social problems also encountered by writers in the GDR, again suggesting communism's and capitalism's common heritage. For example, in essays about Karoline von Günderrode, Bettine von Arnim, and Heinrich von Kleist, as well as in a fictional narrative entitled No Place on Earth (1979), Wolf describes how Romantic artists' longings for self-realization and community clashed with the economic interests of an emerging industrialized society, causing their contributions to go largely unnoticed or unappreciated. This corresponds to the situation in the GDR, where government officials often defamed or exiled artists and intellectuals committed to positive social change. Wolf maintains that the sense of being neither needed nor valued caused both Romantic and GDR writers to regard their world as unbearable. In No Place on Earth (an obvious reference to the Greek word for utopia, ou topos, which means "no place, no where"), Kleist and Günderrode's despair is mitigated somewhat by the suggestion that future generations might solve the problems they face: "To think that we may be understood by beings who have not yet been born" (110). But the promise of a future utopia is slim and countered with a strong dose of despondency.

In her study of the Romantics, Wolf also discovered that industrialization negatively affected gender roles, since men's search for employment outside the home devalued the domestic work that they and their wives had once done together and that the wives continued to perform. While many steps toward women's emancipation have been taken since the early nineteenth century, what have come to be known as "women's concerns" are still regarded by many as largely irrelevant. Furthermore, the definition of what is socially valuable is often limited to goods and services that can be appraised monetarily or to statistics and facts that can be verified. Absent from this definition, Wolf points out, is not only the domestic work traditionally done by women but also essential life qualities such as "friendliness, grace, fragrance, resonance, dignity, poetry," and "trust" ("Berliner Begegnung" 442).[2] Indeed, Wolf considers the ongoing lack of these sustaining qualities to be responsible for "the deadly despair under which 'civilized' society suffers and which could drive it to its death" (442).

Parallels to ecofeminism are particularly pronounced in Wolf's next major project, entitled *Cassandra: A Novel and Four Essays* (1983). This time, Wolf locates the roots of civilization's despair even farther back in history—in the events surrounding the Trojan War. Like the ancient myth, Wolf's version of Cassandra has the god Apollo grant her the gift of prophecy, only to then curse her—in retaliation for her refusal to be his lover—so that no one will ever believe her words. Wolf then transforms this familiar story into a psychological portrayal of denial, using it to explore why human beings refuse to acknowledge what they know deep within themselves to be true.

The essays, which take the form of two travel reports about her trip to Greece in 1980, a work diary, and a letter, record not only Wolf's research on Cassandra and on the patriarchal appropriation of matriarchal deities but also her reflections about the nuclear buildup taking place in the early 1980s between NATO and communist-bloc countries in Europe. In the novel, the Trojan War serves in part as an allegory for the escalating tensions between the Soviet Union, the United States, and their respective allies, with the Greeks symbolizing the victorious West and the Trojans representing both the leaders and the subjects of the increasingly repressive communist system. Cassandra can at times be seen to represent Wolf or simply all those who warn against impending doom and plead for a sane and caring alternative. Thus on a more universal level, the novel provides a means to examine the causes (and effects) of our civilization's self-destructive behavior.

Most of the themes that recur frequently in these texts—including the interconnectedness of denial and secrets, of the past and present and future, of public and private, and of body and soul—are also prominent in Susan Griffin's *A Chorus of Stones: The Private Life of War* (1992). In this work Griffin traces the development of nuclear weapons and shows how the human tendency to deny what we do not want to know links past with present and public with private. And, like Wolf, Griffin looks to the Trojan conflict as a possible starting point for this all-too-human problem:

> I am not free of the condition I describe here. I cannot be certain how far back in human history the habit of denial can be traced. But it is at least as old as I am. In our common history, I have found it in the legends surrounding the battle of Troy, and in my own family I have traced it three generations back, to that recent time past when there had been no world wars and my grandparents were young. All that I was taught at home or in school was colored by denial, and thus it became so familiar to me that I did not see it. Only now have I begun to recognize that there were many closely guarded family secrets that I kept, and many that were kept from me. (3)

By saying that denial is both "at least as old as I am" and at least as old as the Trojan War, Griffin is implying that her history goes back to the beginning of time, that everyone's does, that we carry within us what our ancestors have done and what has been done to them. We are taught in school that wars are public affairs, but clearly they involve the private lives of all those affected by them—the suffering of individuals, untold in history books, but passed on through the generations.

In Wolf's novel *Cassandra* we also see how the private and the public are linked through denial. As the favorite daughter of the Trojan king Priam, Cassandra has been granted the coveted position of priest, with the expectation that she will run the temple according to her family's wishes. Yet because of her prophetic abilities she gradually sees that supporting the court's policy will help neither the people nor the city she loves. As a result she becomes caught up in a conflict of conscience, torn, on the one hand, by her allegiance to her family and state and, on the other, by her awareness, deep within, of the true situation. Her visionary trances—in which she expresses the truth via a voice that emerges from her soul and in which her body trembles and her mouth salivates—are usually preceded by her discovery of a closely guarded family secret that, had she been in better touch with her inner wisdom, she would have known all along. For example, she should have known (and did know on another level) that she had a brother named Paris whom her father had ordered killed when he was an infant, but who had been spared by a shepherd; that this brother did not capture and bring home the beautiful Helen, wife of the Spartan king Menelaus, as the people were led to believe; and that the war they were fighting was based on the lie that he had done so. In Wolf's psychologically motivated depiction, then, Cassandra's initial lack of conscious knowledge about these situations was due both to the court's decision to have the information kept secret and to her desire not to know it—not to have her illusions shattered.

For Cassandra, failing to reveal these secrets was even worse than discovering them. She was particularly ashamed of herself when, in learning that Helen was not in Troy, she controlled her prophetic outburst enough to protect Eumelos, the head of the secret police, whom she despised more than anyone but who represented her father's court: "For when I shrieked, why did I shriek: 'We are lost!'? Why not: 'Trojans, there is no Helen!'? I know why not, I knew even then. The Eumelos in me forbade me" (69). Cassandra censored herself to protect the court, with whom she was aligned and in whom she still, to an ever-lessening degree, believed. Having encountered her own self-censor many times, Wolf uses Cassandra to depict the harm it can cause. In this and other passages, she suggests that we could prevent wars if we did not let ourselves be deceived by our governments, if we did not let ourselves be blinded by our ideals, and if we did not remain silent to fit in.

Sometimes we repress family secrets because acknowledging them would interfere with our ability to love someone who is dear to us but who has nonetheless caused us great pain. This situation is reflected in Griffin's account of Clytemnestra, who forgot, until she heard of Agamemnon's plan to sacrifice Iphigenia, that he had already murdered another child of hers. Griffin reports that

> the great general had abducted Clytemnestra when she was already married. He had slain her husband and then torn her child from her (the text as set down by Euripides reads *from her breast*) and smashed it to the ground before her eyes. This is as violent an image as I can imagine, yet Clytemnestra all but erased it from her memory. She said she grew to love this man. . . . She remembered the death of her first child only when she learned that her daughter [Iphigenie] was . . . to be immolated as a sacrifice to Artemis . . . so that he [Agamemnon] could wage his war. (37–38)

In this account, Clytemnestra had repressed the truth for so long because it was too painful to acknowledge.[3] In some situations people are unable to communicate what they know, either because there is a conspiracy to silence them or because what they have to tell "does not fit into the scheme of things as they are understood to be" (46). If the secrets are very great, the person with access to them may suffer extreme anguish or physical trauma or may be able to speak only through an unconscious medium, such as a dream or a trance. Such was Cassandra's experience, as described by Wolf. Such was also the experience of a young navy ensign who was assigned to work in an atomic weapons plant in Tennessee during World War II, as described by Griffin. Neither he nor any of his co-workers consciously knew they were making the material to be used in atomic weapons, yet he began to have terrible nightmares. Griffin writes: "Is he the repository for the unspoken fears of others? He begins to rave about a terrible weapon that will soon bring about the end of the world. Because his ravings are close to the truth, the navy builds a special wing of the hospital at Oak Ridge for him. . . . [He] is given continual sedation. Whenever he begins to speak, he receives another injection. His family is told that he is on a long mission at sea" (89).

While this ensign perceived and stored in the unconscious regions of his mind/body something he was not supposed to know, the scientists who worked on the Manhattan project became knowing members of a conspiracy of silence. Sworn to secrecy, these men were not allowed to say anything to their families or friends about the work they were doing. This created an apparent split between the public and the private since the men went on trips without telling their wives where they were going, and the wives hosted parties without knowing what they were celebrating. As Griffin points out, not being allowed to talk about one subject with your partner creates a "chain reaction," so that you remain silent on many others. Describing an imagined sexual encounter between Enrico Fermi and his wife, Griffin asks: "At this moment, where is his secret? Does he let it go, believe it never happened? Bury it deeper inside himself, in a wordless place, in a place described only by formula and the vocabulary of science, a vocabulary he keeps apart from all the words he uses at home: *breast, leaf, river, doorbell, cup, child, love*? Fermi. Does he ever tell his secret to himself in this plain language?" (83).

This plain language is the language of everyday life. It belongs to what we normally refer to as the private realm, the world of ordinary experience, the world to which women have often been relegated. In her work diary, Wolf addresses the connection between women and everyday life when describing the *Iliad*: "The line the narrator pursues is that of male action. Everyday life, the world of women, shines through only in the gaps between the descriptions of battle" (233). Wolf's work, on the other hand, is filled with depictions of the commonplace: of a meal well prepared and enjoyed with friends; of the ritual of morning coffee; of the friendly clerk who sells her a new electric plate; and of the landscape she loves best, which she can see through the window of her study when in the country for the summer and which she hopes will fill her gaze during the moment of her death.

But all these endearing details of everyday life are threatened by the decisions reached in the "public realm"—for instance, by the scientists and politicians who determine that nuclear weapons are an appropriate means of self-defense. Unfortunately, these people make decisions that have a lasting impact on everyday concerns, yet do not base them on personal observation and sensory experience, but on "reports, charts, statistics, secret intelligence, films, consultations with men as isolated as themselves, political calculation, and the demands of staying in power" (257). These professionals are, Wolf continues, "men who do not know people, who deliver them to destruction; who by inclination or training can endure the icy atmosphere at the tip of the pyramid. Solitary power affords them the protection they have not received, and could not receive, from everyday life, where they would rub shoulders and skins with normal people" (257).

As part of her attempt to uncover the roots of our current condition, Wolf depicts in her account of the Trojan War the solidification of patriarchy. Before the war begins, some of the women, including Cassandra and her mother, Hecuba, are members of the council that advises the king. As the war progresses, however, all women are excluded from these meetings, their contributions no longer desired. This change is accompanied by others that make the Trojans—in Wolf's version an originally honorable and peace-loving people—lose their connection to all they once held sacred, including their moral principles. As a result, the Trojan men begin treating "their" women as objects—they rape them, steal them, imprison them, trade them as commodities, or use them as bargaining chips—so that Cassandra gradually realizes that Troy had, in its attempt to defeat the enemy, become the enemy: "Now I, Hecuba the queen, the unhappy Polyxena, all my sisters, indeed all the women in Troy, were seized by ambivalence: they had to hate Troy even while they wished it the victory" (79).

But besides the official, male-dominated Troy, Wolf posits an alternative female society that gains strength as the war continues. It consists of women from all social classes (slaves, free citizens, and royalty) and "all" nationalities (both Trojan and Greek—an allusion, I think, to citizens today who were raised in different political systems but have common longings). The community also cares for a changing contingent of men who, wounded or disillusioned by the war, come for healing. And it welcomes visitors such as Aeneas, Cassandra's male lover, and his father, Anchises, a wise old man who gives loving counsel to everyone who asks for it.

The women live in the caves outside Troy, on the banks of the Scamander River. Some of them worship the Earth Goddess Cybele, statues and drawings of whom have remained carved in the cave walls since prehistoric times. Cassandra is introduced to these women in stages, surprised at first to learn of their existence, envious of the loving way they treat each other, wanting but not daring to be a part of their group. Finally, when her connection to the court has been completely shattered, they restore her to health and provide her with a new home and reason for existence: "Between killing and dying there is a third alternative: living" (118).

This community of like-minded women is a way for Wolf to create a positive connection between the present and the past. We are linked to our ancestors not only by denial, guilt, and atrocities, she suggests, but also by our ability to coop-erate and care for each other. Even though this community is about to be de-stroyed by the invading Greeks, its members feel that their limited time togeth-er is worthwhile, all the more so if their existence will be discovered by future generations and if that discovery will spread a sense of hope that a society based on partnership can be achieved. Cassandra recalls her life in the caves:

> We did not stop learning. Each shared [her] own special knowledge with the oth-er.[4] I learned to make pots, clay vessels. I invented a pattern to paint on them, black and red. We used to tell each other our dreams; many of us were amazed at how much they revealed about us. But more than anything else we talked about those who would come after us. What they would be like. Whether they would still know who we were. Whether they would repair our omissions, rectify our mistakes. We racked our brains trying to think of a way we could leave them a message, but did not know any script to write in. We etched animals, people, ourselves inside the rock caves, which we sealed off before the Greeks came. We pressed our hands side by side into the soft clay. We called that immortalizing our memory, and laughed. (133)

In this description Wolf posits an earlier community of women who knew their utopian experiment would be short-lived in their present moment, but who hoped that future counterparts would discover the evidence of their ex-istence and be inspired. In this way, Wolf is using fiction to substantiate the longings that archeological evidence has evoked among feminists in recent years, especially—it seems to me—among ecofeminists in North America. For example, the concept of a partnership-based society that Riane Eisler advo-cates in *The Chalice and the Blade* (1987) was partly inspired by the work of the archeologist Marija Gimbutas, who claims to have discovered the existence of prepatriarchal communities that were peaceful, did not subordinate wom-en to men, and did not see the earth as an object for exploitation and domi-nation, but instead were egalitarian, worshipped an immanent nature goddess rather than a transcendental god, and recognized our planet as a living sys-tem designed to maintain life.[5]

Another ecofeminist who has been inspired by the ideals attributed to such prehistorical societies is Starhawk. Perhaps this is why her novel *The Fifth Sacred Thing* (1993) kept entering my mind as I reread *Cassandra*. Despite their very different literary styles, these two works contain numerous similarities. Simply put, both depict a struggle between good and evil (or utopia and reality) and offer comparable portrayals of future life as the authors would like it to be. Also, in both novels magic or the healing arts play an important role, wise old men and women counsel the young, the protagonists often have loving relationships with individuals of both genders, and the protagonists are endowed with such strength of character that they can endure great suffering and still appreciate life and feel a responsibility toward it.

Also evident in both these works is the authors' preference for an immanent rather than a transcendent spirituality. This is particularly important to Starhawk, who acknowledges that she has been inspired by "woman-valuing, matristic, Goddess-centered" religions such as witchcraft and "New Paganism," which reject the commonly held view that God is superior to and separate from nature (*Dreaming* xii–xiii). Instead of viewing God as a father who looms above us in heaven, Starhawk believes in a divinity who is within and around us, in nature: "who lies coiled in the heart of every cell of every living thing, who is the spark of every nerve and the life of every breath" (xiv). Although this divinity is frequently represented as female—the Earth Goddess—the power "she" yields is within everyone: "When the spirit is immanent, when each of us is the Goddess, is God, we have an inalienable right to be here and to be alive. We have a value that can't be taken away from us, that doesn't have to be earned, that doesn't have to be acquired" ("Power" 76). This kind of value is central to the change ecofeminists want to create, since it prevents the hierarchical ranking that allows people to consider themselves superior to those who are in a different ethnicity, class, gender, or species.

It may be going too far to suggest that Wolf shares Starhawk's spiritual orientation, since she has never yet embraced goddess-centered religions or the worship of any deity.[6] Nevertheless, Wolf is like Starhawk in that she rejects the notion that a male god rules the Earth, and she criticizes patriarchal religions that exclude women and nature from the spiritual realm. In her second travel report Wolf maintains that this patriarchal way of thinking "does not seek to love Mother Nature but to fathom her secrets in order to dominate her, and to erect the astounding structure of a world of mind remote from nature, from which women are henceforth excluded" (*Cassandra* 216). Wolf also criticizes the materialist worldview that denies the existence of anything it cannot account for and that therefore is unable to perceive "the smiling vital force that is able to generate itself from itself over and over: the undivided, spirit in life, life in spirit" (107).

In much of her work, Wolf assigns life-affirming properties not only to the spiritual components of our everyday activities but also to poetry and art. She therefore laments the negative effect that technological development can have on literature. This concern, common also to North American ecofeminists,[7] is apparent in Wolf's 1987 fictionalized account of the nuclear meltdown in Chernobyl entitled *Accident: A Day's News*. In this novel, life-enhancing and life-destroying technologies are juxtaposed by interspersing the narrator's thoughts and psychic revelations about the neurosurgery her brother is undergoing with her reactions to the news of the Chernobyl disaster. While the narrator is grateful to modern science for providing even the possibility of saving her brother's life, she is horrified by the realization that scientific discoveries could also destroy the planet. As she listens to news reports about the cloud of radioactive rain, familiar lines of nature poetry enter her mind, offering painful reminders of the connection between human and nonhuman life. This juxtaposition of what she hears and thinks causes the narrator to realize that much of the language and imagery commonly used to describe nature has become obsolete as a result of the nuclear accident. This is true, she suggests, of the word *exploded* to depict the suddenness with which blossoms appear on the cherry trees each spring (3); of the phrase *the radiant sky* to express appreciation of a sunset's stunning beauty (21–22); and of the word *cloud,* which, unlike in her grandmother's day, no longer provides "a picture in the sky to stir the imagination" ("Hurrying clouds like the ships of the sky / Oh, could I sail with you as you fly") (9). Since radiation-laden clouds threaten the groundwater, the narrator recognizes that "perhaps the problem of what to do with the libraries full of nature poems is not the most urgent" (37). Still, her reflections underscore the relationship between literature and the environment by illustrating the harm technology can cause both.

The narrator does not regard all the literary passages that occur to her on this fateful day as outmoded, however. Rather, she sees in the Grimms' fairy tale "Brother and Sister" the anticipation of human-caused ecological disaster. This view becomes apparent as the narrator, while checking the trees in the nearby woods for signs of disease, recalls both the tale and a conversation she had recently had with her brother. In the conversation, she had complained to her brother about the burden of living under "false alternatives." By this she had meant that all the major industries pollute and that we therefore seem to have no choice but to live either "with radioactivity or the dying woods" (71). In response, her brother had pointed out that such unfortunate situations could be rectified only if we were willing to sacrifice certain "creature comforts," such as, I presume, our desire to stay warm when it is cold, to see when it is dark, and to reach destinations quickly though they are distant.

The narrator's recollection of the fairy tale serves to illustrate the ideas discussed in the conversation with her brother. In the tale, the brother and sister run away from their stepmother because she mistreats them. In retaliation, the stepmother (who is also a witch), casts a spell on all the brooks in the region, so that whichever child drinks from them first shall turn into a wild beast and endanger the life of the other child. In recalling this story, the narrator implies that human beings are so bent on satisfying their desires (or on obtaining the comforts to which they have become accustomed), that they do so even at the risk of destroying themselves. The tale thus provides further illustration of the "false alternatives" human beings create when they develop technologies that contaminate the planet: we can either be destroyed by the brook if we drink from it or die of thirst if we do not.

As Wolf's interpretation of the fairy tale shows, her main focus in *Accident* is on the "insane thinking" that has led our civilization to the brink of disaster and that endangers our children's future. This is also a central theme in her 1996 novel *Medea*. In this feminist revision of the classical myth, Medea does not kill her brother when helping Jason secure the Golden Fleece, and she does not murder her own children in a fit of jealousy after Jason abandons her to marry the Corinthian king's daughter, Glauke. Instead, Medea's brother Absyrtos is murdered so that his father, Aietes, may continue to rule Colchis, just as Glauke's sister, Iphinoe, is beheaded so that her father, Creon, may continue to reign in Corinth. Thus the reputation of these competing nations is based on the same horrendous crime, showing that these leaders' desire for power outweighs their concern for their children. The story provides a clear analogy to heads of nations, corporations, and institutions today who, in their quest for ever more wealth, power, or fame, do not consider the deadly consequences of their actions on future generations.

Wolf's Medea becomes the court's enemy when she uncovers the long-held and closely guarded secret of Iphinoe's murder. To turn the public against her, the court accuses Medea of her brother's death, of being a sorcerer who causes the pestilence that kills many Corinthians, and of castrating one of the court's assistants (an act actually committed by a group of Colchis women in retaliation for his cutting down one of the trees in their sacred grove). After Medea is exiled, her children, who are not permitted to go with her, are stoned to death by a mob bent on ridding Corinth of any trace of her evil influence. The story surrounding the children's death is later changed so that Medea is also said to be responsible for these murders. Any citizen who knows this not to be true has no choice but to remain silent, for fear of retaliation. By changing the myth in this way, Wolf accuses governmental leaders of deliberately deceiving the public for personal gain. More importantly, Wolf challenges the mythic portrayal of Medea as sorcerer and murderer, suggesting that she and other powerful female figures have been slandered to perpetuate patriarchal power.

There are many themes that this novel shares with Wolf's other works of fiction, as well as with Griffin's *A Chorus of Stones* and Starhawk's *The Fifth Sacred Thing*. These include the pain of repressed secrets and the portrayal of strong women with profound healing abilities. Like Cassandra and Karoline von Günderrode, Medea does not know whether there will ever be a world in which she can feel at home. Yet she does offer a "true" alternative to life as she has experienced it. She suggests that people should work for the common good and keep open energy sources "that connect human beings to all other life forms and that must flow freely, if life is not to stagnate" (123).[8]

Certainly, Wolf's desire to transcend dualistic, combative thinking and to embrace life's connecting spirit is shared by many. Despite her detractors, Wolf continues to inspire "sister travelers" who share her vision of a society that is based on cooperation and partnership and that is free of the violence and oppression characteristic of today's social systems. As I hope this essay has shown, Wolf's efforts complement those of ecofeminists, thereby establishing some of the common ground needed for building a liberated society.

Notes

1. This controversy began with Wolf's ill-timed publication of *What Remains* (1990). In this work, Wolf depicts a day in the life of a GDR writer who is being shadowed by employees of the East German secret police. Because she began writing the work in the late 1970s and did not finish it until the Berlin Wall came down, Western critics, most notably Marcel Reich-Ranicki, Frank Schirrmacher, and Ulrich Greiner, suddenly accused her of cowardice and opportunism. Several anthologies of the debate have been compiled; see Anz and Deiritz and Klauss.

2. As far as I know, "Berliner Begegnung" has not been translated; the translations used here are mine.

3. Since Wolf's account of Agamemnon and Clytemnestra's relationship is derived from the version by Aeschylus and not Euripides, it does not include reference to Agamemnon's murder of this first child.

4. In Jan van Heurck's translation of this sentence the pronoun *his* is used where I have put *her* in brackets. I have done so because Wolf herself uses *her* (*ihr*) and the female form of *each person* (*jede*) and because the community Wolf describes consists only of women, making the "generic" masculine form seem particularly out of place.

5. Gimbutas's claims concerning the existence of such prepatriarchal societies are being called into question by some feminists. See, for example, Foley.

6. In the alternative female society on the banks of the Scamander, Cassandra (often a "stand-in" for Wolf) never actually worships the Earth Goddess Cybele herself, but does not mind if the other women do.

7. For ecofeminist views on connections between technology, literature, and the environment, see, for example, Murphy and Warren. In addition, Susan Griffin's pio-

neering work, *Woman and Nature: The Roaring inside Her,* establishes many important connections between women, language, and nature.

8. Translation mine.

Works Cited

Anz, Thomas, ed. *"Es geht nicht um Christa Wolf": Der Literaturstreit im vereinten Deutschland.* Munich: Edition Spangenberg, 1991.

Deiritz, Karl, and Hannes Klauss, eds. *Der deutsch-deutsche Literaturstreit oder "Freunde, Es spricht sich schlecht mit gebundener Zunge."* Hamburg: Luchterhand, 1991.

Eisler, Riane. *The Chalice and the Blade: Our History, Our Future.* San Francisco: Harper, 1988.

Foley, Helene P. "A Question of Origins: Goddess Cults Greek and Modern." *Women's Studies: An Interdisciplinary Journal* 23.3 (1994): 193–215.

Gimbutas, Marija. *The Language of the Goddess: Unearthing the Hidden Symbols of Western Civilization.* New York: Harper and Row, 1989.

Griffin, Susan. *A Chorus of Stones: The Private Life of War.* New York: Doubleday, 1992.

———. "On Women, Animals, and Nature: An Interview with Eco-Feminist Susan Griffin." Interview with David Macauley. *American Philosophical Association Newsletter* 90.3 (1991): 116–27.

———. *Woman and Nature: The Roaring inside Her.* New York: Harper and Row, 1978.

Murphy, Patrick D. *Literature, Nature, and Other: Ecofeminist Critiques.* Albany: State University of New York Press, 1995.

Starhawk. *Dreaming the Dark: Magic, Sex, and Politics.* Boston: Beacon Press, 1982.

———. *The Fifth Sacred Thing.* New York: Bantam Books, 1993.

———. "Power, Authority, and Mystery: Ecofeminism and Earth-Based Spirituality." *Reweaving the World: The Emergence of Ecofeminism.* Ed. Irene Diamond and Gloria Feman Orenstein. San Francisco: Sierra Club Books, 1990. 73–86.

Warren, Karen J., ed. *Ecological Feminist Philosophies.* Bloomington: Indiana University Press, 1996.

Wolf, Christa. *Accident: A Day's News.* Trans. Heike Schwarzbauer and Rick Takvorian. New York: Farrar, Straus, and Giroux, 1989.

———. "Berliner Begegnung." *Die Dimension des Autors. Aufsätze, Essays, Gespräche, Reden. 1959–1985.* Vol. 1. Berlin: Aufbau-Verlag, 1986. 438–42.

———. *Cassandra: A Novel and Four Essays.* Trans. Jan van Heurck. New York: Farrar, Straus, and Giroux, 1984.

———. *Medea: Stimmen.* Frankfurt am Main: Luchterhand, 1996.

———. *No Place on Earth.* Trans. Jan van Heurck. New York: Farrar, Straus, and Giroux, 1982.

———. *What Remains and Other Stories.* Trans. Heike Schwarzbauer and Rick Takvorian. New York: Farrar, Straus, and Giroux, 1993.

10

Grass-Roots Ecofeminism:
Activating Utopia

Cathleen McGuire and Colleen McGuire

SEARCH YOUR ARMCHAIR DICTIONARY for the definition of *utopia* and you are liable to find a description of this sort: "An idealistic goal for perfection; impractical reformist social theory." Were the public, including many in the progressive community, to indulge in a casual conversation on the tenets of ecofeminism, a collective cry of "Utopian!" might well arise. Ecofeminism does indeed resemble a "mode of utopian consciousness," in that it "brings the imaginative possibilities of what is not into the concrete realm of what could be" (Bartkoski 10). We regard ecofeminists as pragmatic visionaries and feel it is our business to "activate utopia." Deflecting marginalization and charges of naiveté, we maintain a firm conviction that ecofeminism offers a vital, down-to-earth philosophy and practice for negotiating a peaceful, green transition into the twenty-first century and beyond.

Background

Prior to founding Ecofeminist Visions Emerging (EVE), the two of us had a long history of anti-imperialist and anti-racist activism. Not surprisingly, we have been feminists since we were teething. By the late 1980s, our political focus began to gravitate toward an exciting new version of feminism. We did not discover ecofeminism through lectures, discussions with other women, seminars, or conferences, primarily because there were so few ecofeminist forums at that time. Rather, our introduction came purely through written materials.[1] Longing to explore ecofeminism in community with other women, in February 1991, with the Gulf War galvanizing activists everywhere, we created EVE.[2]

At that time, the women's movement was struggling to stay afloat in a discouraging, reactionary time warp. American women were reluctant to utter the *F* word in public. Only the stalwart openly identified as feminist. Some theorists had begun to use a confounding new term: *postfeminism.* The designation seemed to suggest cavalierly that either feminism had by and large insinuated itself into the body politic and was irrelevant or, worse, that it had somehow failed, had disappointed women, and was an annoying stigma to get past, post, beyond.

In this relatively dormant feminist climate we assumed our newly formed women's group would remain a lone outpost. Shortly after the creation of EVE, however, a tsunami of gender issues and events flooded the public landscape: Anita Hill, Operation Rescue, Lorena Bobbitt, Camille Paglia, William Kennedy Smith, *Thelma and Louise,* the new *Ms.,* and Susan Faludi's *Backlash.* As a result, large numbers of women were introduced to or became reengaged in spirited feminist activism. It was during this heady reemergence of feminism from early 1991 to late 1993 that EVE flourished.

Yet, we were dissatisfied with much of nineties feminism, having mistakenly assumed it would be ecofeminist at heart. Feminism this time around had clearly learned a thing or two about the politics of diversity, but we were bewildered that it was not making direct connections with the environment, animals, nature, or spirituality. Moreover, much to the dismay of our feminist (let alone ecofeminist) sensibilities, many feminists were championing such patriarchal provinces as pornography and biotechnology. A specific distinction between feminism and ecofeminism was illuminated during the Gulf War. Many mainstream feminists advocated women's equal right to participate in all levels of military operations. In contrast, ecofeminists opposed any association with a war machine that unleashed terror and death on civilians and a hellish assault on nature.

In reaction, we often found—and continue to find—stronger allies in the ecology movement than among feminists. And yet, many environmentalists disappoint us with their desultory development of a race, class, and gender politic. Similarly, those in other progressive groups often demonstrate an inability or an unwillingness to make connections between struggles—a hallmark of ecofeminism. The following incidents, witnessed by us, illustrate our point:

—A white animal rights protester carrying a sign at a march in Washington that read "Experiment on Convicts Not Animals";

—A black prisoners' rights activist stating at a lawyers conference, "I don't give a damn about saving any whales";

—Gulf War anti-imperialist activists intentionally excluding the environmental link in their public policy statements;

—A feminist fundraiser at which meat was served and women unselfconsciously wore fur;

—Numerous women's spirituality gatherings at which Native American traditions were expropriated by nonindigenous women.

While active in several single-issue organizations, we nonetheless desired a forum where we could experiment with a kaleidoscope of theories. An ecofeminist study group in a nonpartisan setting seemed like it might provide a safe haven for inquiry. In creating EVE, a childhood memory surfaced as a metaphor for what we hoped to accomplish. As young girls we used to make potholders at Girl Scouts camp, for 4–H arts and crafts projects, or when visiting our grandmother. The cotton loops came in a rainbow of colors. Stretching them across that square metal frame, we would interlace the strands to produce a comfortable blend. As with those homespun potholders, we hoped through EVE to weave together a grass-roots assemblage of multidimensional interests and create a meaningful whole.

Grass-Roots Pedagogy

EVE's primary activity was its monthly ecofeminist study group.[3] While there is nothing especially novel about forming a study group, as far as we know EVE's was probably the first and (at that time) the only study group in the country devoted exclusively to ecofeminism. Through EVE, women came together and developed grass-roots intellectual theory. We use the term *grass-roots* to distinguish ourselves from scholars whose work, while indisputably more rigorous, is written in an academese frequently inaccessible to lay people. We use the word *intellectual* because our gatherings were focused and serious, not mere gabfests of gut opinions.

Influenced by our involvement in a variety of political and spiritual circles, we sought to inject EVE with a politic of sensitivity and a balance of power. We wanted to walk our talk and do the right thing. Our standards prompted endless debates between us on how to organize the study group most democratically. Egalitarianism, safe speech, and respect for difference—presumably also core features of a utopian society—are a few of the principles we aspired to uphold.[4] We strived to put our ideals into practice here, now, today. Process *matters*. By acting utopian, one activates utopia.

As anchors for the study group, we organized the sessions, selected and circulated the readings, and opened up our apartment for monthly meetings. Despite our initial expectations, women did not step forward to help organize. Sensing the degree of labor involved, most seemed relieved that two energetic bodies had volunteered to keep the study group alive and thriving. The mantle thus remained on our shoulders to make key decisions on the role and scope of leadership, the structure of the meetings, and the nature of the membership.

The study group had no facilitators. The two of us were particularly wary of chairing the meetings since they occurred in our home and we already loomed large as "the face of EVE."[5] Since the gatherings were always small, women generally policed themselves so that no one person dominated the conversation. The experience of figuring out how to hold a collective discussion without a visible leader proved to be a meaningful ecofeminist exercise in and of itself. It lent an anarchic quality to the sessions through which creative ideas organically surfaced.

The most important decision each month was choosing the reading since its theme set the tone for the gatherings. We spent considerable time researching and culling lively material that would educate us, stimulate conversation, and cultivate an ecofeminist consciousness. A few of the myriad topics the group critiqued included urban living, power and oppression, animals, nature as female, Pacific women and nuclear testing, dreams, and sexuality. Few of the participants were students or teachers, people accustomed to reading entire books on a regular basis. In contrast, most of the women did not have the time to read or the money to invest in a different book each month. This compelled us to rely chiefly on essays, a number of which came from *Healing the Wounds: The Promise of Ecofeminism* (Plant) and *Reweaving the World: The Emergence of Ecofeminism* (Diamond and Orenstein). These two books are excellent, easy to-digest anthologies.

A typical study session attracted a half a dozen or so women. While several were core participants, others wove in and out of the study group and frequented EVE's tangential activities as well. The group also saw its share of one-timers who wandered in out of curiosity. Each session represented a heterogeneous cross-section of ecofeminism's constituencies as women from uniquely different points on the ecofeminist continuum came together in one room to theorize. In recalling past EVE study sessions, we marvel at the interesting combination of women engaged in stimulating repartee, as exemplified by the following exchanges:

—An artist and a rainforest activist debating genetic engineering;

—A fertility awareness counselor examining disability rights with a writer;

—A yoga instructor exploring the New Age movement with a Latin American literature major;

—A witch probing the ethics of abortion with a battered women's shelter activist;

—A dancer deconstructing the politics of menstruation with a computer programmer.

Although women from different races, classes, sexual orientations, and age groups consistently came to the study group throughout its three years, it bothered us that overall most of the participants were white. We longed for a dynamic diversity of women. While EVE did not specifically reach out to communities of color, in truth there was no recruitment program for *any* community. Our shoestring operation had no outreach budget. Simply put, EVE was a labor of love.

EVE's vanilla complexion, coupled with the fact that most ecofeminist literature is written by white people, caused us to query whether ecofeminism even speaks to people of color. Or, put another way, is ecofeminism incorrigibly white? If the women of color who did come to EVE are any barometer, their rich contributions indicate that a budding, vibrant grass-roots ecofeminism of color[6] is out there. That women of color were not proportionately represented at EVE meetings in many ways heightened our attention to issues of race. Women of color were not the only community whose increased presence would have enhanced EVE's ecofeminist dialogues. We also would have welcomed far more engagement with mothers, lesbians, senior citizens, disabled women, immigrant women, homeless women, and teenagers, for example.

Men likewise have significant contributions to offer ecofeminism. We encouraged those few males who expressed an interest in attending EVE sessions to form their own ecofeminist study groups or to subscribe to EVE's newsletter. At this stage in history we felt a woman-only space—even as infrequent as once a month—served an important need. Women repeatedly expressed gratitude and relief that a safe, woman-identified "retreat" was available. This does *not* mean, of course, that EVE or ecofeminism is anti-men or that men cannot be ecofeminists.

Buoyed by the energy percolating in the study sessions, we created a newsletter to preserve their conversations. *The EVE Newsletter* was written each month by the two of us and recapitulated in essay form the ideas expressed in the ecofeminist study group discussions. It also featured information about the readings for the upcoming session, a calendar of EVEnts, announcements, and sundry items of general interest. The newsletters kept EVE participants au courant and helped to connect metropolitan New York's scattered ecofeminist community.

Newsletter is a rather grandiose term for our modest kitchen table publication, one whose production and design aspired to an "ecological correctness." *The EVE Newsletter* was printed on a single sheet of recycled paper. Text in ten-point type was squeezed onto both sides so as not to waste paper. When folded, it became the mailing envelope. Adamant that the newsletter be economically accessible to all, subscriptions were frozen to a break-even sliding scale price of four to eight dollars a year. In the three years of EVE's existence, we produced a total of thirty-three newsletters.

Additionally, it is somewhat of a misnomer to characterize the main feature of the newsletters as essays. They were more like minutes of a meeting resulting from a laborious and complex process. It was usually not until long after a session was over and we had reflected extensively on our notes that we were able to distill and transform what had been the free-form thoughts of an unstructured evening of discourse into a flowing, coherent "essay." The writing process was also taxing because we had to ensure that these conversations cum essays made sense to the majority of subscribers who rarely came to the actual sessions and who most likely had not read the "homework."[7] The "voice" of the newsletter was a composite of each woman's contribution. Faithful to the spirit of their words, we never wrote anything that had not been conceptually raised at the sessions. In honor of the essential collectivity of the discussions, anonymous attribution seemed appropriate. Needless to say, we were unequipped to preserve the full oral history of the monthly ecofeminist study sessions. To produce a compact and cohesive newsletter, at least half of the ideas and words spoken during the two-hour sessions had to be cut.

There was a distinct pedagogy to the newsletters. Ecofeminist consciousness blossomed among the already converted and took root with the newly initiated. For many of our readers, *The EVE Newsletter* was their primary—if not only—source of ecofeminist information. The newsletter enabled us to share the ideas sparked by women at the sessions with a wider audience and served as a terrific tool to promote ecofeminism in general. One subscriber (whom we never did meet) called to tell us that she and her officemates would eagerly congregate around the water cooler on a regular basis to read and discuss *The EVE Newsletter* together.

In time, the small local body of women who physically showed up each month had expanded into a virtual community of national and international dimensions. Upon receiving the newsletter, women from as far away as Malta, Namibia, and Tasmania were linked into the EVE dialogue. Visitors to New York checked in with EVE to network, say hello, and establish solidarity. EVE had become a quasi-clearinghouse, albeit unintentionally, and to this day people continue to contact us requesting information on ecofeminism. *The EVE Newsletter*'s initial goal of sharing ecofeminism with other interested souls exceeded our wildest expectations. As EVE's most enduring legacy, the newsletters today constitute a documentation of grass-roots ecofeminist theory.

In parsing and scrutinizing ecofeminism in the EVE study group, four points became apparent and undergirded our formulative thoughts.

First, we discovered that as with other movements and philosophies, ecofeminism is not monolithic. Our readings acquainted us with various versions of ecofeminism that could probably be categorized as social ecofeminism, radical ecofeminism, liberal ecofeminism, and spiritual ecofeminism. Since EVE was not beholden to any political party, academic institution, board of directors, or funders, the group was free to harvest the best fruits available from ecofeminism's varied strands. We were also open to and borrowed judiciously from the broad continuum of progressive ideas associated with the politics of oppression,[8] a pre-patriarchal analysis of history,[9] and alternative spirituality.[10]

Second, we were and remain perplexed that some ecofeminists perpetuate an exasperating dualism: narrowly dichotomizing their identity as either political or spiritual. It is unfortunate that these antipodal camps do not accept, or at least respect, the positive aspects each brings to the ecofeminist table. The beauty and allure of ecofeminism is that it has the capacity to incorporate an analysis and a practice of *both* the political and the spiritual. EVE's motto, "For a Spiritual Politic and a Political Spirituality," underscores our radical agenda to synthesize these oppositional forces within both ecofeminism and society at large.

A third point is that ecofeminism is not the be-all and end-all exegesis or universal, totalizing theory. There are other "wisdom traditions"[11] (those of indigenous peoples or Buddhists, for example) in which Western-based models provide little meaning or significance.[12] Proponents of a Eurocentric worldview, however, are achieving planetary hegemony at an alarming pace and therefore the Western paradigm merits urgent attention. We assert that *from within a Western framework,* ecofeminism offers a singularly powerful and comprehensive vision for attaining peace, harmony, and prosperity on political, social, and spiritual levels—minimum criteria for any utopia.[13]

Fourth, it bears repeating that the philosophy ecofeminists espouse is not necessarily new. In one way or another, its essence has almost always existed in the collective consciousness. Ecofeminism's unique contribution at this point is in coalescing and popularizing ancient and modern wisdom.

Feminist Utopian Visions

As this background suggests, ecofeminism's wide and deep analysis lends itself to the utopian "what-if" scenario. As such, ecofeminists are well-suited to critique the feminist utopian novel. In this essay we will compare *Woman on the Edge of Time* by Marge Piercy and *The Fifth Sacred Thing* by Starhawk. In doing so, we will elucidate and critique ecofeminism's feminist roots, as well as its relationship to contemporary feminism. This in turn allows us to demonstrate our position that ecofeminism extends beyond feminism. Its "transfeminism" binds it to a larger community of catholic dimensions.

Feminist literary criticism has long credited fiction with providing the female writer a venue for social commentary unfettered by the dictates of nonfiction scholarship. The feminist utopian novel extends that license as "a place where theories of power can be addressed through the construction of narratives that test and stretch the boundaries of power in its operational details" (Bartkoski 5). Its cousins, science fiction and mythopoetic writing, likewise afford women a forum to interrogate past and present worlds and thereby through the power of language reimagine a sublime future.[14]

Since the upsurge of the genre around 1915, when Charlotte Perkins Gilman wrote *Herland,* feminist utopian authors have carved a modest, but significant niche in feminist literary history.[15] Frances Bartkoski's critique, however, seems to imply that the genre suffers from a reputation of mediocrity: "The utopian voice is always tendentious; it has designs on the reader. Often its didactic points are made in the form of long monologues and polemics and are just those aspects by which literary critics have often deemed it a marginal kind of fiction— a crossbreed of tract made palatable as literature through a poorly and hastily constructed romance" (Bartkoski 9). We feel both *Woman on the Edge of Time* and *The Fifth Sacred Thing* succumb to this stylistic shortcoming: their political messages eclipse their aesthetic lyricism. These books are remembered less for their literary magic than for their evocative utopian visions.

Another criticism of the utopian author is an inability to escape the present. While all writers are products of a particular historical moment, writers of utopian literature tend to broadcast their time period. This may be explained by the writers' predisposition to right societal wrongs. Hence, utopian novels tend to proliferate during ages of sweeping dissent, change, and turmoil. *Woman on the Edge of Time* and *The Fifth Sacred Thing* mirror the charged feminism of the decades in which they were published. Piercy spotlights the radical feminism popular during the second wave of feminism. Almost twenty years later, Starhawk's book is couched in unequivocal 1990s ecofeminist terms.

Woman on the Edge of Time was one of the few entire books the ecofeminist study group tackled. Our discussion was memorialized in the September 7, 1992, issue of *The EVE Newsletter,* which is reprinted here in its entirety. Through this verbatim reproduction, one can glimpse the process by which the readings became jumping-off points for investigating and advancing ecofeminist perspectives:

> Marge Piercy's inspiring science fiction novel is about a working class Chicana who has been committed to a mental institution and is struggling to avoid a ruthless lobotomy. Able to channel into the year 2137, she encounters a utopia distinctly ecofeminist in character. To her horror, she also stumbles into a competing techno dystopia. Although all the women at this session truly enjoyed Piercy's work, we had

numerous criticisms. One woman noted that the book reflects certain radical feminist ideas of the 70s that differ from those that have evolved into contemporary ecofeminism. The clearest example was Piercy's vision of a future in which humans are created in biogenetic labs; women are no longer birthgivers. This harks back to 70s feminist Shulamith Firestone, among others, who saw science as a way to free females from the shackles of birthing. All of us felt that women's ability to give birth is sacred and that technological birthing is an anathema. Although we welcomed Piercy's imaginative world in which males likewise parent, stripping women of their innate power to give life was not seen as a constructive way to equalize gender relations. One woman deplored the idea of taking away from women. If equality is the goal, she preferred a utopia in which men also give birth.

Several woman felt that had Piercy written her book today, she surely would not have constructed a society in which animals are hunted and eaten by humans. In Piercy's utopia interspecies communication exists through a higher form of language, an animal advocate participates in the grassroots government, and nonanimal food is plentiful (though, regrettably, genetically engineered). Given this scenario, some women found it incongruous that her characters would kill and eat those with whom they are friends. Were she to compose this book in the 90s, the popularity (and ecofeminist support) of today's animal rights and vegetarian movements would seemingly have influenced Piercy to imagine a more thorough non-speciesist society. [None of us had read Piercy's *He, She, It.*]

Several women commented on Piercy's positive depiction of death as a natural passage in the cycle of life. Ecofeminists (as well as prepatriarchal peoples and most current indigenous cultures) regard death with respect, and not a force to be feared or controlled as it is under patriarchy. One woman thought it curious that in a society that accepts death positively Piercy would perceive the death penalty as a means of punishing the incorrigibly violent. Another woman, however, said that in a culture which recognizes multiple rebirths of the soul, there exists a spiritual logic in ending a life so that another more life affirming incarnation can inhabit that energy space.

Piercy's future juxtaposed a nature-based utopia with a frightening, aggressively technological dystopia. One woman said that it seemed appropriate for Piercy to locate her dystopia in what is now New York City. Other women, however, strongly rejected the book's claim that cities do not work, noting, for example, that most urban centers provide public transportation options. One woman added that 40% of all mass transportation in the U.S. is located in New York City alone. By contrast, outside most cities auto dependency is the depressing norm—a *car*mageddon in the making. Other women added that people are part of nature, that people live in cities, and that we can and should reclaim the cities. One woman exclaimed that the privileged elite who control most urban planning don't prioritize the emotional, spiritual, and aesthetic need for green space because they are in a position to purchase nature retreats. Since large portions of metropolitan populations are people of color, another woman implied that it may even be racist to advocate abandoning cities. Some women felt that instead of fleeing to the country, we should be concentrating on bringing the country back into our cities. One woman, a gardener, called for massive infusions of greenery to replace the omnipresent concrete. Another woman felt that even though small-town life may be a refuge from big-city ills, rampant consumerism by inhabitants there is no more earth-friendly than the environmental problems of the megalopolis.

One woman appreciated Piercy's concept of ample leisure time. Along with good health, she said self-defined time is her most cherished want/need. It is through her own time that she is able to give birth to new realities most creatively and radically. The more time we spend in the corporate workplace, the more our visionary minds are distracted and stultified—and the further we enable the possibility of a patriarchal dystopia. Although economically difficult, she felt her active commitment to disengage from the dysfunctional corporate paradigm constitutes a direct contribution toward the realization of a society based on ecofeminist ethics.

A long-term effect of the EVE study group was to sharpen participants' ability to critique with an ecofeminist eye. For example, in reading *The Fifth Sacred Thing* the two of us recalled the study group's 1992 discussion of *Woman on the Edge of Time* and were able to make some insightful comparisons. While both books are essentially ecofeminist, we noted discernible differences between the nascent ecofeminism of the seventies and the more mature ecofeminism of the nineties. A critical ecofeminist lens helped us to formulate an analysis for articulating the roots and evolution of ecofeminism. We shall elaborate on this through a comparative analysis, but first a brief summary of *The Fifth Sacred Thing*.

When an anti-nuclear peace activist who is also a green witch decides to write a novel, you can bet the story will involve a heavy dose of politics and spirituality. Starhawk self-identifies as an ecofeminist and her first work of fiction, *The Fifth Sacred Thing,* provides her a perfect laboratory for conjuring a utopian future.

In the year 2048, two diametrically opposed societies in California are approaching High Noon. The "good guys" live in and around San Francisco, where people are conscientious, compassionate, and have respect for multicultural diversity, communalism, nature, elders, psychic skills, and the integrity of nonhuman animals. Examples abound, sometimes several per page, of the North's evolved lifestyle and consciousness. In stark contrast, greater Los Angeles is home to a wealthy white elite who aggrandize scarce natural resources, especially water, through sheer brute military force over a cowered, unenlightened populace. The South's swollen underclass has been inculcated to accept as natural law the skewed hierarchy of power, to subsist on twenty-first-century junk food, and to relate to one another with the social graces of homo erectus.

In the novel's predictable Manichean plot, the "bad guys" invade the Bay area, forcing the peaceful citizenry to debate at length whether to respond with passive resistance or armed struggle. Through this plot device, Starhawk effectively conveys a basic tenet of ecofeminism: process matters. The utopia/dystopia juxtaposition provides Starhawk a forum to spell out her radical visions and critique the values of late twentieth-century capitalism. For example, there is no ambiguity about which society is permeated by a harsh, unrelenting pornography and which one celebrates a profound primal erotica based on mutual respect. The treatment of a mysterious virus threatening both regions is similarly clear. The South traffics in an arsenal of pharmaceutical drugs manufactured to neutralize the disease. The herbal/spirit healers of the North, on the other hand, invoke the transformative power of chi to become at one with the virus; they dissipate its energy by working with it, not against it.

Regrettably, Starhawk's prose is pedestrian and the plot seems tailored for a television movie-of-the-week audience. But in spite of its literary shortcomings, *The Fifth Sacred Thing* is an attractive vehicle for introducing mainstream readers, especially young people, to spiritual politics.

A Comparative Analysis

The most influential of ecofeminism's roots was the radical feminism of the seventies (distinct from nineties radical feminism) as personified in *Woman on the Edge of Time*. Paradoxically, this same radical feminism was the repository of certain troublesome theories that made the evolution of ecofeminism ineluctable.[16]

Marge Piercy and Starhawk share feminism's basic analysis of racism, classism, and sexism, and they portray these issues in creative, principled ways. The protagonist in each book, a woman of color, lives in a utopia of proud multiculturalism, an intolerance of racism, fluid gender and sexual identities, community parenting, an absence of hunger, and a governing process attuned to nonhierarchical power dynamics. Since race, class, and gender are admirably covered by each author, examining the nuances of their different approaches does not further an understanding of ecofeminism's roots and, by extension, its role in contemporary struggle at large.

Rather, it is in the nexus between nature and technology that the authors most starkly demarcate the differences between seventies radical feminism and ecofeminism, specifically through biotechnology. Whereas Starhawk relegates biotechnology to the dystopic realm, Piercy incorporates it. Fresh organic food is ubiquitous in Starhawk's Northern communities, while chemically manufactured foodstuff prevails in the South. Although produce is harvested from the earth in Piercy's East Coast utopian village, most of it is inherently artificial, the by-product of genetic engineering. The demarcation is at its most decisive in the confluence of technology and women's bodies. Midwifery and natural births abound in *The Fifth Sacred Thing,* and women's role in the process is honored. For Starhawk, genetic tampering of humans is anathema and belongs in the dystopic South. By comparison, Piercy situates biotechnology in her utopian world, where it is harnessed to break "the bond between genes and culture" (104). Babies are "seeded" in scientifically controlled "brooders." Men are genetically mutated to breast-feed. A female character explains, "as long as we were biologically enchained, we'd never be equal" (105).

Biological determinism preoccupied radical feminists in the seventies. Because the birth control pill helped jump-start the women's liberation movement, many women looked to science for further solutions to their problems. If technology were wrested from the oppressive hands of patriarchy, so the dogma held, then the fruits of science could liberate women and in turn society. Large numbers of radical feminists flirted with this thinking, and *Woman on the Edge of Time* reflects the ideology's popularity.[17]

In the second half of the nineties, ecofeminism remains distinctly different from mainstream liberal/left feminism, radical feminism, and multicultural or identity feminism and yet borrows prudently from each. Most other feminists have exhibited a historical reluctance to enlarge their focus to include other issues (race, lesbianism, nature), fearing that "women's issues" will get lost in the shuffle. Further, feminists of all stripes are often dismissive of ecofeminism (Gaard 1994). Of the many topics that set ecofeminism on a different footing from other feminisms, three in particular are germane here: spirituality, biotechnology, and the environment.

Certain sectors of seventies radical feminism imparted ecofeminism with a vibrant spirituality, from which all too many feminists today remain aloof, if not hostile.[18] The Cartesian world of mainstream feminists separates nature from human spirituality; for a quintessentially spiritual ecofeminist like Starhawk, they are one and the same. Her utopian characters deeply connect with Gaia; the power of nature permeates their entire being. The residents of Piercy's Mattapoisett likewise embody an earth-based biophilic spirituality, grounded in a corporeal oneness with nature. As with indigenous cultures, ritual is interwoven into the very fabric of their daily lives. Starhawk's title, *The Fifth Sacred Thing,* accentuates this entwinement of nature and spirit. Its heroine, Madrone, explains, "We say that there are Four Sacred Things [earth, air, fire, and water], and the fifth is spirit. And when you live in right relation to the four, you gain the power to contact the fifth" (300).

Biotechnology as depicted in *Woman on the Edge of Time* holds many contemporary feminists in thrall. While establishment feminists are to be applauded for their activism on behalf of women's health and reproductive rights, ecofeminists are aghast that they tether themselves to the pharmaceutical industrial complex for "solutions." Genetic engineering is another area rife with contestation between feminists and ecofeminists. Perhaps feminism's aforementioned tendency to keep spirituality (especially earth-based spirituality) at arm's length explains its abiding relationship with high technology. Ecofeminists are keenly opposed to the corporate hegemony of allopathic medicine, and for reasons much deeper than its notorious history of misogyny.[19]

Despite their more recent dedication to race, class, and gender issues, most feminists ignore the environment.[20] Indeed, the feminists who organized the 1995 United Nations Fourth World Conference on Women in Beijing were practically *anti*-environmental (McGuire). The lifestyles of surprisingly large numbers of current feminists do not even incorporate such basic habits as recycling, eating organic, or purchasing eco-friendly products. To ecofeminists these practices are not mere lip service, but make a genuine difference. *Woman on the Edge of Time* and *The Fifth Sacred Thing* treat readers to inspiring portraits of societies where nonpolluting mass transportation, clean energy sources, low impact technology, and composting are de rigueur. In addition to multiculturally rich communities, each author promotes *bio*diversity.

In sum, our comparative analysis of spirituality, biotechnology, and the environment as depicted in *Woman on the Edge of Time* and *The Fifth Sacred Thing* illustrates how clearly ecofeminism differs from other contemporary feminisms. We contend that ecofeminism—a metafeminism, if you will—encompasses a much broader vision for planetary transformation.

Conclusion

Reconciling prescient vision with mainstream sensibilities is the paradox of utopian consciousness. For example, activists have been pressuring big business to adopt earth-friendly policies for years. Amid much green hoopla, McDonald's Corporation, Time Warner Inc., Prudential Insurance, and Johnson and Johnson issued a 246-page report in December 1995 detailing twenty-two environmental recommendations corporations can consider when purchasing paper supplies (Holusha). Twenty-five years ago an agenda even this basic would have been dismissed as impractical, not cost-effective, and idealistic—in a word, *utopian*.

Utopian intentions guide paradigmatic change. They energized the people who came into contact with EVE. Although small in number, the EVE participants then impacted ecofeminism and helped the life soup in this big cauldron to finally boil. With ecofeminist visions already emerging, EVE women offered fresh spice to the brew. A politic of hope combined with a spirit of resolve—and a pinch of humor—is our ecofeminist recipe for activating utopia.

Notes

1. The following literature had an early influence on our personal ecofeminist development: Merchant; Sjöö and Mor; Daly; the writings of Ynestra King; and *woman of power* magazine.

2. Throughout this essay, a decentered, polymorphic voice is used. *We* refers variously to ourselves personally, to the entity EVE, to the women of EVE collectively, and to the ecofeminist community in general. While such a diffused subjectivity may be confusing, it reflects the degree to which these relationships are indeed intertwined.

3. EVE was created to be a support and consciousness-raising group with an ecofeminist focus. In addition to the ecofeminist study sessions, EVE offered a "guerrilla graffiti squad," a menstrual circle, a group in which women read aloud together Mary Daly's *Gyn/Ecology,* and EVEnts, special activities EVE sponsored or promoted. Sponsored EVEnts included a workshop on fertility awareness and the screening of a video on violence against women. Promoted EVEnts included a play by Virginia Woolf, a summer solstice gathering, a reading by bell hooks, a lecture by Helen Caldicott, and a program sponsored by GABRIELA Network on the impact of U.S. military bases on Philippine women.

4. We realize that having vision and a consciousness is the relatively easy part; *execution* of that vision is the Sisyphean struggle.

5. Our decision not to facilitate the study groups arose from a desire for a classless, communal egalitarianism. We harbored a vague, although not entirely groundless, fear that taking the reins was somehow patriarchal. In retrospect, we have come to recognize that there is such a thing as "the tyranny of structurelessness" and that mindful leadership has value.

6. While we use the term *ecofeminism of color,* we are aware that neither it nor its corollary, *feminism of color,* is frequently used. Perhaps *womanism,* an alternative term used by some women of color, will spawn the usage of *ecowomanism*—but that is most emphatically not our call to make.

7. In deference to EVE's grass-roots constituency, we endeavored to substitute abstruse concepts like *white supremacist capitalist patriarchy* with simpler terms (without resorting to cant), but our efforts were not always successful.

8. Social justice movements address, at a minimum, issues of racism, class struggle, sexism, heterosexism, sexual identity, disability rights, imperialism, AIDS, environmental racism, (deep) ecology, bioregionalism, speciesism, and anthropocentrism.

9. Many ecofeminists find it instructive to examine the period before men began monopolizing power (approximately five thousand years ago). Skeptics often dismiss the study of prehistory as unscientific and utopian. Many ecofeminists, however, advocate for a more open-minded excavation of our prepatriarchal roots. If we are to forge a just

and balanced world, men and women alike must look to the full spectrum of human presence on earth for clues to a time when gender equality and an unalienated relationship with nature may well have existed. This is not necessarily to legitimate or sentimentalize some past paradise, but rather to allow ancient memory to fuel our imaginations as we explore new, life-affirming possibilities for the future of our planet.

10. By "alternative spirituality," we refer to a vast, nonlinear catch-all category that defies easy compartmentalization. This incredibly diverse, metaphysical melange includes everything from nonmonotheistic spiritual practices such as paganism, Eastern religions, Wicca, Yoruba traditions, shamanism, and mysticism to more physical/emotional modalities sometimes referred to as the human potential movement. Under this rubric one finds yoga, psychic development, twelve-step programs, acupuncture, past life regression, dream work, hypnosis, near-death experience, astrology, tarot cards, runes, palmistry, creative visualization, est, reiki, feng shui, extraterrestrial consciousness, herbal healing, art therapy, chakra balancing, Rolfing, meditation, t'ai chi, ritual dance, reflexology, hallucinogenics, and journal writing. Even sexuality—the unleashing of powerful, mysterious energies—is at times a form of sacredness that can fall within the domain of alternative spirituality (as recognized since ancient times by practitioners of tantric sex). By no means is this list exhaustive. Also, it goes without saying that to identify as ecofeminist does not imply an affiliation with any of the above practices. Conversely, mere adherence to any of the above does not qualify one as ecofeminist.

11. The concept *wisdom tradition* is taken from Spretnak.

12. Ecofeminism, born from classically Western roots, actually has a great deal in common with the ontologies of non-Western wisdom traditions.

13. Strictly speaking, at present there is no official organization dedicated to promoting ecofeminism as a cause. Rather, ecofeminists are active in a variety of political and spiritual forums that tend to focus on single issues, a logical modus operandi for accomplishing specific aims. Single issue activism is fine; single issue thinking is not. Because ecofeminism embraces so many constituencies, it would be impossible to partake in every movement, fight every struggle. The point is to bring to one's work—whatever the front—an overarching vision as exemplified by ecofeminism's interdisciplinary approach.

14. Two mythopoetic works with an ecofeminist flavor that resonate with us are Walker and Cleage. A personal favorite woman-identified science fiction novel is Gomez.

15. The second wave of feminism in particular spawned books with utopian themes. Some of the more acclaimed are Gearhart, Le Guin, Russ, Wittig, and Atwood.

16. Radical feminism was born during the second wave of feminism and is distinct from other branches of feminism. Within seventies radical feminism, different tendencies surfaced, two of which have been referred to as radical *cultural* feminism and radical *rationalist* feminism (see King). The former revels in muliebrity; woman as woman is elevated and celebrated, especially in an identification with nature. In contrast, radical rationalist feminism views the woman-nature connection, and in turn female biology, as the locus of women's historical oppression.

Taxonomies of feminism have been criticized as unnecessary hairsplitting and potentially divisive, yet they can also serve to map a history and clarify differing points of view. A case in point is the dissection of seventies radical feminism to illuminate its role as midwife to ecofeminism. Cultural feminists repudiated the faith and hope in science and technology expressed by rationalist feminists. In opposition to the machine, they celebrated spirituality and an embodied affinity with Mother Earth. One of cultural feminism's most important contributions to ecofeminism was its critical analysis of nature. From this nucleus evolved a core thesis of ecofeminism: the domination of nature and the domination of women are fundamentally connected. Cultural feminism, however, had a tendency toward separatism and universalizing women's experience. These positions are not in sync with ecofeminism's commitment to dismantle dualist thinking and dominant/subordinate power relations. Rationalist feminism bequeathed to ecofeminism a mature analysis of hierarchy and the politics of oppression. To our mind, ecofeminism appropriated the best of seventies radical feminist thought—spirituality, an analysis of nature, and an analysis of hierarchy and the politics of oppression—and left behind the worst—separatism, universalizing women's experience, and faith in science and technology.

Nineties radical feminism is not necessarily the linear heir to seventies radical feminism. The term *radical feminism* today is a catch-all classification for feminists who do not fit into the liberal, mainstream mold (e.g., pro-pornography feminists who self-identify as radical feminists). While *radical feminism* includes those who still maintain the seventies definition of *radical feminism*, it also often includes feminists who are radical but have agendas that are different from, if not at odds with, those associated with the original meaning of the term.

17. Donna J. Haraway, a biologist, historian of science, and socialist feminist, appears to be the heir apparent to second wave feminists who saw in technology the potential for liberation. In her disturbing "Cyborg Manifesto," she states that "science and technology provide fresh sources of power" for transgressive resistance (165). In brokering a reconstructed organicism with an impending brave new world she labels the "informatics of domination," Haraway proffers the cyborg, a hybrid of machine and organism (161). The cyborg persona portends "great riches for feminists in explicitly embracing the possibilities inherent in the breakdown of clean distinctions between organism and machine and similar distinctions structuring the Western self" (174). Reducing ecofeminism to an ideology mired in the interrogation of duality, Haraway fashions "cyborg imagery" as a "way out of the maze of dualisms in which we have explained our bodies and our tools to ourselves" (181). In what seems to be an oblique reference to one of Starhawk's books Haraway asserts, "Though both are bound in the spiral dance, I would rather be a cyborg than a goddess" (181).

18. Katha Pollitt, a leading feminist, claims that the Left is "drenched in religion" (9). Yet, Pollitt's popularity as an atheist affirms the degree to which an anti-spiritual sentiment is pervasive in the leftist community and, by extension, the feminist community.

19. While mainstream feminists are wisely cautious of the drugs, therapies, and alleged cures promoted in the marketplace, their hesitations do not spring from the same

politics vocalized by ecofeminists. The dangers of reproductive technologies and the side effects associated with treatments of illnesses specific to women are all too often ignored by mainstream feminists:

—Despite the regulations of the Food and Drug Administration, researchers do not uncover the harm caused by many drug protocols until they are in use. Ecofeminists deplore how women's bodies are serving as laboratories for experimentation.

—Virtually all medical research involves animal testing. Ecofeminists cannot sanction elevating one group's health over another's.

—Pharmaceutical corporations manufacture products supposedly to benefit women's health. Yet only ecofeminists point out that throughout the world, these factories pollute and poison the very environments in which the customers live.

20. Ecofeminism is much more than tacking an interest in nature onto feminism. *Ms.* magazine's ecofeminist column fell prey to this misconception.

Works Cited

Atwood, Margaret. *The Handmaid's Tale.* Boston: Houghton Mifflin, 1986.

Bartkoski, Frances. *Feminist Utopias.* Lincoln: University of Nebraska Press, 1989.

Cleage, Pearl. "In the Time before the Men Came: The Past as Prologue." *Mad at Miles: A Blackwoman's Guide to Truth.* Southfield, Mich.: Cleage Group, 1990. 6–12.

Daly, Mary. *Gyn/Ecology: The Metaethics of Radical Feminism.* Boston: Beacon Press, 1978.

Diamond, Irene, and Gloria Feman Orenstein, eds. *Reweaving the World: The Emergence of Ecofeminism.* San Francisco: Sierra Club Books, 1990.

Gaard, Greta. "Misunderstanding Ecofeminism." *Z Papers* 3.1 (1994): 20–24.

Gearhart, Sally Miller. *The Wanderground: Stories of the Hill Women.* Watertown, Mass.: Persephone Press, 1978.

Gomez, Jewelle. *The Gilda Stories.* Ithaca: Firebrand Books, 1991.

Haraway, Donna J. "A Cyborg Manifesto: Science, Technology, and Socialist-Feminism in the Late Twentieth Century." *Simians, Cyborgs, and Women: The Reinvention of Nature.* New York: Routledge, 1991. 149–81.

Holusha, John. "Companies Vow to Consider Environment in Buying Paper." *New York Times* Dec. 20, 1995: D5.

King, Ynestra. "Healing the Wounds: Feminism, Ecology, and the Nature/Culture Dualism." *Reweaving the World: The Emergence of Ecofeminism.* Ed. Irene Diamond and Gloria Feman Orenstein. San Francisco: Sierra Club Books, 1990. 106–21.

Le Guin, Ursula. *The Left Hand of Darkness.* New York: Ace Books, 1969.

McGuire, Cathleen. "Beijing '95: A Pale Green." *The Feminist for Animal Rights Newsletter* 9.3–4 (1995–96): 1, 10–11, 13.

Merchant, Carolyn. *The Death of Nature: Women, Ecology, and the Scientific Revolution.* San Francisco: Harper and Row, 1981.

Piercy, Marge. *Woman on the Edge of Time.* New York: Fawcett Crest Books, 1976.

Plant, Judith, ed. *Healing the Wounds: The Promise of Ecofeminism.* Philadelphia: New Society Publishers, 1989.

Pollitt, Katha. "No God, No Master." *The Nation* Jan. 22, 1996: 9.

Russ, Joanna. *The Female Man.* New York: Bantam Books, 1975.

Sjöö, Monica, and Barbara Mor. *The Great Cosmic Mother: Rediscovering the Religion of the Earth.* San Francisco: Harper and Row, 1987.

Spretnak, Charlene. *States of Grace: The Recovery of Meaning in the Postmodern Age.* San Francisco: HarperCollins, 1991.

Starhawk. *The Fifth Sacred Thing.* New York: Bantam Books, 1993.

Walker, Alice. *Temple of My Familiar.* New York: Pocket Books, 1989.

Wittig, Monique. *Les Guérilleres.* Trans. David LeVay. Boston: Beacon Press, 1985.

11

Deep Response:
An Ecofeminist, Dialogical Approach to
Introductory Literature Classrooms

John Paul Tassoni

I WANT MY LITERATURE STUDENTS to be ecofeminists. Ecofeminism offers a better approach to life than the anthropomorphic, androcentric conceptions of nature that dominate Western culture. Because it offers such a better life for our planet, I want students to become active forces in the construction and maintenance of the heterarchical, holistic societies that ecofeminists promote.

However, I am against teachers who impose their values on students. Such impositions reinforce the very sort of monologic, hierarchical relationships that ecofeminists resist. Teachers who force their views on their classes subordinate the interests and concerns of students to their own. Furthermore, such teachers promote passivity in their students, who are encouraged to parrot their instructors' ideas, rather than critically examine their own ideas and those of others.

My goal is to be counterhegemonic, not totalitarian. I want to persuade my students to scrutinize their inherited values and those of ecofeminists, and I want them to voluntarily embrace ecofeminism as more conducive to healthy human and nonhuman relations.

Although the subversion of oppressive Western tenets does represent a principal aim of ecofeminists (see Warren 6–8), ecofeminists need to remain open to conflicting viewpoints; they cannot perpetuate the very monologic conceptions of truth and hierarchy they seek to resist. By closing themselves off from alternative viewpoints—even androcentric, anthropomorphic ones—ecofeminists would close themselves off from the kinds of self-critical introspection they need to respond locally—in persuasive, rather than coercive ways—on behalf of feminist and environmental concerns. In other words, by remaining open to opposing viewpoints, ecofeminists can continually examine and re-examine their own goals; at the same time, they can participate in productive debates with those who might oppose and those who might not understand their aims. In my literature classrooms, I promote ecofeminism as an ongoing dialogue, one taking place among its advocates as well as with those who may not affirm its principles.

My teaching, then, employs what Patricia Bizzell would call "a pedagogy of persuasion." Reflecting the dialogic methods of educators such as Bizzell, Ira Shor, Henry Giroux, and Paulo Freire, the classrooms in which I promote ecofeminist values are not sites of monologue: the students who object to, who are baffled by, and who are suspicious of ecofeminist ideas are taken seriously, and the students who accept these ideas continue to develop and revise their thinking in dialogues with me and with other class members. "In this pedagogy," Bizzell writes, teachers are "authorized to attempt to persuade students to try on [what the teachers perceive to be democratic] values,[1] while at the same time the students also exercise persuasion, on [the teacher] and their peers, where they see changes being needed in the cultural awareness" (198). I introduce ecofeminism to my literature classes because I have been authorized by my university to promote critical thinking and active citizenship. I have a responsibility to expand my students' areas of concern and sense of heterarchy as much as I possibly can, and no approach to life and literature offers a vision as expansive and as egalitarian as that of ecofeminism.

In this essay, I will describe methods of dialogic pedagogy that can be used in the teaching of ecofeminist theory. I will narrate some of my own experiences teaching ecofeminism several years ago in an introductory literature course at a state university. I will describe this particular class for three reasons. First, the dialogues about ecofeminism I had with students in this course demonstrate the extent to which an ecofeminist, dialogical approach to literary study can help teachers and students engage issues of both local and global importance. Second, my experiences with this class—not altogether successful—suggest further ways of dialogizing the classroom so that students might be persuaded to "try on" ecofeminist principles. And third, while it perhaps represents the greatest hope for a counterhegemonic, dialogic, ecofeminist pedagogy, the introductory, nonmajor literature course has been a neglected area of scholarship.

Overall, I will argue that an ecofeminist, dialogical approach to introductory literature classrooms can help students engage critically with and consider alternatives to those aspects of our society that undermine egalitarian relations not only between humans—alternatives for which Bizzell's pedagogy aims— but also between humans and nonhumans and among the various other forms of life on the planet.

~

In my introductory college literature classes—courses I hope will help students read and write discourses vital to their needs as critical citizens—issues of gender tend to be among the first that students broach. My attention to gender issues, which strongly emphasizes ecofeminist concerns, together with the dialogical pedagogies of educators such as Giroux, Shor, Bizzell, and Freire have given me hope for the cultural work that can be done in and through introductory literature classrooms. After all, most of the students who take these classes will not enroll in advanced literature courses; it is in the introductory course that ecofeminist teachers have a chance to reach students who will go on to become chemists, accountants, mathematicians, and dropouts—those who may have little chance for the sustained consideration of cultural issues that literature courses offer (see Cahalan and Downing 8). So, as Patrick D. Murphy does in his essay "Coyote Midwife in the Classroom: Introducing Literature with Feminist Dialogics," I will admit up front that my "introductory literature course is not really 'about' literature." My introductory course, rather, uses literature "as a study example" (163), as a point of departure from which class members might critically examine the attitudes and beliefs that influence them and the world around them.

This is an important distinction to make because in many respects formalist, New Critical doctrines still dominate introductory courses in literature. These doctrines treat texts as self-contained artifacts and promote little, if any, critical consideration of the material conditions surrounding the interpretations, compositions, and receptions of literature. At least two factors contribute to the persistence of such doctrines: many teachers perceive the course as a place in which students learn the "basics" of literature, such as setting, plot, and character; many teachers believe contemporary critical theories, such as post-structuralism and ecofeminism, represent complexities beyond the grasp of freshman and sophomore students.

However, James M. Cahalan and David B. Downing's *Practicing Theory in Introductory College Literature Classrooms* (1991) raises significant questions about the "basics" of literary study. Essays in this collection identify the ideological dimensions of New Criticism and undermine claims its advocates might make for its primacy as a literary tool. Formalist and New Critical approaches to literature, various writers in this collection show, have no more claim to the foundation of literary study than, say, approaches such as Marxism and feminism. In addition, the writers make convincing arguments for introductory courses that are responsive to the social and political issues foregrounded in critical theory. Rather than fixate on textual analyses to the exclusion of sociohistorical factors surrounding compositions, receptions, and interpretations of literary works, introductory literature classrooms can help students examine the various discourses of gender, race, and class that affect them socially, historically, politically, and academically.

Despite such collections, the implications of an ecofeminist approach to the introductory classroom have yet to be examined. It is, however, important that this gap in pedagogy scholarship be filled, because an ecofeminist approach—particularly an ecofeminist, dialogical approach—to literature and life can help teachers and students engage cultural concerns that a formalist vocabulary, as well as the vocabulary of many contemporary critical theories (see Love 202), might otherwise ignore.

∼

I stress the dialogical intentions of my class because teachers cannot adequately address the need for social change indicated by ecofeminists within the traditional framework of the literature classroom. What I mean by *traditional* are those practices related to what Freire describes as the banking method of education (58), an approach to which the New Criticism has been highly adaptable (Cahalan and Downing 6). In its extreme form, banking-method teaching treats students as empty receptacles obligated to receive the information their instructors deposit into their minds. These deposits are intended to accrue interest, serving as cultural capital that in the short run helps students earn A's for the course and in the long run heralds students' solvency in mainstream culture. Such a pedagogy allows little, if any, room for students' critical reflection on the material. Rather, teachers represent knowledge as a set of uncontested truths and compel students to recite (in the classroom, on exams, in research papers) the "true meaning" of texts, those interpretations (usually foregrounding formalistic, New Critical elements) determined by the teacher and previous scholars.

Perhaps the major drawback of the banking method is that it effaces students' own cultural experiences, thus limiting the discourses to which the academy must become accountable and limiting, as well, the opportunities for change such discourses might suggest. In this manner, the banking method works against the democratic promise of open admissions policies: not only does it impede the development of a democratic citizenry by encouraging the uncritical acceptance of information but it also reinforces the academy's own deafness to attitudes and beliefs that might challenge the status quo.

Dialogic pedagogies, however, challenge the banking approach to knowledge. With the dialogic approach, students *and* teachers function as learners, working collaboratively to create and critique course materials. Such a pedagogy reverses the passivity that the banking model encourages in students and inspires them to assume active roles in the reading and writing of their culture. Through the dialogic method, literature classrooms can be transformed into democratic public spheres (see Giroux 309–10) in which students and teachers explore the possibilities of egalitarian human and nonhuman relations and practice the rhetorical strategies necessary to communicate their needs and the needs of "others" within a diverse ecosphere.

Although many literature teachers do encourage discussion in their classrooms, these discussions are often mere preliminaries to the teachers' disclosure of "correct" interpretations. In other words, although many literature courses today little resemble the extreme version of the banking approach Freire describes, elements of the banking method still intercede to curtail dialogue, and as a result, students frequently approach classroom discussions as a form of guessing game wherein they continually guess at "true meanings" until the teacher decides that someone has hit upon them. These interpretations may comprise the unexamined values and assumptions of the dominant gender, race, and class, in which case their function is to maintain the status quo. As C. A. Bowers writes, "in effect, the taken for granted nature of . . . patterns will lead to repeating them, until we either choose to examine them or are forced to confront them because of ecological damage that can no longer be ignored" (126). To put it another way, literature classrooms such as this promote the uncritical acceptance of inherited knowledge over the active decoding and encoding of the metaphorical structures that shape human and nonhuman interactions.

In the same vein, interpretations issued in traditional classrooms may—depending on the instructor—support radical ideas such as those of ecofeminism. However, if students consider these ideas to be but deposits for them to withdraw and spend on demand, they may reinforce the very thoughts and attitudes their teachers seek to resist. Students in traditionally structured classrooms may, to negotiate the demands of their ecofeminist instructors, merely reproduce "correct" answers and, in some cases, even conceal their objections to the answers their instructors' advocate, without ever understanding or even considering the social implications of the answers they write down or say aloud in class. In such cases, some of the students' (and teachers') underlying assumptions of culture may go unaddressed—may continue to support the hierarchical conceptions of human and nonhuman relations that constitute life in Western culture.

On the other hand, students in such classrooms may actually learn to value the radical insights offered by ecofeminists, but class members come to such appreciations within a conceptual framework (the banking method) in which the principles of the powerful (the teacher, the academy) are imposed upon them. They replace one set of truths (patriarchy) with another (ecofeminism), leaving the new truths as resistant to change and as intolerant of difference as the former (see Schilb 263). The danger of having students reach such an understanding of ecofeminist ideas is that they come to it without having to develop the rhetorical capacities to interact with others as speaking subjects. Students exposed to ecofeminism in this manner develop the values but not necessarily the skills they need as critical citizens in a democratic society: they may be able to articulate alternatives to oppressive Western values, but they may become as equally oppressive themselves in presenting their ideas to others.

As an alternative to the banking model, the dialogical approach to literature encourages students to see "others" as speaking subjects, not merely the objects of their attention (Murphy, "Coyote" 164). In the dialogical classroom, knowledge is not represented as static, but as determined between people within a given culture or situation. Dialogic teachers do not merely inform students that knowledge is determined interindividually; they employ classroom practices that reinforce this conception of knowledge and do so in a manner that helps students understand that their determinations of what is valuable and true may have actual effects in the world beyond examination grades.

∽

Other scholars, such as Murphy in "Coyote Midwife," describe dialogic practices in more detail than I have room for here, so in this section I will only touch upon some of their principles and reserve space for a detailed discussion of my students' written responses to our sessions on ecofeminism. In this section I will briefly describe how teachers can dialogize knowledge in literature classrooms by engaging students in the development of curricula and in the criteria for grading. One thing I always do, for instance, is talk with my students about how I have graded certain assignments in the past and ask them, given their particular experiences with the assignments, to suggest things I might emphasize in my assessment of their work. In the spirit of democratizing their classrooms, other teachers ask students to grade one another's work and even go so far as to have students grade their own work. Whatever the case, the object of the dialogical teacher is to have the criteria brought up for discussion, rather than have it imposed upon students as a demarcator of self-evident truths. When students have a say in how they are graded, they can begin to see the means by which "truths" can be negotiated and how the results of these negotiations affect how and what they learn (see Murphy, "Coyote" 166).

Such an understanding opens the teacher's comments on students' writing, on texts, on society to dialogical response, thereby empowering students to develop and practice their own capacities for judgment. Students further exercise these capacities when they take part in the construction of curricula—from determining the direction of class discussion to selecting the texts that they will read. I allow my students to choose at least one novel for the course. Generally, they choose a work I have not read and usually one that has had little, if any, scholarly attention, such as Stephen King's *Misery*. Their involvement in this procedure, like their involvement in establishing criteria for grades, not only sets the stage for discussions about the politics of choice—about what kinds of texts and ideas get included and valued and what kinds get excluded, devalued, or ignored—but it also helps me to demonstrate the limits of my expertise. I need to learn the text with my students and relearn my assumptions about culture according to the interests my students express through their choice and through their interpretations of the reading. As Ira Shor writes in *A Pedagogy of Liberation*, a book he co-authored with Paulo Freire,

> If the dialogical teacher announces that he or she relearns the material in the class, then the learning process itself challenges the unchanging position of the teacher. That is, liberatory learning is a social activity which by itself remakes authority. In this case, authority is the form of existing knowledge as well as the governing behavior of the teacher. . . . These challenges demystify the teacher's power, open it up to change. They impose humility on the existing order. They invite the students to exercise their own powers of reconstruction. (101)

When students select the readings, they can be reasonably sure that *I* have no prefabricated set of correct answers that they must struggle to uncover. Rather, students and I work together to generate meanings in and against the context of other works we have read over the course of the semester. Students do not passively consume "universals" pronounced by a single speaker; we argue the cultural significance of texts and our readings of texts, not what students "need to know for the exam."

The dialogic classroom opens to debate the various perspectives class members bring to literature. One of the more common ways for teachers to foreground these various views is to have class members write responses to their readings and to share these responses in class—sometimes in small groups, sometimes with the class as a whole. Rather than conduct the class according to a preset agenda, the teacher allows discussion to originate from students' own textualizations, and the class together explores the social and cultural implications of their various responses. In this manner, ecofeminists have a much better chance than they would in a traditional lecture format of addressing students' interests, of helping them to develop an internal dialogue—a deep response—concerning their role as readers and writers of culture (see Bauer xi), and of encouraging them to engage and develop not only their own ideas but also those of other students (see Murphy, "Coyote" 172–73).

The advantage of having class members write down their responses is that it offers students a record by which they can chart the changes (or lack of changes) in their perspectives and continually use their earlier responses as resources for future readings and discussions as they participate in dialogues with me, with other class members, with the readings, and with themselves. I often ask my students to write down their initial responses to texts and then to amend or revise their responses after they have read the comments of others and after we have discussed the work in class. I also ask students to comment upon any revisions they might have made (or might not have made) in their subsequent response. In this manner, students in an ecofeminist, dialogical classroom can situate their ideas in terms of broader social and environmental dialogues; whether or not their perspectives change, they are encouraged to become accountable to others for their beliefs.

Such accountability, facilitated through the few methods I describe above, challenges monological, patriarchal, authoritative, "correct" views of the world.[2] In this manner, the aims of the dialogical classroom intersect very much with those of ecofeminists. Like ecofeminists, dialogical teachers promote heterarchical relations through a critical understanding of "others," whether they be fellow class members, teachers, or members of another gender, race, class, or ethnicity. Donald A. McAndrew, examining workshop writing classrooms, draws similar comparisons between writing pedagogy and ecofeminism, comparisons that apply very much to the type of literature classrooms I describe:

> We form communities of readers and writers, reducing the patriarchal dominance of the teacher. We read from a non-hierarchal canon that represents writers of all colors, classes, genders. Students write what is important to them not what is assigned by a dominant teacher; they have ownership and authorship. We don't teach them as much as we nurture and empower. Our classroom has become more like a micro-environment or . . . an ecological niche, as we see its diversity and connectivity as a richness and model of living literacy. (7)

Additionally, an ecofeminist, dialogical approach to literature ensures a fuller consideration of social issues, ensures a consideration of the ways our everyday interactions with one another might reinforce, challenge, or change conditions on this planet.

∽

When I introduced ecofeminist ideas into what I had considered to be a dialogical classroom, students and I expanded our discourse to encompass topics ranging from those commonly cited by ecofeminists, such as connections between human interpersonal relations and current ecological crises, to those of more particular concern to me as a teacher of English, such as the connections between my students' attitudes toward the course and the responsibilities of democratic citizenship. I learned many things in that introductory literature class and have adjusted my pedagogy accordingly in subsequent courses, but looking back on those few sessions that focused on ecofeminism, I can think of nothing I learned more than the range of concerns that ecofeminism addresses and the need to address such concerns within a chain of pedagogical practices committed to a dialogic critique and creation of culture.

For the particular week of classes I narrate here, I assigned my students two short stories. I chose the texts because I felt they complemented each other nicely in regard to ecofeminist concerns. For the Tuesday class, students were to have read and written responses to Antonio Moravia's "The Chase," and for Thursday, they were to have read Angela Carter's "Peter and the Wolf." For this second period, they were to have written a response to the following set of questions: "How are women and nonhuman nature perceived in Angela Carter's 'Peter and the Wolf'? How is this perception similar to or different from those exhibited in Moravia's 'The Chase'? In either of these works, are there comparisons/contrasts between human and nonhuman nature? Are these comparisons/contrasts or this lack of comparisons/contrasts beneficial or harmful to those involved in the works and to culture in general? If so, in what ways?" Although I normally do not issue such directive questions to my classes, I was not afraid of imposing my interpretation of the texts or my narrative of ecofeminism on these students. Even though I was in fact limiting the context within which students could read the texts (in fact triggering a discussion of ecofeminism), I felt comfortable that I had arranged my class, and particularly these sessions on ecofeminism, so that our discussion of the issues could proceed from the students' assumptions about the theory. I also informed class members why I was assigning them the questions—to help us get started on a study of ecofeminism, which I briefly defined—and told them that they still had the option to write responses of their own if they felt my questions excluded any insights they might otherwise have on the texts.

Nonetheless, even before students had encountered my directive questions, their consideration of "The Chase" led us into many areas of concern to ecofeminists. Briefly, Moravia's story is about a distressed husband. Throughout his first-person account, the husband laments what he views as his wife's loss of vitality, which he describes as a "wildness." One day he follows her, noticing as his "chase" proceeds that her wildness seems to be returning. He discovers the cause of this to be a male lover, whom she meets and embraces passionately in the street. The narrator is at first compelled to confront the couple, but soon decides against it, deciding to leave the luster of his wife's wild beauty unscathed. What I initially saw in this story was the explicit association of woman and nonhuman nature and how the institution of marriage seemed to eschew this woman's needs as an individual. I thought the story might provoke some interesting dialogue about gender relations, particularly in marriage, and about human/nonhuman relations, as suggested by the man's "chase."

What became immediately apparent in our class discussion on the story was that students held the woman in "The Chase" completely responsible for the failure of the marriage, with the strongest indictment coming from the women in the class. In fact, the first woman to speak referred to the man's wife as a "dog" because of her extramarital affair. Another woman in the class commented that "she needs to feel guilty; she needs to be put in her place." After asking these students to elaborate more on their statements, I attempted to defend the woman's actions, pointing out that we were not getting her side of the story and indicating that the husband throughout seems oblivious to what she is thinking. Many students still, however, blamed her because she had not forced herself to be heard. One male student even suggested that since "The Chase" represented the husband's first-person point of view, he would be obviously articulate enough to understand her needs if she would only speak up. I suggested that his understanding of her as something wild might be impeding his sympathy for her needs, making her needs secondary to his own. As the session progressed, I felt that criticism of the woman's actions lessened, but many in the class were still concerned with defending the position of the man, even feeling that he should have attacked his wife's lover. Although I would not exactly characterize our debates as ecofeminist, our class's reading of "The Chase" addressed many of the Western assumptions challenged by ecofeminists: the irrationality and unreliability of women as creatures of nature, the superiority of moral laws and social institutions put forth by humans, the valuation of physical conflict over cooperation and negotiation. I identified these issues for my students and mentioned that they were principal concerns of ecofeminism, which we would discuss in more detail in our next session.

The second session began with students reading their responses to my questions. Students, therefore, came into class already having grappled with issues important to ecofeminists: to various degrees the students had developed positions on which to reflect critically and to use to challenge ecofeminist ideas as I made my arguments. For this session, students were working with Carter's "Peter and the Wolf." This story is about a young girl raised by wolves and her series of encounters with her male cousin, Peter. The wolf-woman is very much a part of wolf culture; the cousin evolves more and more into "civilized," human culture, even leaving his village at the story's end to pursue a career as a member of the clergy. I like this story for its juxtaposition of wolf life and human culture, particularly its depiction of Peter's inability to understand his cousin's wildness, which is very much tied to her femininity.

The students had a good time with this story and were certainly less antagonistic toward its female character. Among the topics they brought up were the differences between nonhuman and human "ideologies" (the girl becomes acculturated to wolf life, just as Peter is to human civilization, and each "culture" holds different values), the ways humans see themselves as superior (characters saw the woman's life amongst the wolves as unfortunate), and conceptions of female/nonhuman sexuality (Peter is unable to come to terms with his cousin's mysterious sexual organ). I told my students that I was interested in these topics because they had led us into many ecofeminist concerns. Our observations had pointed to the fictionality of human truths, and the demystification of such truths helps us to see where changes might be made in oppressive social constructs. Our reading had also indicated some of the particular and harmful aspects of "human ideology": hierarchical conceptions of human/nonhuman relations and the understanding of women as things beyond reason represent perspectives that patriarchally raised men use to legitimate their domination of women and the environment.

At this time I also passed out photocopies bearing the following principles of ecofeminist thought outlined by Ynestra King in "Toward an Ecological Feminism and a Feminist Ecology." I briefly discussed these tenets in the context of the discussions our class had had over the past two sessions:

1. The building of Western industrial civilization in opposition to nature interacts dialectically with and reinforces the subjugation of women because women are believed to be closer to nature in this culture against nature.

2. Life on earth is an interconnected web, not a hierarchy. There is not a natural hierarchy, but a multitiered human hierarchy projected onto nature and then used to justify social domination. . . .

3. A healthy, balanced ecosystem, including human and nonhuman inhabitants, must maintain diversity. . . . Biological simplification, i.e., wiping out of whole species, corresponds to reducing human diversity into faceless workers, or to the homogenization of taste and culture through mass consumer markets. . . . We need a decentralized global movement founded on common interests but celebrating diversity and opposing all forms of domination and violence. Potentially, ecofeminism is such a movement.

4. The survival of the species necessitates a renewed understanding of our relationship to nature . . . ; it necessitates a challenging of the nature-culture dualism and a corresponding radical restructuring of human society according to feminist and ecological principles. (King 119–20)

This brief presentation took the form of a dialogue, with students interjecting their thoughts throughout. I then asked students to amend their written responses with any thoughts they might be having in reaction to our week of discussion. When the session was over, I collected their response statements and headed to my office, where I would continue our dialogue on paper.

∽

An ecofeminist, dialogical pedagogy makes environmental awareness an integral part of what McAndrew calls a classroom's "living literacy"—a practice that takes dialogics even beyond that performed by Mikhail Bakhtin, whose writings underlie many of the practices discussed here (see Ward 174–78). Bakhtin writes, "outside society and, consequently, outside objective socioeconomic conditions, there is no such thing as a human being. Only as a part of a social whole, only in and through a social class, does the human person become historically real and culturally productive" (15). An *ecofeminist,* dialogical pedagogy takes this conception of the human and this conception of the historically real and culturally productive a step (in fact, countless steps) further. Where, as Murphy points out, Bakhtin (and, we might add, dialogical pedagogues) "in [their] effort to reinsert the human being into history and culture . . . artificially remove . . . that being from the environment" ("Prolegomenon" 46), an ecofeminist perspective "break[s] dialogics out of the anthropocentrism in which Bakhtin performs it" (48). The aim of my ecofeminist approach to my students' written responses was to help them and to help me expand our notions of dialogic relations.

As I commented on my students' responses, then, I was trying to use my ecofeminist viewpoint to "break" my class's dialogue "out of the anthropocentrism" that pervades Western civilization. Of course, this was no small feat, and I cannot with any certainty say I was successful. But I can say that the ecofeminist perspective offered me a position from which I could consistently call my students' attention to interpersonal *and* environmental concerns. Doing this, I could at least begin to bring my students to a point where they could "try on" ecofeminist values and weigh them against their inherited ones.

Some students responded favorably to my discussion on ecofeminism, and I tried to use my reading of their statements to get them to examine further the implications of the theory. I wanted them to strengthen their stance, especially where they revealed only surface understandings of ecofeminism (which was to be expected, given the relatively short period of time we had spent on the subject) or attempts to please their teacher (which was also to be expected, given the amount of time many students spend in traditional classrooms). For instance, I noticed that students who expressed interest in ecofeminism rarely considered the nonhuman emphasis of the theory when they revised their responses. "Well," wrote one student, "I would kind of like to change my view on 'The Chase.' I see better now that he was not listening to her and didn't care for what she had to say. She was listening to him by doing the physical things he wanted to but he was not listening to her by talking to her." The student's response displays a sensitivity to the lack of dialogue between Moravia's characters, a sensitivity to the ways the husband may be at once silencing and reconstructing his wife according to his own ideals. However, the student's response does not attend to other consequences of the husband's ideals: Moravia's speaker sees not only his wife but also nonhuman nature as the prey of men. The character's conception of his wife curtails dialogue within his marriage and displays humankind's monologic approach to "other" life in general.

That the student forsook discussion of the environment in favor of a discussion of gender relations may have been because so few readings in our anthology had lent themselves to a discussion of environmental issues. Simply, the student was better prepared to discuss gender. In this light, her example suggests further the need to bring ecofeminist issues into the classroom: an ecofeminist reading can expand the perimeters of our discourse in ways that a focus on gender relations does not. Had I introduced the ecofeminist perspective earlier in our semester, many of the works we encountered in our anthology, whether they attended to images of nonhuman nature or not, may have provoked discussions of environmental concerns, which could have helped students to see the connections between human interrelationships and the fate of our planet. I felt it was important to ask class members who took stances such as this student's, "Is it important as well that he might think all things wild undeserving of dialogue?"

I also noticed that the responses of students who reacted favorably to ecofeminist theory often reflected assumptions complicitous with patriarchal domination. A male student, for instance, wrote, "Instead of trying to change nature as the family tried to change the girl [in "Peter and the Wolf"] we should let it take its course and live life like it was supposed to." He also asks, at the conclusion of his amended response: "Just because we don't understand, does that give us the right to change both women and nature to something we do understand?" This student's position reflects a critical awareness of human epistemology, particularly the degrees to which our values shape our reality. In place of our aggressive epistemology, he believes men "should always listen to what [women and nonhuman nature] are saying." Such a position lends itself to a productive dialogue, but I was concerned that the student had opened his amended response qualifyingly: "I believe the girl in 'Peter and the Wolf' would have had a much better life being human." Although he acknowledges the need for dialogue, the student nevertheless assumes a position of superiority: the wolf-woman in Carter's story should follow the (wolf) course in life she has been allotted, but this course bears the marks of inferiority; she "would have had a much better life being human." I felt compelled to ask this student: "What's wrong with the girl's life as it is?" and "What's so great about being human?" It is doubtful that humans can construct and maintain dialogic relations with nonhuman nature so long as they assume their superiority.

I worked especially hard at identifying such underlying assumptions, which ultimately might curtail students' appreciation of ecofeminism. One student, for instance, amended her position statement with the words: "Sometimes I feel ecofeminists tend to go overboard." She agreed that "fundamental changes must be made" in society if humans are to manage a healthy relationship with their planet; however, she believed that some of the comments her classmates made in the name of ecofeminism were "ridiculous." In particular, she saw little sense in comparing the smokestack of a nearby cogeneration plant to a penis, as had one speaker, and she belittled the attempts of some feminists to change the spelling of words, such as *women* to *womyn* All in all, the student dwelled on these aspects of what she termed "extremist" ecofeminism. In neither her initial nor her amended response did she devote analysis to those "fundamental" social structures she felt were in need of change, and she made no comment on the cultural transformations that ecofeminists propose.

In my written response to the student's paper, I commented on her criticisms of feminist and ecofeminist thought: indeed, this woman is not the only person ever to find letter changing and phallus hunting excessive, and I wrote to let her know that I agreed with her to a certain extent, that an overemphasis on these particular points may trivialize some of the more dire concerns of ecofeminists. But at the same time I told her that I thought dialogue about such apparently trivial things could produce, eventually, big changes in society. I wrote that I was also worried that her attention to these elements might have distracted her from some vital issues. Reading the student's response statement from an ecofeminist perspective, I began to question her initial assumption, feeling that it might exhibit a complicitous relation with elements in society that reinforce the oppression of women and nonhuman nature.

Particularly, I was concerned that the students' connection between ecofeminists and "overboard" replicated elements of Western hierarchical society that associate men with rationality and culture and women with irrationality and nonhuman nature. Over the last couple of millennia, such a social structure has subordinated women and the nonhuman nature with which women have been associated. Meanwhile, the notion that any position can be "overboard" assumes that the prevailing social structure must remain intact and suggests that it is the responsibility of individuals to remain "on board." Such an assumption characterizes alternatives to the status quo as crazy, dangerous, or, at least, inconsequential. Given the depletion of the rainforest in Brazil and recent attempts to overturn *Roe vs. Wade,* the student's willingness to go down with her ship portends consequences of which she might not have been aware.

I hoped to engage her in a dialogue that would direct her toward a more critical involvement with her own position: "What is 'overboard'?" "Can 'overboard' be something good?" "Whose interests do we serve by following rules of behavior that keep us on board?" "Where is this ship headed?" I also was sure to ask her why she found the attention to symbolism excessive, but not that we need to make "fundamental changes" in our society: "Isn't this a lot more 'excessive' than playing with language?" Again, the purpose of these questions was not to indoctrinate the student, but to initiate an internal dialogue on her part, to question her current position so that she might interrogate some of the underlying assumptions on which she had constructed her arguments.

In some instances, students' rereadings of their responses did indeed display interrogations of their assumptions. An initial response by one student, for example, evidenced an uncritical view of associations between women and nonhuman nature: "In 'The Chase' the woman was 'wild.' The girl in 'Peter and the Wolf' was also 'wild.' I believe this is the way these two authors perceive women, and the way many of us men perceive women. They are creatures that can't be trusted and just do things (most things) without any thought. This is where I tie in the nature aspect. It is the nature of all women no matter what environment they are in to act 'wild.'" Amongst this conundrum of patriarchal assumptions is the implicit valuation of masculinist reason over the supposed irrationality of women and nonhuman nature. The student assumes the "natural" superiority of men as the bestowers of meanings and values, as the rulers of creation on guard against all things female and nonhuman, "wild" things that cannot be trusted. Reading this response, I thought of Michael E. Zimmerman's claim that "so long as patriarchally raised men fear and hate women, and so long as men conceive of nature as female, men will continue in their attempts to deny what they consider to be the feminine/natural within themselves and to control what they regard as the feminine/natural outside themselves" (24).

Over two millenniums old, such assumptions do not often come undone in one ninety-minute literature class. However, the student's reply to his response suggests the relativization of his position: "I was pretty lost in my response to 'Peter and the Wolf.' After the discussion on ecofeminism I understand more of what you were looking for. I know I am a pig headed conservative type of guy but I just don't see it happening. I'm for equal rights but changing our way of life to cater to the environment is a little crazy. I feel we should recycle and be conscious of our resources but there has to be a point to stop. I really don't know what I mean, I think I'm just lost?" After the discussion on ecofeminism, the student's position no longer bears the marks of a universal. Aware of an alternative discourse, the student now identifies himself as "conservative," and he expresses an uncertainty about his opinions. The gratuitous question mark with which he concludes his response seems to highlight a sudden and somewhat inarticulate confusion. Despite the assertiveness of his previous remarks ("I just don't see it happening "; "changing our way of life . . . is a little crazy"; "there has to be a point to stop"), the student in the end appears indecisive, nagged by some unmentioned (or unmentionable) principle as he wanders "lost" ("overboard"?) amongst his own assumptions.

The student's indecisiveness could reflect the vacillation of his current position. But his revision also displays the entrenchment of oppressive Western values and the need for expanded discussion of ecofeminist principles in undergraduate classes. Although classroom dialogue destabilizes the student's assumptions, he nevertheless reaffirms some diehard tenets of patriarchal culture. For one thing, the similar ways that Western culture has oppressed both women *and* nonhuman nature receive little consideration in his amended response. The student advocates "equal rights," but refuses to compromise his privileged position as human to "cater to the environment." In other words, the student perceives humans as distinct from and superior to other life on the planet. As ecofeminists have argued, this perception reinforces not just the oppression of nonhuman nature but also that of women, who "are believed to be closer to nature in this culture against nature" (King 119). In my attempts to persuade him to "try on" ecofeminist principles, I pointed these things out to him and asked him, "Who decides at what point to stop?" and "Why is 'catering to the environment' crazy?"

The responses also helped me to understand the ways the classroom shaped students' responses. Sticking with the above example, I found disturbing the student's acknowledgment that he composed his response while conscious of "what [I was] looking for." Considering this statement, I was forced to read the student's vacillating position in an additional light. It was not so much, I figured, that his conservatism was under threat, but that he was struggling with ways to affirm his conservative beliefs without offending me. I had worked hard at dialogizing my classroom, but elements of my course still disrupted a free exchange of ideas.

~

Remarks such as this student's have convinced me just how necessary it is to talk to students about the class. It is a mistake to assume that students' examinations of ideas are entirely unmediated, that the classroom setting has no effect on their thinking. Talking with students about the class has helped me to remain critical about my courses, to become accountable to students, and to be open to change. One of the changes I have made as a result of my experiences in this class involves the use of the response statements.

At the time, I was grading one response statement from each student each week. I would pose questions on individual statements, rate the student's response on a scale from one to ten, return it to the writer, and then move on to the next reading and the next set of responses. Under such circumstances, it is understandable why the above student felt he needed to give me what I was looking for: his grade might have depended on it. Borrowing from composition theory, I now structure the use of responses so that they may reflect a continual dialogue: students keep journals that represent their initial responses to texts, the comments that I and other class members make on their responses, and any additional entries the writer considers pertinent. I grade these response journals only at the end of the term, after I read and comment on them throughout the semester, and what I "look for" is students' commitment to issues raised in class.

Also, I now read my students' responses from an ecofeminist standpoint throughout the semester, so that this dialogue has a chance to unfold. In the class I describe above, students did not have the time or space to stake out their claims as intellectuals, as I did not allow them the opportunity to examine more of the complexities of ecofeminism, such as questions over attempts to establish the relative values of the individual parts of nature (Kheel 139), the (dis)advantages of working within a dualistic paradigm (144–45; King 123), and the ecofeminist critiques of deep ecology (Salleh) and other versions of feminism (Warren 8–17). As a result, I found myself more in the role of the enlightened instructor bringing his news to the duped masses than an equal participant in a cultural dialogue.

A dialogic pedagogy should situate the teacher in the role of learner as well as instructor. I did learn a lot about my students and their beliefs; however, our week-long discussion had allowed us only to scratch the surface of ecofeminist issues. My students had not learned enough about ecofeminism to enter into a debate that could be considered democratic, and my authority as "teacher-as-acculturator," as Bizzell would call it, was never as "provisional, shifting, and changing" as it ought to have been (200). In the limited amount of space and time I had allotted students to consider ecofeminism, a negotiation over values never materialized, or at least not to any great extent.

Since I wanted my students to become ecofeminists, it was not enough to simply identify the assumptions they held that might disrupt their appreciation of ecofeminist ideas. We needed to explore the assumptions that would take the place of the anthropocentric, anthropomorphic ones I was asking them to discard, needed to make sure the values I wanted students to embrace could remain as heterarchical and dialogic as patriarchy has been hierarchical and monologic. We needed to read more, write more, and talk more about the social and ecological crises ecofeminists address, and we needed to read, write, and talk more about the alternatives they propose. In an ecofeminist, dialogical literature class such crises can be addressed, and deep changes in the social fabric can become the course's principle concern.

Notes

I would like to thank Robin Pennell and Margery Vagt, who helped me organize the class sessions described in this essay and who allowed me to use their notes, which were invaluable.

1. My conception of "democracy" considers nonhuman nature amongst the "people" the term denotes. Ecofeminism, and particularly ecofeminist dialogics, as described by Murphy, represents attempts to facilitate the "coming into verbal being of both sides of the [humanity/nature] dyad" ("Prolegomenon" 48). In this sense, ecofeminist dialogics reflects the democratic impulse described by Bizzell, although it represents a radically expanded view of the participants typically involved in democratic processes.

2. One thing that is difficult for me to describe, however, is the response that students might have to such challenges by different teachers. I have heard criticisms about dialogic, democratic pedagogies from women and minority instructors who sometimes feel that their attempts to share power with their students are viewed as marks of inferiority. (I have also heard the same criticisms from graduate teaching assistants who feel that their youth acts against them in negotiations of authority in the classroom.) And I have heard from minority and women teachers who have had their attempts to include multicultural and feminist readings in their curricula looked upon suspiciously as ways to impose their own interests on their students.

As a white man, I fit very well the image of the person many students expect to see in their college classroom, and I think my subject position helps students to read my dialogic, ecofeminist pedagogy as something other than a lack of knowledge about the material, an invitation to adopt an "anything goes" attitude toward the class, or an unwarranted use of my authority to advocate the causes of my own race and gender at the expense of white males. On the other hand, on occasion I have been challenged as a man attempting to speak for women and therefore discounted (although I think of my pedagogy as an attempt to create the conditions in which marginalized voices can come into dialogue—not as an attempt to speak for an "other").

Ideally, the dialogic method makes such challenges the object of discussion. In the same sense, an instructor's accountability for her practices can help to dispel notions that dialogic classes are devoid of purpose or design. With the dialogic method, students and teachers can reflect on the cultural and institutional implications of their attitudes and beliefs (the ways, for instance, interpretations of the woman teacher's self-interest might undermine feminist attempts to make life better for women *and* men or the ways such interpretations, as they come to be reflected on student evaluations of teachers, might make teachers hesitant to employ dialogic, democratic practices).

My point is that the gender, race, and age of the teacher (as well of those of the students) can determine the students' perceptions of ecofeminist principles and that while I continue to recommend the dialogic method as a way to address such determinants, I must also caution that the approaches and the responses to ecofeminism that I discuss throughout this essay may have entirely different impacts depending upon the subject position of the teacher.

Works Cited

Bakhtin, M. M. *Freudianism: A Marxist Critique.* Trans. I. R. Titunik. Ed. I. R. Titunik and Neal H. Bruss. New York: Academic Press, 1976.

Bauer, Dale M. *Feminist Dialogics: A Theory of Failed Community.* Albany: State University of New York Press, 1988.

Bizzell, Patricia. "The Teacher's Authority: Negotiating Difference in the Classroom." *Changing Classroom Practices: Resources for Literary and Cultural Studies.* Ed. David B. Downing. Urbana, Ill.: National Council of Teachers of English, 1994. 194–201.

Bowers, C. A. "A Batesonian Perspective on Education and the Bonds of Language: Cultural Literacy in the Technological Age." *Studies in the Humanities* 15.2 (1988): 108–29.

Cahalan, James M., and David B. Downing, eds. *Practicing Theory in Introductory Literature Courses.* Urbana, Ill.: National Council of Teachers of English, 1991.

Carter, Angela. *Saints and Strangers: Short Stories by Angela Carter.* New York: Penguin, 1987.

Freire, Paulo. *Pedagogy of the Oppressed.* Trans. Myra Bergman Ramos. New York: Continuum, 1970.

Giroux, Henry A. "Textual Authority and the Role of Teachers as Public Intellectuals."

Social Issues in the English Classroom. Ed. C. Mark Hurlbert and Samuel Totten. Urbana, Ill.: National Council of Teachers of English, 1992. 304–21.

Kheel, Marti. "The Liberation of Nature: A Circular Affair." *Environmental Ethics* 7.2 (1985): 135–49.

King, Ynestra. "Toward an Ecological Feminism and a Feminist Ecology." *Machina Ex Dea: Feminist Perspectives on Technology.* Ed. Joan Rothschild. New York: Pergamon Press, 1983. 118–29.

Love, Glen A. "Revaluing Nature: Toward an Ecological Criticism. *Western American Literature* 25.3 (1990): 201–15.

McAndrew, Donald A. "Ecofeminism and the Teaching of Writing." Conference on College Composition and Communication. Boston. Mar. 21, 1991.

Moravia, Antonio. "The Chase." *Literature: The Human Experience.* Ed. Richard Abcarian and Marvin Klotz. 5th ed. New York: St. Martin's Press, 1990. 746–49.

Murphy, Patrick D. "Coyote Midwife in the Classroom: Introducing Literature with Feminist Dialogics." *Practicing Theory in Introductory College Literature Courses.* Ed. James M. Cahalan and David B. Downing. Urbana, Ill.: National Council of Teachers of English, 1991. 161–76.

———. "Prolegomenon for an Ecofeminist Dialogics." *Feminism, Bakhtin, and the Dialogic.* Ed. Dale M. Bauer and Susan Jaret McKinstry. Albany: State University of New York Press, 1991. 39 56.

Salleh, Ariel. "Deeper than Deep Ecology: The Eco-Feminist Connection." *Environmental Ethics* 6.4 (1984): 339–45.

Schilb, John. "Pedagogy of the Oppressors?" *Gendered Subjects: The Dynamics of Feminist Teaching.* Ed. Margo Culley and Catherine Portuges. Boston: Routledge, 1985. 253 64.

Shor, Ira, and Paulo Freire. *A Pedagogy for Liberation: Dialogues on Transforming Education.* South Hadley, Mass.: Bergin and Garvey, 1987.

Ward, Irene. *Literacy, Ideology, and Dialogue: Towards a Dialogic Pedagogy.* Teacher Empowerment and School Reform Series. Albany: State University of New York Press, 1994.

Warren, Karen. "Feminism and Ecology: Making Connections." *Environmental Ethics* 9.1 (1987): 3–20.

Zimmerman, Michael E. "Feminism, Deep Ecology, and Environmental Ethics." *Environmental Ethics* 9.1 (Spring 1987): 21–44.

12

Hiking without a Map:
Reflections on Teaching Ecofeminist Literary Criticism

Greta Gaard

OVER THE LAST DECADE, ecofeminist theory has been developed by philosophers, scientists, activists, and academics around the world. Based on our activism and research, many ecofeminists believe the urgency of modern social and ecological conditions offers sufficient motivation for academics to become activists and to bring an awareness of the need for social and ecological justice to every class we teach. In designing my first course on ecofeminist literary criticism, however, I felt less like an ecofeminist theorist and more like a backpacker without a topo map. I knew the theory of ecofeminism, but had never applied it—nor seen it applied—to the terrain of literary criticism.[1] What kinds of students would such a course attract, and how would grading and evaluation be structured? What texts could be used to bring into dialogue the diversity of ecofeminist perspectives? What might be the central questions generated through such an approach? And finally, what would be gained from taking an ecofeminist approach to literary criticism?

Walking the Talk: Audience, Syllabus Design, and Evaluation

I decided to start my planning with the students. Since an upper-division course titled Ecofeminist Literary Criticism was likely to attract students with backgrounds in literary criticism, women's studies, environmental philosophy, or even outdoor education, I could not assume students would have a familiarity with ecofeminist theory; moreover, I could not assume students would have a familiarity with any more than one of the aforementioned disciplines. Clearly, the course needed to be structured in such a way that students could benefit from the interdisciplinarity of their colleagues and used a method of teaching that encouraged students to teach and to learn from each other. No doubt we would have to begin with presentations on feminism, ecofeminism, and strategies for reading literature, but after a few weeks we should be able to proceed with the practice itself; since I had no desire to define the path of ecofeminist literary criticism before we began, I decided we would build the road as we traveled.

To walk the talk, I would have to create a method of grading and evaluation that embodied feminist ideas about student-centered learning, Green values that indicated that the means embody the ends, and ecofeminist ideas about the importance of community and relationships. Fortunately, in this area there was some precedent, and I followed guidelines from feminist pedagogy, liberation pedagogy, and individual ecofeminist teachers as well.[2] Since this would be a small class (under twenty students), I invited students to select graded events from several clusters of possibilities involving class participation, journal writing, short responsive essays, longer academic essays, and group projects, and to assign percentages to each of their selections. To enhance the interdisciplinary learning potential for the students, I built into the required assignments two cycles of writing and responsive writing. In these cycles, students would bring to class five copies of a one- or two-page essay responding to some aspect of the reading; the papers would be distributed in groups and discussed and the students would then write a responsive piece of one or two pages addressing the ideas presented by their peers.

Selecting the Texts, Setting the Route

Once I had considered who might enroll and how to proceed with the course instruction, I had to complete the book orders. To fulfill the goals of literary criticism, I wanted the texts throughout the course to cover a variety of genres—expository "nature" essays, postmodern experimental narratives, novels, short stories, poetry, academic criticism. To begin the course, however, I wanted texts that would quickly introduce students to the central ideas and debates within ecofeminism or invite students to raise questions that would elicit from me whatever perspectives were absent from those texts. For a foundation in ecofeminism, I wanted to cover such topics as the much-debated "woman-nature connection," the several branches of ecofeminist theory, a brief history of feminist theories and environmentalism in the United States, the ecofeminism–deep ecology debates, the question of the self/other relationship, the importance of locating theory in terms of cultural contexts, and the various analyses of the root causes of social and environmental injustices—and I wanted to cover all this in the first two weeks, since we had to confine our explorations to the limits of a ten-week term. Finally, I wanted to create clusters of texts throughout the course so that students would be able to recognize and to enter into dialogue with the various perspectives on each of these issues. For these purposes, I decided Susan Griffin's *Woman and Nature,* Edward Abbey's *Desert Solitaire,* and Leslie Marmon Silko's *Ceremony* would provide a sufficient contrast in perspectives to introduce the course.

With Griffin, Abbey, and Silko, I would be able to initiate a discussion of ecofeminist literary criticism in regard to prose—postmodern narrative, "nature writing," novel—while simultaneously locating that discussion in terms of gender and culture. To continue that discussion in terms of poetry, I decided to choose two Pulitzer prize–winning collections—Mary Oliver's *American Primitive* and Gary Snyder's *Turtle Island*—and to draw selected poems from Rayna Green's collection, *That's What She Said: Contemporary Poetry and Fiction by Native American Women.* I expected this configuration would allow us to address the culture/nature and human/nature relationships specifically in terms of gender and culture and to explore from a variety of perspectives what it would mean to be an inhabitant of the land. These readings would take the class through week five.

For the second half of the term, I wanted to complicate the gender/nature/ culture relationship with other variables, to interrogate various constructions and uses of the term *nature,* and to explore literary constructions of identity and the uses of language from an ecofeminist perspective. For these purposes, I paired Toni Morrison's *The Bluest Eye* with Leslie Feinberg's *Stone Butch Blues,* expecting that Morrison's novel would foreground the influence of race in exploring these questions and Feinberg's novel would emphasize sexuality. To bring in ecofeminist critiques of science, biotechnology, and animal experimentation, I chose Mary Shelley's *Frankenstein* and Ursula Le Guin's *Buffalo Gals and Other Animal Presences.* In all these books, but particularly with Le Guin, I hoped that students would be drawn to investigate the various ways that language has shaped human/nature relationships. As soon as the term began, of course, my careful plans were quickly taken up and modified through actual classroom practice—so much the better, for as any hiker knows, the map is not the territory.

The Expedition

Ecofeminist Literary Criticism was offered during the winter 1995 term as a once-only special topics course through women's studies and positioned to draw both advanced undergraduates and M.A. students; hence, the enrollment of only six students was typical for a course of this type on our campus. Of the six, one (the only man) dropped the course after the first week due to time constraints, leaving us with five women: two graduate students and two seniors, majoring in art history, English, social work, and women's studies; the fifth woman directed the rock climbing program on our campus. Three of the students had taken my ecofeminist theories course in the past, and two of these had crossed over from a private college to do so. Yet with all this background, students had a hard time knowing how to approach the texts, and at their request I created one- or two-page questionnaires on each of the texts, as a means of encouraging discussion (and keeping myself from lecturing). Because these sheets were created each week of the class, I was able to devise questions that would both respond to and advance the current debates taking place in the classroom. I also supplied a few selections of related criticism or commentary after students had written position papers for each text. As the class progressed, then, the questionnaires offered less guidance, and the students took over by creating their own lists of questions for shaping an ecofeminist literary critique.

As the first text of the course, Susan Griffin's *Woman and Nature* helped students articulate some basic questions that set the groundwork for what lay ahead:

—What is the root cause of the problem described by this writer?

—In solving or responding to this problem, what is the role of language? Of vision, seeing, or perspective? What is the role of emotion? Of anger?

—Where is the erotic in the text? How is it portrayed?

—How does the text redefine key terms, terms you think would be central to ecofeminist literary criticism?

—What's missing?

Students agreed[3] that, from Griffin's perspective, the root cause of the problem was two-fold, as described in "Book One: Matter" and "Book Two: Separation": first, a devaluation of nature and of all those things seen as part of nature (women, the body, animals, emotions, sexuality, procreation) and a simultaneous elevation of an otherworldly patriarchal God, science, reason, and all things associated with these; second, a radical separation of the valued from the devalued, manifested as the separation of self from other, humans from nature, intellect from emotion. *Woman and Nature* is the story of naming and responding to this problem through language: whereas the voice of patriarchal authority (masquerading as emotionless objectivity through the use of the passive voice) dominates the first two books of the text, the subordinated voices of women and nature (presented in italic), speaking first of self-doubt and the experiences of subordination, are transformed in "Book Three: Passage" and, asserting "we name ourselves" (226), fill the pages by the end of "Book Four: Her Vision."

In this transformation from subordination to liberation, we found, the free expression of emotion and particularly anger was crucial. For example, from studies of emotionology we found that although normative gender dualisms assign emotion to women and reason to men, significantly, one emotion is allowed to men and denied to women: anger (Stearns and Stearns). To experience anger, and focus it at its source, one must be able to name directly the source of one's anger, but the language for anger is denied to women and to other oppressed groups (Scheman). Through "His Cataclysm: The Universe Shudders," Griffin describes the destructive force of the patriarchal God, a force wielded by patriarchal medicine, science, and technology as well. In this section, the italicized voice "rage[s] for no visible reason" at the pervasiveness of patriarchal destruction, with a "fury . . . that will not die" (135). The anger of the subordinate voices is unfocused and rages without end because expressing anger directly requires naming the object of that anger—and this naming, this kind of language, is not yet available to these voices. Once the subordinated "Sees through Her Own Eyes" in "Book Four: Her Vision," the anger of the subordinate voices is described soon thereafter, in the three sections of "Our Ancient Rages"—"Turbulence," "Cataclysm," "Consequences." In "Turbulence," women's fury is described as a way of responding to injustice, a form of self-defense, or a means of protecting loved ones. "Cataclysm" and "Consequences" develop that definition, describing the fury of both women and nature not as a form of vengeance but simply as a refusal to accept the destructive force of tyranny and a means of returning that energy back to its source: "We say everything comes back" and "There are consequences. You cannot cut the trees from the mountainside without a flood" (186). Instead of fearing her own anger, the woman/mountain in "Cataclysm" comes "to see this anger-that-was-so-long-denied as a blessing" (185). Naming this anger is a result of refusing to see through the eyes of the dominator and reclaiming "Her Vision."

Using Audre Lorde's definition of the erotic as "an assertion of the lifeforce of women" (55), students found that the erotic in *Woman and Nature* increased as the italicized voices gained prominence. The book's utopian ending gives full expression to those voices and to the erotic in the text, naming the interconnections of woman and earth, woman and animal, woman and woman. The erotic communion of light that metaphorically joins the lovers and connects them with the earth is an ecstatic affirmation and celebration of life. But students argued that Griffin's solution offered healing only for the dominated voices of women and nature; without a strategy for healing the oppressor, students believed, Griffin's book could offer only partial solutions to the problem of alienation. We read Carol Cantrell's argument that the "central movement" of *Women and Nature* is "the gradual inhabiting of language by women" (230) and Patrick D. Murphy's examination of the ways that Griffin uses a "dialogical structure of narration" (43), but students maintained that Griffin's narrator, while continuing the dialogue with more receptive others, has nonetheless cut the dominant voice out of the dialogue by the book's conclusion, thereby not solving the source of the problem but rather implying a separatist solution. Hence, students proposed, a final question for our list should be, "What—or who—is missing?"

We found some of what was missing from Griffin by reading Abbey, and there were many reasons for doing so. First, confining the scope of ecofeminist literary criticism to only those texts perceived as "ecofeminist" or even "feminist" artificially limits the potential of such a perspective. Second, such a paired reading illuminated Abbey's patriarchal biases for everyone, even those students who thought they were quite familiar with his writing, and dispelled the last vestiges of disbelief other students might have felt in reading Griffin. I listened as students catalogued the inconsistencies between Abbey's stated goals and actual practices, along with various examples of his blatant racism, sexism, and persistent feminizing of nature. But a ten-week course in feminist criticism hardly affords the time to read texts only to denounce them for their oppressive assumptions or descriptions—the list of texts that could or should be so examined might comprise an entire baccalaureate program—and after a sufficient time devoted to such discussion, students began asking the questions I had hoped for: "How can *Desert Solitaire* assist us in shaping an ecofeminist literary critique?" "What new questions does this book prompt us to consider?" "What terms does it invite us to redefine?" "And how does the vision of this book—the description of the problem and the proposed solution—compare with Griffin's book?"

Abbey's emphasis on the threat of population and the need to preserve wilderness characterizes much of deep ecology and inspired a conversation about the comparative positions of ecofeminism and deep ecology; while Abbey's positions on population and the status of Native Americans were easily dismissed, students agreed that ecofeminism has yet to develop a critique of wilderness and that reading Abbey's book from an ecofeminist perspective could be useful in beginning a conversation about what that critique might entail. Moreover, by describing at least part of the problem as capitalism—"an economic system which can only expand or expire" (145)—Abbey emphasizes an aspect of the dominant culture we had not explicitly noticed being described in Griffin's work. And after noting his racist and sexist remarks, students acknowledged that Abbey's descriptions of nature, anecdotes, and theorizing nonetheless characterized what we have been taught to call "nature writing." In fact, the form itself—the autobiographical narrative essay—was familiar to us from Thoreau, Muir, Leopold, even Dillard. But was not Griffin's book also "nature writing"? The entire category was called into question by this comparison, and remained so for the rest of the term.

As in *Woman and Nature*, Abbey's solution to the problem involves a reconnection with nature, but it is a reconnection quite different from Griffin's: whereas Griffin locates the problem as originating in culture itself, and thus requiring a transformation of social relationships as well as culture/nature relations, Abbey locates the problem primarily in the relationship between wilderness and civilization, and hence his solution addresses various ways to correct that relationship. In "Down the River," Abbey reports "enjoying a very intimate relation with the river: only a layer of fabric between [his body] and the water," and describes his return to wilderness as "a rebirth backward in time and into primeval liberty," a return to the womb (176–77). But while Abbey continues to feminize the earth, he is not particularly interested in reconnecting with or liberating individual women, who embody the womb. In fact, wilderness seems like an all-male bastion—and here students referred to the "All-Man He-Male" magazines Abbey finds, "with the best pictures torn out by some scoundrel" (194)—which is one reason Abbey professes to prefer wilderness to human society (177, 183). From an ecofeminist perspective, students argued that a writer who detests women and yet feminizes nature cannot be said either to love the earth or to offer a liberatory vision. In one respect, Abbey's male separatist utopia parallels Griffin's, in that both writers provide solutions only for their respective constituencies. Again we asked the question, "Who—or what—was missing?" We were ready to examine the role of culture in shaping the relationship between humans and nature.

In reading Leslie Marmon Silko's *Ceremony*, students considered the ways that an addictive culture affects its members differently, based on such variables as race, class, and gender. The series of separations or dualisms of Western culture we explored in this novel were ones central to an ecofeminist critique: self/other, culture/nature, human/animal, white/nonwhite. As in Griffin's work, we also looked for descriptions of the erotic and the body, the recognition and expression of anger, and the relationship of identity and place. Finally, we looked at the narrative structure itself, which in its very form—interweaving of story and myth, along with disparate times and places—conveyed the message of fundamental interconnectedness. To complement the novel, we also read criticism from Paula Gunn Allen, Andrea Smith, and Leslie Marmon Silko that helped students understand the worldview of certain Native American cultures.

An ecofeminist reading of *Ceremony* clearly shows the problem statement of the novel—and the problem here, as in Griffin's work, is separation. Tayo, the protagonist, has been separated from his cultural heritage as a Laguna Pueblo Indian. After enlisting in the white man's war in Vietnam, Tayo is disconnected from his homeland. He is cut off from the most precious members of his family—his uncle Josiah, his brother Rocky, and his mother. Moreover, he feels separated from the earth. Students observed that, in the context of this novel, but possibly true for other contexts as well, identity is shaped through relationships—to place, to people, to animals, to the earth—and that Tayo's loss of identity is a product of the separations he experiences. It is also tied to his loss of language. In the white people's hospital, Tayo tells the white doctor about himself: "He can't talk to you. He is invisible. His words are formed with an invisible tongue, they have no sound" (15). The story itself, a healing ceremony, narrates his return to identity and to language, a movement from silence to speech comparable to the movement described in *Woman and Nature*. As in Griffin's book, Tayo's journey involves reclaiming and naming the real objects of his anger, rejecting separation and dualisms by recognizing the fundamental interconnectedness of all life on earth. Once Tayo begins reconnecting the severed pieces, he is able to regain the authority of his own experiences and feelings and to name the appropriate source and objects of his anger. Hence, in both *Woman and Nature* and *Ceremony*, students found that coming into language is seen as a reclaiming of power for those subordinated by race or gender. We also noticed that *Ceremony* brings into perspective something that was missing from the works by both Griffin and Abbey—that indigenous cultures have been colonized along with women and the land.

Here in Minnesota, a state variously famous for either our ten thousand lakes or our ten thousand treatment centers, students are particularly aware of topics involving addiction and recovery; many have read Earnie Larson, Stanton Peele, or Charlotte Kasl by the time they reach graduate school. Hence, students were quick to notice how Tayo's problem of separation is the problem of an addict functioning in an addictive culture. Using the feminist insight that "the personal is political," students commented on the way that both alcohol and the model of addiction function to privatize what they saw as a political problem. By repressing feelings and separating people from the erotic, from each other, and from the earth, addiction serves the dominant culture by keeping people powerless and oppressed. In *Ceremony*, Tayo connects the personal with the political through the help of the medicine man's story and ceremony; Tayo is then able to name the source of his pain and his anger and to begin the journey of healing. The process is completed when Tayo realizes "the way all the stories fit together—the old stories, the war stories, their stories— to become the story that was still being told" (246). Through narrative, we found, the connection between self and other was restored.

Students discussed the different audiences for the works by Griffin, Abbey, and Silko in terms of genre, style, and content. We considered which text would be most rhetorically effective in awakening an ecological or ecofeminist awareness in specific groups of people. As with the other books, we noticed how *Ceremony* redefines certain key terms such as *nature* and *self,* since many of the characters' quest for an acceptable identity (according to white culture) involved a colonization of their inner natures and a rejection of their self-identity for a socially prescribed identity. Compared with both Griffin's and Abbey's books, students decided, Silko's *Ceremony* offers a more comprehensive solution to the problem, one that is both personal and political. Recognizing the importance of cultural context (Allen; Silko "Landscape"; Smith), students discussed the likelihood and the means of translating Silko's solution into a nonnative cultural context. With this foundation in comparative prose readings, we turned to poetry.

We read Mary Oliver's *American Primitive,* Gary Snyder's *Turtle Island,* and poems by Paula Gunn Allen, Joy Harjo, and Wendy Rose (Green). Many of these poets suggested that the problem of reconnecting with nature could be approached by listening to nature, asserting that nature has a voice and a language that humans now ignore. We found eating to be a central metaphor in the poetry of Snyder and Oliver and explored the ways that eating was variously described as communion, connection, domination, and annihilation; these descriptions we then compared with ecofeminist writings about vegetarianism and the woman/animal connection in Western cultures (Adams "Feminist"). Through Oliver's poetry, we looked at the way that the self/other connection with nature became erotic, full of life and celebration. We compared that connection with Snyder's poetry to discover various ways that gender seemed to alter the relationships of self/other and human/nature and with the poetry by indigenous women to discover that culture was another shaping variable. With this group of poets, students added several new topics to their growing list of questions that ecofeminist literary critics might ask.

Listening to the voice of nature has been widely suggested as one means of reconnecting humans with nature, and this theme runs throughout the poems of the Native American women we read; from their perspective, it seems, nature has a language and a voice of its own. For example, in "Remember," Joy Harjo writes of listening to nature and to the voice of nature, and in "For Alva Benson, and for All Those Who Have Learned to Speak," the earth speaks, the human body speaks, and people speak; each has a language and the potential to understand one another's speech. But this poem's protagonist notices that "the people in the towns and in the cities" have been "learning not to hear the ground" and hence, "She learned to speak for the ground" (Green

153). In "Naming Power," Wendy Rose seems to say that the loss of language is a consequence of colonization and perhaps the reclaiming of language will be a path to reclaiming identity, authority, and power. Finally, the loss of communication between the earth and the people is also observed in Paula Gunn Allen's poem "Kopis'taya." Allen says because of their colonization and the alienation required for their membership and survival in Western culture, the people have ceased to trust the reality and the validity of "the voices / that come shadowed on the air" (Green 32). Urging the people to listen, Allen concludes, "the spirit voices are singing."

Listening to nature or speaking for nature is a theme not confined to these Native American women poets but is also articulated by both Snyder and Oliver. For example, Snyder explores "The Uses of Light" from the various speaking perspectives of stones, trees, a moth, and a deer. The poem's concluding stanza suggests that shifting perspectives affords vast new vistas. Similarly, in one of the "Plain Talk" essays appended at the end of *Turtle Island*, Snyder suggests not only that nature speaks and has language but also that we must listen because we may already be receiving "non-negotiable demands about our stay on earth" (108). For Oliver, the language of nature is found through the experience of it. In "First Snow," for example, Oliver reports that the snow articulates a "white rhetoric" and "oracular fever" that "call[s] us back to *why, how, / whence* such beauty and *what* the meaning" (26), but the only way to answer such questions is to experience the snow directly. Perhaps not unlike many other writers, Oliver is certain her dog has language, and in "Spring" her dog not just reports the smells of nature and the activity of animals but counsels her to experience these for herself: "he says / each secret body is the richest advisor" (45). While students agreed the dog's advice seemed ideal if not romantic, we remained divided over these poems: one group of students was not convinced that nature had a language; another group, convinced of nature's language, remained doubtful that humans were capable of listening or of verifying the accuracy of what they had heard. One skeptic maintained that nature has language and that humans have heard it: the problem is that humans do not care. On this topic, and throughout the course, we continued a consideration of the possibilities and the limitations of dialogue as a means of reconnecting humans with nature.

Another contested method of reconnecting with nature we found was eating, a theme articulated primarily in the poems of Oliver and Snyder. Oliver seems at peace with the "mournful, unalterable fact" of predation in "In the Pinewoods, Crows and Owl," and even celebrates "those powerfully leaping / immaculate / meat-eaters" in "Bluefish." In poems describing her consumption of other animals, Oliver emphasizes the scarcity of food in winter as be-

ing a justification for her behavior ("Cold Poem" stanza 5) and seems to advocate vegetarianism in the summer (stanza 2). In the only poem that could be
called a hunting poem ("The Fish"), Oliver uses eating as a metaphor of communion and transubstantiation, wherein her act of consuming the "other"
offers a form of resurrection for both eater and eaten. Students questioned
Oliver's stance here, arguing that eating the "other" effectively annihilates the
separate identity of the "other" and that Oliver uses metaphor as a way of avoiding that realization. If so, the same technique is also at work in Snyder's poems.

In "The Hudsonian Curlew," Snyder begins discussing camping on the beach
in section one, describes vultures in section two, and reports humans shoot-
ing the same birds they have just admired in section three. To the students, this
succession of topics seemed like an attempt to naturalize the hunters' behavior through a metaphor comparing humans to animal predators; compared
to Oliver's "Cold Poem," we found Snyder does not offer any urgent reasons
for killing as necessary to the humans' survival. In sections four and five Snyder describes in detail the defeathering, skinning, gutting, and other activities
in preparation for consumption of the birds in section six. In section seven,
however, the poet awakens at dawn to see three other curlew calling and walking on the beach. Here, students used Carol Adams's concept of the mass term
("Feminist") to describe the way that this poem denies the death of the two
individual birds by ending with the image that shows "there's always more,"
as if the same birds are still alive. In a poem ostensibly describing a means of
reconnecting with nature, students argued, Snyder achieves quite the opposite effect. Through these poems and others, students found that species can
be a particularly good indicator of a writer's understanding of the relationships between self and other, culture and nature, and the writer's overall environmental ethic; hence, examining the relationships among human and
nonhuman animals was added to their list of focus questions for ecofeminist
literary criticism.

Finally we looked at the contexts in which these writers gendered the hu-
man/nature relationship and the ways that gender shapes humans' relationships with the natural world. In "The Honey Tree," for example, Oliver's use
of language confuses the identity of the tree with that of a beloved and the act
of eating honey becomes an act of lovemaking, a celebration of desire and
appetite for external nature and erotic nature alike. In her description of the
honey tree Oliver feminizes nature and, if the narrator of the poem is indeed
a woman, seems to celebrate lesbian lovemaking through the metaphor of
eating honey from the "secret rip" (81). The erotic relationship of woman-as-
human with woman-as-nature is reinscribed in the volume's concluding

poem, "The Gardens." There, as in "The Honey Tree," the beloved seems to be both woman and nature simultaneously—sea creature, animal, tree, woman. The poem's conclusion—and the conclusion of the volume—seems to echo "the roaring inside her" first described by Griffin:

> the boughs of your body
> leading deeper into the trees,
> over the white fields,
> the rivers of bone,
> the shouting,
> the answering, the rousing
> great run toward the interior,
> the unseen, the unknowable
> center.
>   (87)

Instead of dissecting or dismembering woman/nature like a scientist or a predator, students decided that Oliver approaches as a lover whose "nature" is like *nature*.

What does it mean for a woman to depict nature as female? Is the meaning different if a man uses the same metaphor? To explore these questions, we looked at poems by Harjo and by Snyder in which earth is female. In "The Blanket around Her," Harjo exhorts, "remember who you are / woman / it is the whole earth" (127). Harjo's poem "Remember" urges the reader to remember all the relationships that shape her life: relationships to parents, the earth, plants, animals, the elements. As in Silko's *Ceremony*, in Harjo's poetry feminizing nature reminds her of her connections to the whole of life, connections that shape her identity and on which her survival depends. In contrast, the separation of seer and seen, along with the supine and thus apparently passive posture of the women in Snyder's "Charms," led students to argue that the narrator is a speaker whose language objectifies women and for whom the essentialized quality of gender transcends culture and species. Moreover, the relation of "charm" or "enchantment" between active and articulate seer and passive, silent, and recumbent female "seen" has not proven to be liberatory for women. Just like Abbey, who goes to the desert to see but not necessarily to save nature, students criticized "Charms" for its description of a romantic relationship that requires no action on the part of the speaking seer and offers no empowerment or active agency for the silent seen.

The students' reading was further articulated through an analysis of "The Bath." In this poem, Snyder uses variants of the italicized refrain "is this our body?" and "this is our body" to convey the sacred and joyful bonds of family relations. Through repeated readings of the poem, students argued that the referent of "this" in the refrain indicated either the son or the mother and that "our" named a possession that began with the narrator and emanated outwards. In short, the students argued, the relationship of interconnection was not one in which independence became interdependence; rather, the unique identities of the son and the mother were subsumed in the identity of the father. As ecofeminists have explained, there are a number of ways the self/other relationship can be bridged, but many of these destroy the unique identity of the other (Plumwood). If the poet describes the interconnectedness of his relationships with his family members in a way that subsumes their unique identities, what implications does this have for the poet's environmental ethic? Students looked at "Prayer for the Great Family" and speculated that it would be possible for the poet to transfer this colonizing attitude to nature, since the poet perceives the rest of nature as a kind of extended family.

We concluded that the way Oliver feminizes and eroticizes the human/nature relationship nonetheless allows for an interpenetration of identities in which the unique positions of both nature and woman are maintained. In effect, Oliver's description of woman/nature differs from Snyder's in several ways: Oliver's woman/nature is an active agent; she is singular, rather than generic or universal; and Oliver's final position is not to admire or to absorb her but to join with her in a way that Oliver's own identity is momentarily subsumed. To the students, the relationship described in Oliver's poems seemed to involve a reciprocal dialogue between two different subjects, a relation of interconnection described by ecofeminists. In contrast, the relation of human to woman/nature as described in Snyder's poems involved subsuming the identities of woman/nature, a problem ecofeminists have found characterizes and hampers the perspective of deep ecologists. For an example of human/nature interconnection that involves both a man and a female gendered nature, students returned to Silko's *Ceremony* and concluded that the contexts of both culture and gender influence whether the female gendering of nature will be oppressive or liberatory. The importance of other contextual variables in shaping human/nature relationships was an insight we found reinforced in the novels that followed.

The questions surrounding the relationship of cultures and natures, though addressed throughout the course, gained special significance in the two novels we read next: Toni Morrison's *The Bluest Eye* and Leslie Feinberg's *Stone Butch Blues*. Both novels show how the prejudices of the dominant culture are internalized in the psychology of the oppressed. Through the repeated association of women and nature, animals and nature, nonwhite people and nature, and sexuality and nature, both novels redefine what it means for dominant Western culture to colonize nature. And in these novels, as in the poetry, the relationship between nature and the erotic takes on new significance.

Set in Lorain, Ohio, *The Bluest Eye* tells the story of Pecola Breedlove, a black girl whose desire for blue eyes symbolizes her desire for acceptance and self-worth in a racist culture, where whiteness is the standard of beauty. On a metaphoric level, the blue eyes signify not merely feminine beauty but the white perspective, which blacks and whites alike in the novel seem to agree is superior. Pecola's wish for blue eyes thus functions as a form of internalized oppression, an artificially induced desire to subordinate her own nature—her physical self and her unique perspective—to the authority of dominant culture. As Toni Morrison comments in the novel's afterword, the book can be seen as "a speculation on the disruption of 'nature' as being a social disruption with tragic individual consequences in which the reader, as part of the population of the text, is implicated" (214).

Following Morrison's lead, students read the novel as culture's assault on nature, manifested through the dominant white culture's assault on the "nature" of black women; hence, the novel challenged us to rethink our definitions of "nature" and the "natural." For if the nature of feminine beauty is defined only in terms of whiteness, then there will always be something "wrong" with black women, something less than womanly (Christian). The closer that women are to the white feminine ideal of beauty, the more they gain in social status and approval. That there is nothing inherently "natural" about the distinctions or values between races can be seen by how much effort has to be expended in policing the various boundaries of difference: for example, Geraldine is careful to explain to her son Junior the "difference between colored people and niggers," although the "line . . . was not always clear . . . and the watch had to be constant" (87). Like Tayo's mother, Geraldine strives to conform to white ideals of beauty, using the right beauty products and the right manners but learning most of all "how to get rid of the funkiness. The dreadful funkiness of passion, the funkiness of nature, the funkiness of the wide range of human emotions" (83). Just as the dominant culture decrees the proper nature of women and the definitions of women's beauty, it also destroys the erotic in nature.

For Morrison, nature's erotic potential is diminished into banal sexual encounters when the power dynamic between humans or between humans and nature is unbalanced. Of the three sexual encounters in the novel—Cholly and Darlene as adolescents, Cholly and Pauline in the early years of their marriage, and Cholly and Pecola—students argued that only equality is repeatedly eroti-cized. For example, Pauline describes both her initial meeting with Cholly and their early lovemaking as a rainbow of color that is pure sensuality, but once the fighting and the drinking take over their relationship, the erotic diminishes. Similarly, Cholly and Darlene's newfound sexuality occurs one evening after a spring rain, on a walk to "a wild vineyard where the muscadine grew" (145). For these two teenagers, the newness of spring accents the newness of their bodies and their sexuality, which is interrupted by the presence of two white male hunters. What began as an erotic and mutual encounter between equals ends as a rape, with the white hunters using their guns to force Cholly to con-tinue intercourse with Darlene. When Cholly's rape of Pecola is finally de-scribed, it is through a drunkenness in which he confuses memories of his early relationship with Pauline and his present acts with his daughter. In these in-stances and others, we traced the ways that anger is directed downward along the lines of social hierarchies and oppressions, rather than upward, at the real objects of anger.

Students found that comparing the causes of anger with the actual recipi-ents of anger in the novel is a means of unraveling social hierarchies of race, age, gender, and species. As we had already learned, emotion and particularly anger is an aspect of nature and the natural and as such is repeatedly distort-ed, repressed, and controlled. After Cholly and Darlene's sexual encounter, for example, Cholly ends up hating Darlene. Like Tayo's friends in the bar, Chol-ly is unable to focus his anger at the appropriate source and instead both in-ternalizes it and misdirects it onto a subordinate member of his own race. Junior's anger at his mother's lack of affection for him is misdirected instead toward her favored pet, the cat. Junior later generalizes his anger into bully-ing girls and picks out Pecola because she is ugly and alone. The episode in which Junior kills the cat and blames its death on Pecola shows the way that anger in a hierarchical society is directed downward, onto those with less and less power and privilege. Pecola is the recipient of Junior's anger because of her less powerful status in terms of both her gender and her color (she is blacker than he is); thus, anger passed down along the social hierarchies of race, gen-der, and age accumulates a force with the potential to kill the least powerful—who are, in this novel, the members of nonhuman species.

Morrison's repeated association of women and animals in their simulta-neous degradation is best illuminated by an ecofeminist reading, for the gen-der/species dualism is another manifestation of the culture/nature dualism. Unlike the Dick and Jane fable that introduces the novel, the real cat and dog in the novel are killed as a result of their association with Pecola. One vege-tarian feminist student compiled a number of references associating race and species as a means of subordinating both: in the delivery room, for example, the doctors come to Pauline Breedlove and tell each other, "now these here women you don't have any trouble with. They deliver right away and with no pain. Just like horses" (125). Or, when Cholly loses the house he has rented for his family, the community decides "he had joined the animals; was, indeed, an old dog, a snake, a ratty nigger" (18). And Cholly and Darlene's sexual encounter is interrupted by not just any white men, but white hunters—ostensibly out with their guns to hunt animals, they end up hunting blacks instead. This student's examples succeeded in persuading the class that, in a culture that subordinates nature and animals, being seen as "closer to nature" or to animals is detrimental to blacks, just as it has been detrimental to women.

Through discussions of this novel and the poetry preceding it, students found that the human body they had previously regarded as "natural" could be seen as a site of cultural construction and potential colonization. Human relations with "outer" nature—plants, mountains, animals, lakes—were further complicated by and reflected in human relations with "inner" nature. Based on this understanding, students rejected the binary pairs human/nature and culture/nature that had previously guided their analyses, choosing instead the metaphor of Rubik's Cube as a better way of describing the shifting relations of human/nature based on the intersections of gender/race/class. What we found was that like gender, race has been "naturalized," or made to seem a natural characteristic, when in fact it may be a social construct, a part of the nature of a human self that has been variously constructed and even colonized. Another piece of their analytical puzzle was soon to be discovered through our next novel.

Stone Butch Blues brought in a new factor for consideration: the place of sexuality, and of transgendered identities, in ecofeminist literary criticism. The question first articulated in regard to *The Bluest Eye*—"What could be considered natural if one's own body or one's own race is regarded as a cultural construct?"—took on additional significance here. In this portion of the class, students drew on queer theories and ecofeminist theories to explore the boundaries of a queer ecofeminism. Using Feinberg's critique of the relationship between oppressions of class and sexuality, students compared the ways that multiple identities of race, class, gender, and sexuality shaped their own relationships with nature and their concepts of nature and of self (Feinberg "Transgender").

Winner of both the 1994 Lambda Literary Award for best small press book and the 1994 American Library Association Lesbian/Gay Book Award for fiction, *Stone Butch Blues* interrogates the naturalness of the relationship between gender and sexuality through the life of narrator Jess Goldberg. From her childhood to her coming out as a butch lesbian in Buffalo and her later explorations of transgendered identity through breast reduction surgery and hormone injections, Jess is a character in search of a physical identity that expresses her true self, and a community that values that identity. "I didn't want to be different," Jess begins, and from the start the book captures a central theme of white Western culture: difference as problem. The question that echoes throughout her life—"Woman or man?"—is a question that articulates the way that gender dualisms organize the world. Neither one gender extreme or another, Jess literally embodies the borderland; in Gloria Anzaldúa's terms, Jess is a mestiza, a border-crosser, and for her refusal to remain within the prescribed boundaries of gender and sexuality, Jess is brutally and repeatedly punished.

The "stone" of the novel's title refers to an emotional shut-down, a wall of protective anger and disassociation that protects butch lesbians from experiencing overwhelming emotional pain, since they cannot escape the violence and rage directed at them for their mere existence as gender and sexual outlaws. Once it is in place, the stone wall functions like "a home alarm system that [does not] seem to have an on-off switch" (94). As we learned from studies of emotionology, human emotions are not like a piano on which notes can be played one at a time; rather, emotions are either available or not, and opening up to the experience of sexual desire requires opening up to the experience of the whole range of emotions (Stearns and Stearns). Hence, butches who shut down emotionally to keep out the pain may be unable to open up erotically. Their protection becomes a stone wall that keeps pain out as much as it keeps their other feelings trapped inside. Students saw many similarities between *Stone Butch Blues* and *Ceremony,* particularly in the way that the protagonists must struggle against an addictive culture that denies emotions and the erotic and devalues all those associated with nature and the natural—women, people of color, animals, and queers.

Jess's relationships with nature and animals serve as a refuge for her, and here, as in the poetry we read, speaking with and listening to the language of nature is seen as a path to liberation. As a child, Jess often visits the dog kennels near a field where she can escape the taunts of her peers. She asks animals the question that the dominant culture repeatedly asks her—"Are you a boy or a girl?"—to which the dog replies, "Ruff, ruff!" and the crow replies, "Caw, caw!" In the language of nature, each animal speaks its own identity as the only answer to such a binary question, and Jess concludes, "nature held me close and seemed to find no fault with me" (17). When she is captured in a bar raid and the police gang rape her in a jail cell, Jess again finds refuge in nature by imagining herself "standing in the desert," her first home and birthplace, where "the scent of sage was overpowering" and a golden eagle screams above her (62–63); of course, what she hears as the eagle's scream is also her own. Jess identifies with the golden eagle again when she decides to begin taking hormones and realizes she must stop seeing her friend's children since they will not understand the changes in her body. She attempts to explain her situation by taking the children to the zoo and showing them the golden eagles: "You know there's not many eagles left. The food they eat got all poisoned with chemicals, and sometimes people shot at them. . . . [To protect themselves, the eagles] flew high up into the mountains, way up above the clouds and they're going to stay up there and fly around in the wind until it's safe to come visit" (167). As Jess's metaphoric explanation makes clear, the dominant culture is violent and toxic for animal nature and sexual nature alike.

Students grappled with the implications of Jess's choice to alter her body through breast reduction surgery and the injection of male sex hormones, possibly because the body has been considered a locus of identity, a pure site of nature that should not be tampered with. We recalled that in *The Bluest Eye,* Pecola's desire to alter her body is a form of internalized oppression, a response to racist definitions of beauty that Black Liberation has since worked hard to challenge. In the 1970s (the decade in which Jess's transgendered experience formally begins), feminists saw transgender as part of transsexuality and saw both as a form of privatizing a political problem, blaming the "victim" instead of the culture (Raymond; Steinem). But in *Stone Butch Blues,* Jess's desire to alter her body is not an attempt to conform to external social standards; rather, it is a struggle to shape her body so that it articulates the identity and the image of herself she has held all along.

As in the other books we read, here once again the problem is the oppression of nature, and students agreed that liberation for Jess—as it was for Tayo or would have been for Claudia—means finding her own "nature" and having the community support to express that nature. The female body she is born with, and the social sex roles and behaviors associated with it in the dominant culture, do not reflect Jess's true nature. To explore this idea, we looked at postmodern analyses of sexual identity (Butler; Gaard), which is often seen to include many independent yet interactive components, such as biological identity, gender identity, social sex role, sexual orientation, and sexual practices (Shively and De Cecco; Zemsky); we also looked at studies of the many possible combinations of chromosomes in nature and the way that medical science forces the diversity of nature into the binarism of two cultural genders through sex reassignment surgery for infants (Kessler and McKenna). Using these critiques, students agreed that Jess's nature was apparent in four of out five of these components of sexual identity; her decision to take hormones and undergo surgery was a decision to align her biological identity with the rest of her nature. *Stone Butch Blues* encouraged students to reconceptualize their definitions of the "natural" by replacing dominant culture's binary definition of gender with the idea of gender as a continuum and by recognizing the social construction of nature in the idea of the body and biological identity as one's own or only "true nature."

To end the class, I wanted to bring in ecofeminist critiques of science, particularly Vandana Shiva's work on biotechnology, but also ecofeminist critiques of animal experimentation. We read Mary Shelley's *Frankenstein* and used the novel to explore Western culture's fear of nature, a theme that had been introduced in Griffin's *Woman and Nature* and had resurfaced throughout the term. Told through the device of three embedded narratives, *Frankenstein* depicts the role of science in Western man's pursuit for control over nature: the first layer of narrative is a series of letters written by the North Pole explorer Robert Walton to his sister; Walton relates Victor Frankenstein's narrative, Victor relates the Creature's story, and the Creature tells the story of the DeLacey family and of Safie. After discussing their responses to the novel, students read and applied analyses from Shiva's work ("Biotechnology"; "Reductionism"), examining the patriarchal appropriation of motherhood through mythology, along with its modern manifestation in biotechnology.

Although at first Walton's journey to the North Pole might appear to be motivated by a love for nature and a desire to explore the wilderness, the embedded narrative structure soon reveals that Walton and Victor share Western culture's drive for domination of nature. In both their narratives, science is masculinized, nature is feminized, and the pursuit of scientific knowledge becomes the metaphoric rape of virginal nature. Analogous to heterosexual rape and patriarchal marriage, the desired outcome of Victor's scientific experimentation is his control of "the elixir of life" (45)—fertility itself. Unlike Walton's mere desire for "glory," Victor wants to be a god: "A new species would bless me as its creator and source; many happy and excellent natures would owe their being to me. No father could claim the gratitude of his child so completely as I should deserve theirs" (55). And here is the problem: mere fatherhood is not enough; the male/scientific appropriation of motherhood is desired. As students wryly observed, Victor's task of "prepar[ing] a frame" for the life he was now able to bestow, "with all its intricacies of fibres, muscles, and veins" would not have "remained a work of inconceivable difficulty and labour" if he had been able to conceive—that is, if Victor were a woman capable of gestation and childbirth (55). The Creature he makes is thus motherless, a theme that plays a significant role in this novel (Gilbert and Gubar), as it had in *Ceremony* and *The Bluest Eye*.

Students recalled other novels we had read in which mother loss, or the presence of an indifferent mother, had a detrimental effect on the novel's protagonist. In *Ceremony*, for example, Tayo is abandoned by his birth mother, treated harshly by his surrogate mother (Auntie), and alienated from the earth as mother. In *The Bluest Eye*, Pecola is rejected by her mother, Pauline, who favors the white daughter and the white household over her own; in turn, Pauline's mother had also neglected her, failing to respond to the rusty nail through her foot that crippled her for life; and Cholly's mother abandoned him on the railroad tracks shortly after his birth. As Adrienne Rich has written in *Of Woman Born*, every woman in patriarchal culture is "wildly unmothered" because sexism and heterosexism prevent women from having self-esteem and from passing self-esteem on to their daughters; yet the establishment of a satisfactory mother-child relationship is crucial to an individual's development of self-esteem and security in the world. In *Frankenstein*, the mother-loss creates monstrosity because it is here that Mother Nature is replaced by Father Science.

Students previously skeptical about the possibilities of humans entering into a dialogical relationship with nature, or with the "other," see in Frankenstein, conversely, the dangers of rejecting such a relationship. For a central problem in the novel is that Victor resists dialogue with the Creature; once the Creature becomes conscious, Victor flees before the Creature has a chance to speak. At their first meeting over two years later, Victor greets the Creature with "Devil . . . do you dare approach me?" and calls its words "detested" (90). Ultimately, Victor turns from fleeing to pursuing the Creature, in the hope of silencing it completely. In the context of this narrative, students found, the consequences of refusing a reciprocal dialogue with the "other" may be quite destructive to all. As the Creature tells Frankenstein—and as Shiva predicts—when humans ignore the messages of science and nature, the consequences may be beyond human control: "Remember that I have power. . . . You are my creator, but I am your master;—obey!" (142).

We concluded the class by reading Ursula Le Guin's *Buffalo Gals and Other Animal Presences*. Through this book, we continued a discussion of the ways that language mediates the relationship humans can have with nature, their own natures as well as wild nature. Le Guin's text offers a number of entry points for an ecofeminist critique, among them the technical device of shifting point of view, narrating from the viewpoint of the "other"; interrogating the culture/nature relationship through the girl-child/animal relationship (fable); examining the role of language in constructing nature, self, and "other"; interrogating the role of science in constructing nature; comparing the relationship between poetry and prose in their effectiveness in conveying ideas; and explaining the uses of retelling myth and story from a liberatory perspective.[4] As Le Guin writes in her introduction, "In literature as in 'real life,' women, children, and animals are the obscure matter upon which Civilization erects itself, phallologically. That they are Other is . . . the foundation of language, the Father Tongue" (9). But Le Guin proposes to use another kind of language, one that expresses "the continuity, interdependence, and community of all life, all forms of being on earth, [as] a lived fact, made conscious in narrative" (10). The question of speciesism came to the fore during these classes, as students puzzled over ways of revising their analytical Rubik's Cube to account for this variable.

In retrospect, I can think of many other books that offer possibilities for an ecofeminist literary critique. Students found that, rather than limiting their readings, an ecofeminist literary perspective could be invoked for almost any novel to illuminate relationships of power and privilege or to explore the Rubik's Cube of identity and relationships of self and other.

Penciling in the Contours of an Ecofeminist Literary Criticism

By the end of the class, while realizing that others might travel the same terrain and come up with different routes, we had nonetheless mapped what we believed were significant contour lines for ecofeminist literary critics. We rejected the simplistic idea that such an approach would proceed by attempting to apply the label "ecofeminist" to various texts, often in ways that would be anachronistic, culturally imperialist, or simply irrelevant. Regardless of whether the writers identified themselves as ecofeminists, we found that an ecofeminist approach to literary criticism invited an exploration of certain central questions:

1. *Defining nature:* What constitutes "nature" or the "natural" in a text? how does this definition redefine what counts as "nature writing"?

2. *The Rubik's Cube of identity:* In what ways do the various aspects of human identity—particularly gender, race, class, and sexuality—shape human/nature relationships? How does the association of human sexuality, race, class, or gender with nonhuman animal species affect the status of a particular character? How does it affect the animal's position in the text? How does the association of human gender, race, class, or sexuality with nature affect the status of that human? How does it affect the status of nature?

3. *Eating:* How is the act of eating portrayed, and what does its portrayal reveal about specific human/nature relationships?

4. *Emotions/anger:* How can the various expressions of emotion, particularly anger, be traced back to fundamental relationships between self and other?

5. *The erotic:* Where is the erotic expressed in the text? What kind of power relations inhere in its expression? Is the erotic welcomed, celebrated, repressed, or feared?

6. *Formal elements:* Given the ecofeminist valuing of praxis, or the integral relationship of theory and practice, what is the relationship between a text's form and content? Its narrative structure and plot? What does the text's point of view, its audience, and the various metaphors or other literary tropes convey about the relationship between writer and reader? Between self and other?

7. *Language:* What is the role of language in constructing or in healing the relationship between culture and nature, self and other? How does the text (re)define key terms, terms that seem central to an ecofeminist literary criticism?

All of these questions pointed back to the fundamental realization of ecofeminism, namely that our cultural, economic, and ecological crises stem from a separation of self from other. Insofar as an ecofeminist approach to literary criticism can illuminate our understanding of these crises, their sources, and their present functioning, perhaps it can also be used to uncover and to generate the means for healing this fundamental alienation. If so, an ecofeminist perspective has the potential for bringing literary criticism into dialogue with the most important issues of our time.

Notes

Many thanks to the students of Ecofeminist Literary Criticism, whose perceptive readings and lively discussion contributed immeasurably to the ideas expressed in this essay.

1. Since the inception of this essay, Murphy's outstanding collection of ecofeminist literary critiques has been published and has influenced my thinking through later revisions (*Literature*). I am also grateful to Patrick D. Murphy for his constructive criticism on an earlier draft of this essay.

2. See Bunch and Pollack; Culley and Portuges; Freire; Murphy "Coyote." Murphy also sent me a syllabus for his course, Literature, Nature, Other, which influenced my choice of grading criteria.

3. In such a small group of women, we tended to work cooperatively toward consensus; when our interpretations differed, we worked toward an understanding of that difference by creating a larger interpretive framework that could account for differences, instead of competing for the status of who would hold the single correct interpretation. This conversational style is simply a product of white women's socialization (see Kramarae; Helgeson; Tannen; Wood).

4. I have condensed our discussion of Le Guin's stories here because a fuller critique is offered in Armbruster (this volume).

Works Cited

Abbey, Edward. *Desert Solitaire: A Season in the Wilderness.* New York: Ballantine Books, 1968.

Adams, Carol. "The Feminist Traffic in Animals." *Ecofeminism: Women, Animals, Nature.* Ed. Greta Gaard. Philadelphia: Temple University Press, 1993. 195–218.

Allen, Paula Gunn. "The Feminine Landscape of Leslie Marmon Silko's *Ceremony.*" *The Sacred Hoop: Recovering the Feminine in American Indian Traditions.* Boston: Beacon Press, 1986. 118–26.

Anzaldúa, Gloria. *Borderlands/La Frontera: The New Mestiza.* San Francisco: Spinsters/ Aunt Lute Books, 1987.

Bunch, Charlotte, and Sandra Pollack, eds. *Learning Our Way: Essays in Feminist Education.* New York: Crossing Press, 1983.

Butler, Judith. *Gender Trouble: Feminism and the Subversion of Identity.* New York: Routledge, 1990.

Cantrell, Carol H. "Women and Language in Susan Griffin's *Woman and Nature: The Roaring inside Her.*" *Hypatia* 9.3 (1994): 225–38.

Christian, Barbara. "Community and Nature: The Novels of Toni Morrison." *Black Feminist Criticism: Perspectives on Black Women Writers.* New York: Pergamon, 1985. 47–64.

Culley, Margo, and Catherine Portuges, eds. *Gendered Subjects: The Dynamics of Feminist Teaching.* Boston: Routledge, 1985.

Feinberg, Leslie. *Stone Butch Blues.* Ithaca: Firebrand Books, 1993.

———. *Transgender Liberation: A Movement Whose Time Has Come.* New York: World View Forum, 1992.

Freire, Paolo. *Pedagogy of the Oppressed.* Trans. Myra Bergman Ramos. New York: Continuum, 1970.

Gaard, Greta. "Identity Politics as a Comparative Poetics." *Borderwork: Feminist Engagements with Comparative Literature.* Ed. Margaret R. Higonnet. Ithaca: Cornell University Press, 1994. 230–43.

Gilbert, Sandra, and Susan Gubar. "Horror's Twin: Mary Shelley's Monstrous Eve." *The Madwoman in the Attic.* New Haven: Yale University Press, 1979. 213–45.

Green, Rayna, ed. *That's What She Said: Contemporary Poetry and Fiction by Native American Women.* Bloomington: Indiana University Press, 1984.

Griffin, Susan. *Woman and Nature: The Roaring inside Her.* New York: Harper and Row, 1978.

Helgeson, Sally. *The Female Advantage.* New York: Doubleday, 1990.

Kasl, Charlotte Davis. *Women, Sex, and Addiction: A Search for Love and Power.* New York: Ticknor and Fields, 1989.

Kessler, Suzanne J., and Wendy McKenna. *Gender: An Ethnomethodological Approach.* Chicago: University of Chicago Press, 1978.

Kramarae, Cheris. *Women and Men Speaking.* Rowley, Mass.: Newbury House Publishers, 1981.

Larson, Earnie. *Stage 2 Recovery: Life beyond Addiction.* San Francisco: Harper and Row, 1985.

Le Guin, Ursula. *Buffalo Gals and Other Animal Presences.* New York: Penguin Books, 1987.

Lorde, Audre. "Uses of the Erotic: The Erotic as Power." *Sister Outsider: Essays and Speeches.* Trumansburg, N.Y.: Crossing Press, 1984. 53–59.

Morrison, Toni. *The Bluest Eye.* New York: Penguin/Plume, 1970.

Murphy, Patrick D. "Coyote Midwife in the Classroom: Introducing Literature with Feminist Dialogics." *Practicing Theory in Introductory College Literature Courses.* Ed. James M. Cahalan and David B. Downing. Urbana, Ill.: National Council of Teachers of English, 1991. 161–76.

———. *Literature, Nature, and Other: Ecofeminist Critiques.* Albany: State University of New York Press, 1995.

Oliver, Mary. *American Primitive.* Boston: Little, Brown, 1983.

Peele, Stanton. *Diseasing of America: Addiction Treatment out of Control.* Lexington, Mass.: D. C. Heath, 1989.

Plumwood, Val. *Feminism and the Mastery of Nature.* New York: Routledge, 1993.

Raymond, Janice. *The Transsexual Empire.* Boston: Beacon Press, 1979.

Rich, Adrienne. *Of Woman Born: Motherhood as Institution and Experience.* New York: Bantam Books, 1976.

Scheman, Naomi. "Anger and the Politics of Naming." *Women and Language in Literature and Society.* Ed. Sally McConnell-Ginet, Ruth Borker, and Nelly Furman. New York: Praeger Special Studies, 1980. 174–87.

Shelley, Mary. *Frankenstein.* Ed. Johanna M. Smith. Boston: Bedford Books of St. Martin's Press, 1992.

Shiva, Vandana. "Biotechnology and the Environment." *Monocultures of the Mind.* London: Zed Books, 1993. 95–131.

———. "Reductionism and Regeneration: A Crisis in Science." *Ecofeminism.* Maria Mies and Vandana Shiva. London: Zed Books, 1993. 22–35.

Shively, Michael G., and John P. De Cecco. "Components of Sexual Identity." *Journal of Homosexuality* 3.1 (1977): 41–48.

Silko, Leslie Marmon. *Ceremony.* New York: Penguin Books, 1977.

———. "Landscape, History, and the Pueblo Imagination." *Antaeus* 57 (Autumn 1986): 83–94.

Smith, Andrea. "For All Those Who Were Indian in a Former Life." *Ms.* Nov.–Dec. 1991: 44–45.

Snyder, Gary. *Turtle Island.* New York: New Directions, 1974.

Stearns, Carol Zisowitz, and Peter N. Stearns. *Anger: The Struggle for Emotional Control in America's History.* Chicago: University of Chicago Press, 1986.

Steinem, Gloria. "Transsexualism." *Outrageous Acts and Everyday Rebellions.* New York: Holt, Rinchart, and Winston, 1983. 206–10.

Tannen, Deborah. *You Just Don't Understand: Women and Men in Conversation.* New York: Morrow, 1990.

Wood, Julia. *Gendered Lives: Communication, Gender, and Culture.* Belmont, Calif.: Wadsworth Publishers, 1994.

Zemsky, Beth. "Stonewall Remembered." *GLCAC OutFront* 2.4 (1992): 1, 3.

Contributors

STACY ALAIMO is an assistant professor of English at the University of Texas at Arlington. She has published in *Feminist Studies, Legacy,* and the *Electronic Book Review* and is working on a book entitled "Undomesticated Ground: Nature and Feminism in Fiction, Theory, and Culture," in which she examines the conflicts, intersections, and alliances between the discourses of nature and a wide range of feminist theory, literature, and other popular culture texts.

KARLA ARMBRUSTER lives outside of Boulder, Colorado, and teaches American studies and English courses in a residential program at the University of Colorado. She received her Ph.D. in English from Ohio State University in 1996; her dissertation focused on environmental advocacy in American literature and culture. She is currently revising her dissertation into a book as well as pursuing research and teaching interests in environmental literary criticism, bioregionalism and community studies, and women's perspectives on environmental issues.

JOSEPHINE DONOVAN has written about the intersections between feminist and animal defense theory and is the author of numerous books and articles on women's literature and feminist criticism. Most recently she coedited with Carol J. Adams *Animals and Women: Feminist Theoretical Explorations* (1996) and *Beyond Animal Rights: A Feminist Caring Ethic for the Treatment of Animals* (1995). She is a professor of English at the University of Maine.

GRETA GAARD is an associate professor of humanities at Fairhaven College, Western Washington University. She is the editor of *Ecofeminism: Women, An-*

imals, Nature and the author of *Ecological Politics: Ecofeminists and the Greens.* Her grass-roots video productions include "Thinking Green" and "Ecofeminism Now!" Her essays have appeared in *Hypatia, Signs, Environmental Ethics, The Ecologist, Feminist Teacher, Society and Nature,* and elsewhere. Currently, she is at work on a volume of ecofeminist creative nonfiction essays.

BARBARA T. GATES is Alumni Distinguished Professor of English and Women's Studies at the University of Delaware. Currently completing a study of Victorian and Edwardian women and nature entitled "Kindred Nature," she is the author of *Victorian Suicide: Mad Crimes and Sad Histories* and numerous essays and reviews. She is the editor of *Critical Essays on Charlotte Brontë,* the *Journal of Emily Shore,* and, with Ann B. Shteir, *Natural Eloquence: Women Reinscribe Science.*

DEBORAH JANSON is an assistant professor of German at West Virginia University, where she teaches courses on German language and literature, including several seminars focusing on the portrayal of nature in literature. Her interests include the literature of the German Democratic Republic, parallels between Christa Wolf and ecofeminism, ecocritical readings of texts from various periods, and the theme of seduced maidens in German literature since the eighteenth century.

CASSANDRA KIRCHER is an adjunct professor at Elon College, where she teaches composition, literature, and creative writing. She received her Ph.D. from the University of Iowa in 1995; her dissertation, "Women In/On Nature," is a feminist analysis of nature writing by women. Her work in American nature writing has appeared in *Southwestern American Literature* and *ISLE: Interdisciplinary Studies in Literature and Environment.*

CATHLEEN MCGUIRE and COLLEEN MCGUIRE are identical twin sisters who live together in the Hell's Kitchen neighborhood of Manhattan. Colleen is a tenant attorney who has been in private practice for over ten years. Cathleen, a World Wide Web document producer, is creator and webgoddess of EVE Online (http://www.envirolink.org/orgs/eve/).

PATRICK D. MURPHY teaches in the Graduate Program in Literature and Criticism at Indiana University of Pennsylvania. Founding editor of *ISLE: Interdisciplinary Studies in Literature and Environment,* he is the author of *Literature, Nature, and Other: Ecofeminist Critiques* and *Understanding Gary Snyder,* as well as editor or co-editor of eight other books, including *Planetary Writing: International Essays on Nature in Literature*. He is currently arts and the natural environment feature editor of *Organization and Environment*.

KAMALA PLATT is an instructor at Nassau Community College on Long Island and a doctoral student in comparative literature at the University of Texas at Austin. She has received an M.A. in comparative literature from the University of Texas at Austin, an M.A. in interdisciplinary arts from Columbia College in Chicago, and an M.F.A. in creative writing from Bowling Green State University. In her dissertation, "Cultural Poetics in Environmental Justice Movements: Organization, Theories, and Resistance in India and Greater Mexico," she studies the practice, theory, and aesthetics of women generating cultural poetics that promote environmental justice.

DEBORAH SLICER is an associate professor of philosophy at the University of Montana in Missoula. Her essays have appeared in *Hypatia, Environmental Ethics,* and other journals. She teaches environmental philosophy and cofounded and directs a community garden providing organic food to low income women and children.

JOHN PAUL TASSONI is an assistant professor at Miami University in Ohio, where he teaches composition and American literature. His work in American literature and pedagogy appears in books and journals such as *Social Issues in the English Classroom, Nineteenth Century Studies,* and *ISLE: Interdisciplinary Studies in Literature and Environment* With Gail Tayko, he is co-editor of *Sharing Pedagogies: Students and Teachers Write about Dialogic Practices,* a book that privileges students' stories about nontraditional composition and literature classrooms.

Index

254   Index

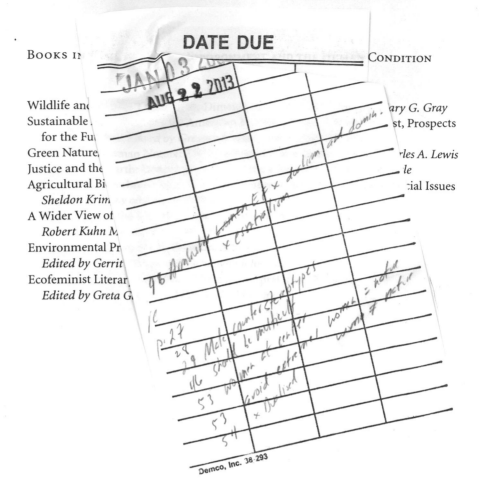

DATE DUE

JAN 03 [...]
AUG 2 2 2013

Wildlife and [...] ary G. Gray
Sustainable [...] st, Prospects
  for the Fu[...]
Green Nature[...] rles A. Lewis
Justice and the [...] le
Agricultural Bi[...] cial Issues
  Sheldon Krim[...]
A Wider View of [...]
  Robert Kuhn M[...]
Environmental Pr[...]
  Edited by Gerrit [...]
Ecofeminist Literar[...]
  Edited by Greta G[...]

Demco, Inc. 38-293